*For my wonderful family:*

*Nick, Tommy, Jackie, Verenda, Austin, and Carter*

# Teaching Children Physical Education

## Becoming a Master Teacher

### Third Edition

## George Graham, PhD
**Pennsylvania State University**

**Human Kinetics**

**Library of Congress Cataloging-in-Publication Data**

Graham, George, 1943-
  Teaching children physical education : becoming a master teacher / George Graham. -- 3rd ed.
    p. cm.
  Includes bibliographical references and index.
  ISBN-13: 978-0-7360-6210-7 (soft cover)
  ISBN-10: 0-7360-6210-6 (soft cover)
  1. Physical education teachers--Training of--United States. 2. Physical education for children--
Study and teaching--United States. I. Title.
  GV363.G68 2008
  372.86'044--dc22
                                    2007043207

ISBN-10: 0-7360-6210-6
ISBN-13: 978-0-7360-6210-7

The Web addresses cited in this text were current as of January 2008, unless otherwise noted.

**Acquisitions Editor:** Scott Wikgren; **Managing Editors:** Bethany J. Bentley and Amy Stahl; **Assistant Editor:** Anne Rumery; **Copyeditor:** John Wentworth; **Proofreader:** Anne Meyer Byler; **Indexer:** Betty Frizzell; **Permission Manager:** Dalene Reeder; **Graphic Designer:** Joe Buck; **Graphic Artist:** Denise Lowry; **Cover Designer:** Keith Blomberg; **Photographer (cover):** © Human Kinetics; **Art Manager:** Kelly Hendren; **Associate Art Manager:** Alan L. Wilborn; **Illustrators:** Dick Flood (cartoons) and Kristin King (mac art); **Printer:** United Graphics

Printed in the United States of America      10   9   8   7   6

The paper in this book is certified under a sustainable forestry program.


**Human Kinetics**
Web site: www.HumanKinetics.com

*United States:* Human Kinetics, P.O. Box 5076, Champaign, IL 61825-5076
800-747-4457
email: humank@hkusa.com

*Canada:* Human Kinetics, 475 Devonshire Road Unit 100, Windsor, ON N8Y 2L5
800-465-7301 (in Canada only)
email: info@hkcanada.com

*Europe:* Human Kinetics, 107 Bradford Road, Stanningley, Leeds LS28 6 AT, United Kingdom
+44 (0) 113 255 5665
email: hk@hkeurope.com

*Australia:* Human Kinetics, 57A Price Avenue, Lower Mitcham, South Australia 5062
08 8372 0999
e-mail: info@hkaustralia.com

*New Zealand:* Human Kinetics, P.O. Box 80, Torrens Park, South Australia 5062
0800 222 062
e-mail: info@hknewzealand.com

# Contents

**Chapter 14  Continuing to Develop as a Teacher          213**

# Preface

One of the truisms in life is that if you can't throw and catch a ball, you probably won't enjoy sports that require those two skills (such as softball, basketball, and ultimate). Teaching is similar. If you don't learn the skills to teach effectively, then you probably won't enjoy, or be successful at, teaching. This book is not about *what* to teach but rather *how* to teach. During my more than 30 years of observing and working with physical educators, I encountered countless teachers who were searching for the perfect games or activities, ones that the children would enjoy and also learn from. All too often, however, they were never able to find the perfect game because the children would not listen long enough, or carefully enough, to understand how to play the game. Thus the perfect game often disintegrated into confusion, uncertainty, and even chaos. This book is different because it focuses solely on the teaching, or pedagogical, skills used by successful children's physical educators.

I have written this book from the perspective of a teacher as opposed to that of a university professor. I have done this for several reasons. The first is that for more than 30 years my work has been focused on children and physical education—and especially those who teach it! When I conduct workshops and make speeches, one of the greatest compliments I receive is that I know kids and know what it is like to teach physical education in elementary schools.

I have also worked hard to stay connected to schools and teachers. It is all too easy to be at a university and lose touch with the realities of teachers' lives and forget what it's like to teach several hundred children a day with barely enough time to eat lunch and use the restroom. As I write this third edition, many states have implemented high-stakes testing with public accountability. Consequently, in addition to everything else they do, some teachers are having to justify their programs more than ever before. While this is not part of their job description, it is a wearying, time-consuming, and often frustrating part of teaching children's physical education as we move further into the 21st century.

We are in the midst of a full-blown obesity epidemic. Experts are predicting that, for the first time ever, this generation of children might live shorter lives than their parents. Thus, in addition to high-stakes testing, many schools are increasingly focused on the health of children. In fact, more and more states are introducing legislation requiring 150 minutes of physical education, not physical activity, a week in elementary schools. If this legislation passes, there will be a need for more children's physical education teachers—especially those who are effective at guiding youngsters in the process of remaining physically active for a lifetime.

I have been fortunate throughout my career to be surrounded by excellent children's physical education teachers who both inspire and impress me with their teaching skills and effectiveness with youngsters. They are truly geniuses with kids! And they are all different. I list some of their names in the acknowledgments on page xiii because I have learned so much from them and, even though they might not know it, their teaching is reflected throughout the book.

In this book, I express the perspective of a teacher while also relying on the teaching research completed in the last 40 years or so. I have applied it to teaching children's physical education so that it will be of value to undergraduates as well as those already teaching. This book is unique in that it focuses on the teaching process—the skills and techniques that successful teachers use to make their classes more interesting and appropriate for children. Future teachers will find the book helpful because it describes and analyzes many of the teaching skills and techniques used by veteran teachers. Topics such as motivation, minimizing discipline problems, and structuring successful learning environments will be of particular interest to novice teachers.

Experienced teachers, in contrast, will discover that some of the techniques they already use are named and described in the book. I hope that veteran teachers will also be challenged to consider some new techniques for structuring their classes, developing lessons, and adjusting tasks for individual children—ideas that will benefit them and the children they teach. We have learned a lot about teaching in the past four decades, and the veterans will find this information both useful and informative.

Because this book is intended for both experienced and beginning teachers, I have included many practical examples in the form of teaching scenarios and vignettes throughout the text. It is obvious that the teaching process (that is, what the teacher actually does) cannot be separated from the content to be taught. For this reason, many of the analyses and descriptions of the various teaching skills include examples of the content (activities or tasks) typically found in children's physical education classes.

# FEATURES OF THE BOOK

Teaching cannot be reduced to a simple formula. There are always decisions to be made—quickly and often. Learning to make those decisions can be done only on your feet. You can read about what teachers do, but until you are actually in the eye of the hurricane, it is difficult to grasp the complexity of choices confronting a teacher. In this book, I explain the decision-making process by separating it into various chapters. Realistically, parts of every chapter in the book will be used in virtually every lesson that is taught. To help you integrate, I have included several features to encourage the type of thinking that teachers do during a lesson.

## Chapter Introductions

Each chapter begins with a brief introduction that sets the stage. This is helpful for connecting one chapter to another and also for understanding the teaching skills and techniques that are discussed in that chapter.

## Chapter Objectives

Each chapter introduction includes a series of objectives that highlight the key points in that chapter. Some books use the word *student* instead of *teacher*. I have used *teacher* instead of *student* because those who are interested in this book are, or will become, teachers.

## Insights

Throughout the book are informal insights or asides. These are based on experiences, my own or those of others, from teaching children in physical education settings. They provide the types of practical, interesting insights that are often not included in a book but help to personalize the book and make it come alive. A sample insight section follows:

# *Mentoring*

I am often struck by the fact that teaching is neither terribly difficult nor mysterious when it involves one-on-one mentoring (such as a mother and daughter, an older and a younger brother, or a grandparent and grandchild). The tasks can easily be changed and accommodated to suit the needs and interests of that child. The problem in school, however, is that teachers are responsible for many children, have limited resources, and work in confined spaces—an awesome task that, viewed in perspective, is done remarkably well.

# DVD

One of the highlights of the third edition is the inclusion of a DVD with the book. This DVD contains brief vignettes of elementary school physical education teachers demonstrating some of the teaching skills described in the book. Although the examples are limited, you will find them useful as a vehicle for understanding the pedagogical skills and how they are actually implemented in real-world teaching situations. The skills that include a vignette on the DVD are indicated by the following icon:

**See Set Induction**

The DVD that accompanies this text provides a brief description of set induction along with an example of how one teacher introduces the technique of "quick feet" dodging a moving object.

As you view the vignettes, you might notice that the clothing worn by the teachers and the children is outdated. That's true. The lessons were taught years ago. Some of the examples used by the teachers might be old, too (such as when they name professional athletes). Try not to let that distract you. The teaching skills used then are every bit as relevant today.

As you view the examples on the DVD, remember that these are taken from actual lessons and thus may not be perfect—but they will enhance your understanding of how the skills might be used in your teaching.

# Reflection Questions

Each chapter concludes with a series of questions for reflection. Because teaching cannot be reduced to a precise formula, the questions help you think about the teaching process and the reasons you teach the way you do. They will also lead you to question some of the ways physical education has been taught in the past—find the good points and remodel those practices that may be counterproductive for children.

Good teachers have a sense of wonder about their teaching. They question whether their techniques worked, how something could have been better, what would happen if another element were introduced, why one way is better than another, whether there are other ways to do something in less time, and how to gain the interest of more children. The reflection questions will increase and deepen your sense of wonder about teaching.

# Chapter Summary and References

Each chapter concludes with a summary or parting thought and a list of the references cited in that chapter.

# OVERVIEW OF CHAPTERS

One of the challenges of writing a book on the process of teaching is figuring out how to describe a process that is intertwined, complex, and nonlinear. When you break out various teaching skills, you tend to oversimplify their use because they are removed from the dynamic context of a lesson. Realistically, however, there is no choice in a book. The DVD vignettes and questions for reflection will restore a sense of context and complexity to the variety of skills that you use to create stimulating lessons for children. Furthermore, after the introductory chapter, chapters are arranged in chronological order, based on the points at which various teaching skills and techniques might be used in a lesson.

Chapter 1 presents discussions of the purpose, challenges, and rewards of children's physical education described in realistic settings. The chapter concludes with a description of the knowledge that successful teachers of children's physical education have and how it looks when translated into practice. The important message of chapter 1 is that this book is about how to teach (that is, the process); it is not a description of activities and games that teachers might use in teaching children.

Planning, the subject of chapter 2, is probably not a favorite subject—but it is a necessary one. The chapter features ideas for planning and sequencing lessons and also for developing yearly plans that are sequential and developmentally appropriate.

Discipline and off-task behavior are often primary concerns of teachers. Chapter 3 describes how you can minimize discipline problems by developing management routines (protocols) that prevent off-task behavior from the very first day of the school year.

Despite all of your good intentions and preparations, some children will manage to be off task. Chapter 4 describes how successful teachers deal with these problems.

A successful beginning to a lesson is often the prelude to a worthwhile class. Chapter 5 discusses this aspect of teaching. Chapter 6 analyzes the ways in which you can provide instruction and use demonstrations to help children better understand and retain important concepts.

A worthwhile topic for discussion among any group of teachers is motivating children. Chapter 7 suggests ways to do this and emphasizes intrinsic, rather than extrinsic, motivation techniques.

One of the premises of this book is that good teachers recognize the differences in children—that one class of third graders is different from the next, and that within any third-grade class, there is a wide range of abilities and interests. This child-centered approach to teaching requires that you be able to accurately observe and interpret the movement of children and then adapt the lessons accordingly. Chapter 8 presents techniques of observing and analyzing children as they move.

Questions regarding the best way to organize the content, when you should change from one task to another, and what to do when the children need to continue working on a task but want to do something else are addressed in chapter 9.

Chapter 10 concerns when and how you can provide useful feedback that is consistent with the focus of the lesson. Chapter 11 examines the teaching skills of asking questions and setting problems for children to solve, emphasizing the importance of cognitive understanding.

Chapter 12 focuses on the affective domain and suggests ways in which you can help children feel good about themselves and about physical activity. Chapter 13 provides a contemporary perspective on assessing (testing) children in schools.

Chapter 14 is the conclusion, covering the importance of teachers' continuing to learn and develop professionally to avoid becoming stagnant and out of touch.

# Acknowledgments

It is snowing hard in central Pennsylvania on this February day, yet I feel a warm glow when I think about all of the teachers I have been fortunate to work with over the years who have, knowingly or unknowingly, contributed to what I have written in the pages that follow.

The most influential people are the elementary school teachers that I have been associated with and who continue to inspire and motivate me. Even though I am now miles away from them, I think of teachers such as Liz Johnson, Sean Fortner, John Pomeroy, Rosa Edwards, Casey Jones, and Shirley Ann Holt/Hale. I don't think they have any idea of how good they really are with kids! They are no different from athletes at the height of their game: They make teaching appear so easy, yet they have worked incredibly hard for years to arrive at the top of their profession. Had I not been able to work with teachers like them, this book would be very different. Although too few recognize these teachers' excellence, they are truly touching the lives of the thousands of youngsters they work with throughout their careers. I am also grateful to the elementary school physical educators in State College, Pennsylvania, who have been so supportive and good to work with: Sean Fortner, Andy Lloyd, Becky Ferguson, and Ann Frederick.

Since the first edition of *Teaching Children Physical Education* was published in 1992, it has been used as the textbook for the American Master Teacher Program (AMTP). As part of this program, workshops have been conducted for more than 2,000 teachers throughout the United States. I am especially appreciative of all the excellent work of the national instructors who have taught these workshops: Marybell Avery, Craig Buschner, Christine Hopple, Dolly Lambdin, Larry Satchwell, Sue Schiemer, and Sandra Stroot. In addition to being excellent teachers, they are incredibly dedicated to effective physical education for children. In the process of conducting these workshops, they spent many weekends on the road and lots of hours in airports. They have been, and continue to be, an inspiration to me in my work. I express my appreciation to another outstanding educator, Eloise Elliott, who served as the director of the AMTP for several years and did an excellent job as an administrator.

The students at Virginia Tech and Penn State are another continuing source of learning and inspiration for me. I have been challenged the most by my doctoral students, who ask such penetrating, complex, and fascinating questions in their quest to become outstanding college professors and researchers. I learned more from them than they'll ever know, and I am grateful for their questions—and apologize for my inability to answer so many of them. But, as I hope they have learned, the most important part of the journey is asking, and continuing to ask, the right questions.

My thinking and writing have been influenced by several professionals who have remained in contact with me and who continue to ask the right questions, albeit from a distance most of the time. They include Mark Manross, Christine Hopple, Marina Bonello, Missy Parker, Steve Palmer, Tom Ratliffe, Ken Bell, and Kim Oliver. I want to acknowledge two university professors who have inspired me for many years with their work ethic, dedication to the profession, and quest to remain on the cutting edge in their thinking and writing even though they are now retired: Daryl Siedentop and Larry Locke.

I want to acknowledge the folks at Human Kinetics who have worked so hard and so well to bring this third edition to press. First I thank Scott Wikgren for his support, keen insights, and willingness to go to bat for this book and also AMTP. Scott and I have worked together for many years on several projects. He works hard from his office in Champaign, Illinois, to advance the new physical education. His title at Human Kinetics is division director of Health, Physical Education, Recreation and Dance, but underneath that title he is a physical educator who knows and values good physical education and is doing his part to spread the word.

I express my appreciation to Bethany Bentley and Amy Stahl at Human Kinetics, who served as the managing editors for the third edition. I especially appreciate their patience. I am grateful to the others who worked on this edition: Anne Rumery, the assistant editor; Joe Buck, the graphic designer; Denise Lowry, the graphic artist; Dalene Reeder, the permissions manager; and the rest of the Human Kinetics team.

## Chapter 1

# Successful Teaching

*Those who can, do. Those who can't, teach. Those who can't teach, teach physical education.*

**Woody Allen**

Woody Allen is right. We do have teachers in our profession who can't (or don't) teach (obviously some of them taught Woody Allen!). As an unfortunate result, a number of adults in the United States recall physical education (PE) classes as painful, humiliating, and virtually worthless experiences.

Fortunately, that is changing. Today we have a new breed of physical educators in the United States who are revolutionizing the way physical education is taught. These revolutionaries teach physical education in ways that make the Woody Allens of the world look forward to physical education with enthusiasm. These teachers care as much about the low-skilled, sensitive, unconfident child as they do about the aggressive, athletic child. And they have found ways to make their classes both pleasant and worthwhile for all children—the low- and the high-skilled, and all those in between.

This book describes and analyzes the techniques, behaviors, skills, and approaches used by successful teachers to develop and teach lessons that are developmentally appropriate—and that result in enjoyable and beneficial learning experiences for children.

## After reading and understanding this chapter, the teacher will be able to

▶ explain why teaching children's physical education is characterized as a dynamic, constantly changing process,

▶ analyze both the obstacles and the benefits of teaching children's physical education,

▶ explain the concept of orchestration as it relates to the selection and use of teaching skills,

▶ describe the distinction between content (what is taught) and the process of teaching (pedagogy), and

▶ delineate the major components of successful children's physical education teaching.

# THE TEACHER, NOT ONLY THE CONTENT

When I think back on all of the teachers who taught me throughout my school years, several come immediately to mind—the good ones and the not so good ones. One of the teachers who pops into memory is my high school trigonometry teacher. I had decided in elementary school that math was not one of my academic strengths. I struggled through required math courses from year to year—until I took a trigonometry course in my senior year. I vividly remember the first day. The teacher informed us that our text would be a college-level trigonometry book. I thought, *I am in big trouble in this course.* Surprisingly, that wasn't so. Although the topic and the textbook were difficult for me, my trig teacher made the material very interesting, and I actually did quite well. Despite my negative attitude at the beginning of the class, I almost enjoyed learning math.

Obviously, it wasn't the subject—trigonometry—that encouraged me to do better than I had expected. It was the teacher—the way he explained concepts, took time with us, never made us feel foolish, structured the content, answered questions with understandable examples, arranged for us to succeed in small steps, and did a plethora of other small things that, when totaled, were the earmarks of a highly effective teacher of trigonometry.

Fortunately, this book isn't about trigonometry. It's about teachers and the kinds of things they do (or don't do) that make learning attainable and enjoyable for students. Trigonometry, reading, or physical education can all be taught in ways that are exciting and educational. However, they can also be taught in ways that are boring, confusing, and distasteful. We are not just concerned with the content to be taught. We are also concerned with the teachers and all of the things they do that make our attempts to learn the material productive and stimulating—so that we learn and enjoy the process.

That might sound as if I am suggesting that the content—and a teacher's knowledge of the content—is unimportant. That isn't true. Good teachers know their subjects thoroughly; it enables them to develop their subjects in ways that are engaging and productive for children. My high school trigonometry teacher understood the subject well, which enabled him to develop lessons that were interesting, enjoyable, and productive.

The distinction between knowing what to teach (the content or curriculum) and knowing how to teach (the process or the performance of the teacher) is an artificial one. Content and process cannot be separated. They are interwoven. But in studying and understanding teaching, this artificial distinction is nevertheless helpful. The chapters that follow describe many of these teaching skills and techniques and provide practical examples of how successful teachers use them to create lessons and programs for children.

Because physical education is a unique subject in schools, teachers use orchestrations of skills that are somewhat different from those used by their colleagues in the classroom. This book delineates many of the teaching skills employed by successful children's physical education teachers and the ways they are used effectively in realistic teaching situations.

# HOW IS CHILDREN'S PHYSICAL EDUCATION DIFFERENT?

Teaching any subject to a class of children is challenging. Teaching children's physical education is probably the most challenging job in an elementary school. There are a number of reasons why this is so: The children are moving rather than anchored in desks; a teacher might work with 5-year-olds one lesson and with 11-year-olds a few minutes later; the range of content to be taught covers the entire spectrum of physical activity; facilities and equipment are often less than ideal. No doubt you can add to this list.

In addition to these factors, there is also a frenetic pace, often with 30 or more children involved simultaneously in activity. Larry Locke (1975), in his now-classic description of a children's physical education lesson, captured the complexity and pace of teaching with a vibrant accuracy that is hard to find in written descriptions. Because this book is about teaching children's physical education in the real world, it seems appropriate to begin by setting the stage with his description of a two-minute observation of a class of 34 fourth-grade children during a gymnastics unit:

> Teacher is working one on one with a student who has an obvious neurological deficit. She wants him to sit on a beam and lift his feet from the floor. Her verbal behaviors fall into categories of reinforcement, instruction, feedback, and encouragement. She gives hands-on manual assistance. Nearby two boys perched on the uneven bars are keeping a group of girls off. Teacher visually monitors the situation but continues work on the beam. At the far end of the gym a large mat is propped up so that students can roll down it from a table top, and the mat is slowly slipping closer to the edge. Teacher visually monitors this but continues work on the beam. Teacher answers three individual inquiries addressed by passing students but continues as before. She glances at a group now playing follow the leader over the horse (this is off-task behavior) but as she does a student enters and indicates he left his milk money the previous period. Teacher nods him to the nearby office to retrieve the money and leaves the beam to stand near the uneven bars. The boys climb down at once. Teacher calls to a student to secure the slipping mat. Notes that the intruder, milk money now in hand, has paused to interact with two girls in the class and, monitoring him, moves quickly to the horse to begin a series of provocative questions designed to reestablish task focus. (Locke, 1975)

This two-minute vignette suggests how complex teaching is—but that's only 120 seconds out of 17,000 the teacher spent that day actually working with children.

## 10,000 Children

An elementary school physical educator typically teaches several hundred children a week—let's assume 350 children a week. Over a 30-year career, that adds up to over 10,000 children. And many teachers work with 500 to 600 children a week! In this business a single effective physical educator can truly make a difference in the lives of many youngsters.

## ANALOGIES OF TEACHING

Teaching is complex. Sometimes it seems as if you are in the eye of a hurricane. Balls, children, and ideas are whirling everywhere with no apparent order—but all demand immediate attention.

Teaching has also been likened to a three-ring circus. The teacher is in the center ring—as the circus master. From this central position the teacher simultaneously directs all three rings and attempts to maintain a pace and variety that hold the interest of the audience.

A third teaching analogy is not related to a hurricane or to a circus—it's that of a composer and conductor of a symphony. There are many ways to arrange and blend the different instruments in an orchestra: the strings, the brass, the woodwinds, the percussion instruments. Some extraordinary works of music are dominated by violins, violas, and cellos. Oboes, bassoons, and flutes might be featured in another piece. Marches and military music are dominated by brass and percussion instruments. The fascinating part of listening to and watching a symphony orchestra is observing the myriad ways the various pieces of the orchestra blend in harmony to form enjoyable, often memorable, works of music.

That is how I see successful children's physical education teachers. They are artists, able to orchestrate teaching skills and develop lessons that are both absorbing and beneficial to children of all ages and abilities. As is true of music, there is no single way to organize and teach a lesson.

# CHANGING AND DYNAMIC

There is no predetermined formula that one can follow precisely to become a successful teacher. Teaching is too unpredictable. One third-grade class is not identical to another. Children are different on Monday morning from the way they are on Friday afternoon. So are teachers! Our understanding of teaching has increased over the years, but knowing what skills, strategies, and tactics to use when and with whom is still an artistic decision that varies from class to class and from teacher to teacher.

True teaching, as distinguished from "rolling out the ball," is not like working on an assembly line—it's constantly changing and dynamic. Schon (1990) uses the phrase "indeterminate zone of practice" to describe the uncertainty and ambiguities faced by teachers. Some professions appear to be driven by rules: When this happens, do this; when that happens, do that. Although one may try to reduce teaching to a precise science or formula, there is always a substantial degree of artistry and judgment involved in every lesson we teach.

One isn't simply born an artist—or a teacher. There are techniques to learn and concepts to understand. A painter, for example, might learn painting techniques for use with water colors, oils, and pastels. In addition, there are concepts that need to be understood and expressed through the chosen medium: harmony of color and light, shading, combining colors to create various hues and tones, perspective, form, unity, and abstraction. The artist selects from among these skills and concepts to express desired meanings on a canvas.

Good teachers follow an approach similar to that of good artists. They acquire a range of skills and techniques, not necessarily at a university, which then allows them to develop and teach lessons that are meaningful and worthwhile for children. Although some of the skills are learned consciously, others seem to be acquired subconsciously. Regardless of how the skills are acquired, successful teachers possess a repertoire of abilities from which they select to consistently and intentionally provide children with developmentally appropriate experiences in physical activity (Graham et al., 1992; Stork & Sanders, 1996).

Our scientific understanding of the skills and techniques used by expert teachers continues to grow (Brophy & Good, 1986; Rink, 1997; Siedentop & Tannehill, 2000; Silverman, 1991). We are learning more about what good teachers do (and don't do) with children. As in virtually any profession, however, knowing when and how to use this information requires an artistic decision.

# DIFFICULT TO CAPTURE IN WORDS

Try to tell someone how to juggle—without demonstrating. You might find it's hard to find the right words and phrases. We might be excellent jugglers ourselves, but words are often inadequate tools for helping someone else learn a skill. Like juggling, teaching children's physical education is a process that is easier to observe than to describe. Good teachers are artists with children, but they have a hard time describing what they do. We can recognize a good teacher when we see one, but it's much harder to explain why that teacher is so much better than another teacher.

One of the techniques used by good teachers is one that I am going to use in this book. I am going to break the complex teaching process into small parts with the hope of providing a more penetrating analysis and deeper understanding. This is possible on paper—but not with 30 children on the playground or in the gym. Writing (and reading) about teaching is a luxury because it allows the reader to pause and reflect on the various aspects of teaching: how they're used, why they're used, and how they might be used differently in various settings.

When we're teaching, we don't have the opportunity to say to a class every few seconds, "Freeze. I want to spend three minutes thinking about what I am going to do next as a teacher." In writing, however, the challenges of teaching—and how they are met by successful teachers—can be described and discussed at a more leisurely pace than the frenetic, urgent one described by Locke (1975).

# THE CHALLENGE OF TEACHING CHILDREN'S PHYSICAL EDUCATION

Teaching any subject in American schools today is a challenge, even when viewed from the perspective of the written word that can be frozen in time. All teachers face obstacles; they also feel great satisfaction when the job is done well.

## The Obstacles

In a single day an elementary school physical education teacher typically works with 7 to 12 classes of children. The ages might range from 5 to 11, the physical abilities from poor to excellent; the needs and interests might vary from children interested in sports and physical fitness to those who have already decided that physical activity is not for them. In addition, many teachers have jump rope programs before school, juggling clubs at lunch, and after-school programs. Some also coach. When an elementary school physical education teacher ends her day, she has typically interacted with several hundred children, several classroom teachers and parents, and one or more principals, secretaries, custodians, and cooks—and she wonders why she is so tired. That's a challenging day.

Needless to say, few teachers complete their days under ideal circumstances. During cold and rainy weather, some teachers' gyms become lunchrooms from 11:15 a.m. to 1:15 p.m., so PE is taught in halls, lobbies, classrooms, and on stages. Some classroom teachers insist on bringing their classes to PE early and arriving late to pick them up; others view PE as a time to help individual children "catch up" on math or reading. Often, these are the children who enjoy physical education the most. Schedules are always a complex conundrum in elementary schools. The result is that a class of fifth graders might be followed by kindergartners, followed by second graders, and then by another fifth-grade class. Field trips and visiting speakers often present surprises to the physical education teacher—especially when the principal and classroom teacher forget to notify the PE teacher, who discovers that his next class has just left on a bus to visit the entomology museum. Equipment budgets of $350 for the year represent yet another challenge to the physical educator, who quickly learns the value of collecting soup labels and attending PTA meetings at budget time.

As virtually any elementary school physical education teacher will attest, these are real challenges. They weren't simply invented to catch the reader's attention. Obviously, however, there are also rewards. If there weren't, we wouldn't be able to find many teachers spending more than one or two years teaching in elementary schools.

## The Benefits

Clearly the primary benefit of teaching is not the pay, or the perks. I have yet to meet a physical education teacher with an expense account or company car. And summers, which appear on paper as two and a half months of "rest and recuperation," are often spent taking courses required for continued certification—or working a second job. What then are the benefits?

One of the most obvious benefits is simply the joy of being with children—the contagious giggles; the naive curiosity; the honesty that makes you sometimes wish you hadn't asked; the exuberance and willingness to try; the hugs around the knees; the barely legible notes that mean "thanks for paying attention to me"; the fact that the bad things that happened today will be forgotten by tomorrow; the refreshing lack of sophistication; the true need of so many of today's children to be with adults who can be trusted for their predictability and caring; the fun that children associate with physical activity and the brief respite from the classroom routine; the touch on the arm that says "I appreciate your caring"; and the opportunity to introduce children to the pleasures that derive from the various forms of moving. These small rewards occur frequently. In fact, as long as we remain sensitive to the children, there are few other jobs that are so gratifying.

A benefit that occurs less frequently is the satisfaction of seeing children grow and develop. It's a sobering thought when teachers who remain at the same school for five or six years observe their classes in May and realize that much of what the 10- and 11-year-olds know, or don't know, is a direct result of the physical education program provided by those teachers.

There's a strong sense of expectation held by successful teachers. They share a common belief that, under the right circumstances, they can make a difference. In physical education they make this difference by introducing children to various forms of physical activity and beginning to build the movement foundation that eventually leads to enjoyment, satisfaction, and the benefits of participation in a physical activity throughout a lifetime (U.S. Department of Health and Human Services, 1996). Many educators are convinced that the foundation of many skills is built or destroyed by the time a child leaves elementary school—in physical education, in math, in art, and in reading.

In many ways a physical educator with a good program does her* part to make the world a better place for children to grow up in. When we help children lead their lives

*The English language offers no truly convenient way to refer to the third person singular without excluding one gender or the other. The contortion "he/she" is both awkward and hard to read. Because both men and women teach children's physical education, we have made the decision to use feminine and masculine pronouns in alternate examples.

in a productive direction, we can feel good about our work. Clearly, this is a benefit of teaching children.

Some will label my comments thus far as optimistic. That's fine. I am an optimist. In fact, to me the terms "pessimism" and "teaching" are incongruous together. If we don't believe we can make a difference as teachers, then how can we accept the responsibility of working with children?

My experience tells me that good children's physical education teachers are optimists who believe fervently in the value of their work. They are also realists, however, recognizing the challenges and difficulties of the job. This book is written for just such teachers, whether you're just beginning your student teaching or are in your 30th year. This book is for those who believe in the importance of physical education for children and are willing to dedicate themselves professionally to providing high-quality programs of physical education for youngsters.

## *Hugs, Giggles, and Touches for the Teacher*

Pick one of your favorite classes, or observe a teacher with a favorite class. During the class, try to be keenly sensitive to all of the ways the children find to say they like the teacher and the program. Be sensitive to the smiles, the touches, the nods, the way they move close to the teacher, all of the ways they find to say, "Watch me!" When the class is over, or as soon as you can, take a few minutes to bask in all of the warm feelings the children have shared.

## THE TEACHER MAKES THE DIFFERENCE

Physical education teachers are really no different from teachers of any subject. We want our students to learn. We also want them to enjoy our classes.

Some physical education teachers emphasize learning motor skills and playing games. Others emphasize the development of physical fitness. Still others place their major emphasis on the development of positive student attitudes toward themselves and physical activity. And, of course, many teachers would list a blend of these purposes for their programs.

It's relatively easy to list goals for a program. It's relatively difficult to accomplish these goals, especially when classes are large and meetings are limited to two or three days a week.

A few years ago we began to understand that teachers who were successful weren't necessarily so because of what they taught. Ten teachers could teach the same unit. Two or three might be highly successful (i.e., the successful teachers' students would report that they had enjoyed the unit, and a posttest would demonstrate that, in fact, they had learned much of what had been taught in the unit). The posttest of students of two or three other teachers might reveal that they hadn't learned anything from the teacher, and they would say that they had disliked the unit. The students of the other four to six teachers might reveal mixed outcomes, with no apparent trend as a result of participating in the unit.

In the past 25 years or so, we have increased our understanding of how those two or three successful teachers worked with their students, so that the students learned from and enjoyed the unit. This book describes and analyzes many of the teaching approaches, behaviors, skills, and techniques (the pedagogical knowledge base) that successful teachers select to create effective lessons.

We don't fully understand the orchestrations of skills and attributes that combine to make teachers successful or effective, but we do know more than we did 30 years ago. We also know that the use of teaching skills is situation-specific and varies according to the content taught and the grade level.

## PEDAGOGY TOOL BOX

One of the ways successful teachers make a difference is by effectively using the tools (skills, techniques, strategies, methods) that they have in their pedagogy tool box. Imagine workers who use a variety of tools in their trade, such as carpenters, plumbers, or car mechanics. If you looked into their tool boxes you would find them chock full of specialized tools that they use in their jobs. With *Teaching Children Physical Education*, we want to assist you in two ways:

1. In filling up your tool box with a variety of tools used by successful physical education teachers
2. In helping you to learn to use the tools effectively in a variety of teaching situations

If a carpenter, for example, has only a hammer and a pair of pliers in his tool box he won't be a successful carpenter. Good carpenters have many tools—and know how to use them. Although you won't be exposed in this book to *all* the teaching tools used by successful teachers, you will be introduced to many of the skills that effective teachers possess. As you begin this book, you already have some tools in your pedagogy tool box. By the time you finish reading, I hope that your number of tools has increased and that you have the knowledge of how they are used by successful teachers.

## WORKING DEFINITION OF "SUCCESSFUL"

The purpose of this book is to define and describe the process of teaching used by successful children's physical educators. The emphasis on "successful" is an important one. This book is about more than simply keeping children "busy, happy, and good" (Placek,

1984) two or three days a week so that classroom teachers can have a planning period. "Successful" implies that children learn and develop positive attitudes, that teachers derive satisfaction from their jobs, and that physical education programs are consistent with the overall focus of a school (figure 1.1).

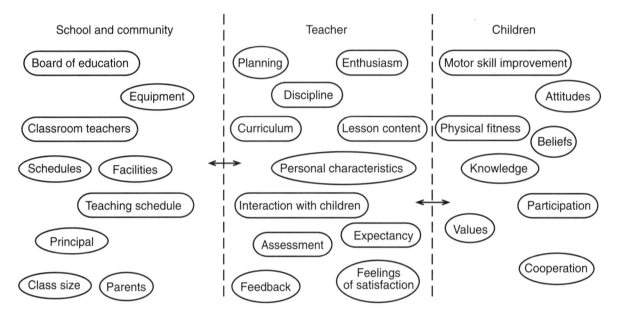

**Figure 1.1**    School and community, teacher, and children: influential factors related to successful programs of physical education.

## The Children's Goals

The first component of successful teaching, obviously, is the children. If a physical education teacher and program are successful, the foundation is built for a child to become a physically educated person. In 1995 the National Association for Sport and Physical Education (NASPE) published national standards for K-12 physical education programs (NASPE, 1995). This document contained a definition of a physically educated person. Box 1.1 contains this definition, which was reviewed by hundreds of physical educators during its development.

## The Teacher's Goals

In addition to the benefits accrued by the children, for any program to be successful, the individuals responsible need to feel a certain sense of satisfaction and accomplishment, as suggested in the definition of someone who is physically educated. For teachers this often means that acts of support and nurture are communicated to them by administrators and parents. As with any profession, when we don't feel supported or cared about as professionals, it is too easy to give up and go through the motions. In physical education jargon, this often leads to "rolling out the ball."

Teachers who continue to plan and develop innovative curriculums, teach actively and enthusiastically, and evaluate and assess hundreds of students must experience a sense of satisfaction if they are going to continue this type of teaching throughout a career (see chapter 14). Interestingly, this doesn't mean that the only way a teacher can be happy is to have ideal conditions. In fact, it seems that part of the job description

Box 1.1

# Characteristics of a Physically Education Person

A physically educated person
- Has learned skills necessary to perform a variety of physical activities
    1. Moves using concepts of body awareness, space awareness, effort, and relationships
    2. Demonstrates competence in a variety of manipulative, locomotor, and nonlocomotor skills
    3. Demonstrates competence in combinations of manipulative, locomotor, and nonlocomotor skills performed individually and with others
    4. Demonstrates competence in many different forms of physical activity
    5. Demonstrates proficiency in a few forms of physical activity
    6. Has learned how to learn new skills
- Is physically fit
    1. Assesses, achieves, and maintains physical fitness
    2. Designs safe, personal fitness programs in accordance with principles of training and conditioning
- Participates regularly in physical activity
    1. Participates in health-enhancing physical activity at least three times a week
    10. Selects and regularly participates in lifetime physical activities
- Knows the implications of and the benefits of involvement in physical activities
    1. Identifies the benefits, costs, and obligations associated with regular participation in physical activity
    2. Recognizes the risk and safety factors associated with regular participation in physical activity
    3. Applies concepts and principles to the development of motor skills
    4. Understands that wellness involves more than being physically fit
    5. Knows the rules, strategies, and appropriate behaviors for selected physical activities
    6. Recognizes that participation in physical activity can lead to multicultural and international understanding
    7. Understands that physical activity provides the opportunity for enjoyment, self-expression, and communication
- Values physical activity and its contributions to a healthful lifestyle
    1. Appreciates the relationships with others that result from participation in physical activity
    19. Respects the role that regular physical activity plays in the pursuit of lifelong health and well-being
    20. Cherishes the feelings that result from regular participation in physical activity

Adapted from *Moving into the Future: National Standards for Physical Education*, with permission from the National Association for Sport and Physical Education (NASPE), 1900 Association Drive, Reston, VA 20191, USA.

for any children's physical education teacher must be to battle continually for improved working conditions and an increased understanding of the importance of physical education for children. For example, many teachers seem to be constantly working toward one or more of the following:

▶ Convincing other teachers and administrators of the value of physical education for children so that classes are not considered "breaks" that can be canceled for field trips, plays, and special events

▶ Obtaining more and better equipment for classes

▶ Attaining realistic teaching loads (e.g., a maximum of seven or eight classes a day)

▶ Arranging teaching schedules that provide reasonable transitions between grades (e.g., not a fifth-grade class followed by a first-grade class followed by a third-grade class)

▶ Lobbying for daily physical education for every child

▶ Limiting class sizes to 30 or fewer students

▶ Securing facilities that are truly designed for physical education

Despite these battles, teachers who are constantly struggling to improve their programs often feel effective. They have developed the understanding that successful physical education involves more than simply teaching children well—it entails other responsibilities, too.

## So You Want to Teach Physical Education?

When college students enter my office and tell me they are thinking about changing their major to physical education, I typically ask four questions:

Do you like physical activity?

Do you like being around kids all day long?

Do you need to make a lot of money?

Are you willing to work in a profession that requires a career-long battle for recognition and support?

Although most students haven't thought about their responses to these questions, I think they are important to ask, because they might help the students start thinking about the characteristics of someone who truly enjoys teaching physical education and finds it a satisfying career—and whether or not they have those characteristics.

## The School's Goal

An important responsibility of any teacher is finding ways to contribute to the overall goals of the school. The goals of good physical education programs (NASPE, 1995) are compatible with the overall goals of good schools—helping children to learn and feel positive about themselves and school and working cooperatively with others toward common purposes. Only when a physical education program is compatible with an overall school program can it be considered successful.

## SUMMARY

"What is it that successful children's physical education teachers actually do when they teach children?" This is the question this book attempts to answer. Our focus will be on the skills and techniques used by good teachers, not on the content of their lessons.

In recent years we have increasingly come to understand that there is no such thing as the perfect lesson that will succeed for every teacher. A good teacher is able to take

virtually any content area and weave it into an interesting and worthwhile experience for children. Unfortunately, an ineffective teacher can take virtually any content, no matter how appealing it might seem to children, and "teach" it in such a way that the children not only fail to learn anything but also fail to enjoy the experience.

This book describes and analyzes the pedagogy of children's physical education—the orchestration of techniques and skills teachers use to involve children in physical activities that are interesting and worthwhile. It is designed for the teacher, or future teacher, whose goal is to help children develop the skills, knowledge, and attitudes to eventually become physically educated adults who enjoy the benefits of physical activity for a lifetime.

## QUESTIONS FOR REFLECTION

1.  When you think about children's physical education, what do you see as the biggest challenges? How do you think you will meet them as a teacher?
2.  Chapter 1 describes a number of benefits of teaching children's physical education. Which of the benefits do you see as the most motivating to you?
3.  If we talked with the children you teach (or plan to teach), what would you like them to say about you as a teacher? What kinds of things might you do to encourage children to feel the way you would like them to feel about you and your program?
4.  Why does the book make a distinction between the teaching process (pedagogy) and the content (what is taught)?
5.  For five minutes, watch another teacher (or a video of yourself) teaching a lesson to children. Write down all the questions you think might be going through that teacher's mind.
6.  Figure 1.1 depicts the influential factors related to successful teaching. How would you revise this figure to better reflect your views?

## REFERENCES

Brophy, J., & Good, T.L. (1986). Teacher behavior and student achievement. In C.M. Wittrock (Ed.), *Handbook of research on teaching.* 3rd ed., 328–375. New York: Macmillan.

Graham, G., Castenada, R., Hopple, C., Manross, M., & Sanders, S. (1992). *Developmentally appropriate physical education practices for children: A position statement of the Council on Physical Education for Children (COPEC).* Reston, VA: National Association for Sport and Physical Education.

Locke, L.F. (1975, Spring). *The ecology of the gymnasium: What the tourist never sees.* Paper presented at the meeting of the Southern Association for Physical Education for College Women, Gatlinburg, TN.

National Association for Sport and Physical Education (NASPE). (1995). *Moving into the future: National standards for physical education.* St. Louis: Mosby.

Placek, J. (1984). A multicase study of teacher planning in physical education. *Journal of Teaching in Physical Education, 4,* 39–49.

Rink, J. (1997). *Teaching physical education for learning.* 3rd ed. New York: McGraw-Hill.

Schon, D.A. (1990). *Educating the reflective practitioner.* San Francisco: Jossey-Bass.

Siedentop, D., & Tannehill, D. (2000). *Developing teaching skills in physical education.* 4th ed. Palo Alto, CA: Mayfield.

Silverman, S. (1991). Research on teaching in physical education. *Research Quarterly for Exercise and Sport, 62,* 352–367.

Stork, S., & Sanders, S. (1996). Developmentally appropriate physical education: A rating scale. *Journal of Physical Education, Recreation and Dance, 67*(6), 52–58.

U.S. Department of Health and Human Services (USDHHS). (1996). *Physical activity and health: A report of the surgeon general.* Atlanta, GA: USDHHS, Centers for Disease Control and Prevention, National Center for Chronic Disease Prevention and Health Promotion.

## Chapter 2

# Planning to Maximize Learning

*While at first-quarter conferences, a kindergarten student brought his parents up to me and said, "Mom and dad, this is Jim Teacher." Mom said, "You mean this is your phys ed teacher?" The kindergarten student answered, "Yes, his name is Jim Teacher."*

**Paul Schumm, Albertville Primary, Albertville, Minnesota**
Reprinted with permission from PE Central (www.pecentral.org).

In the first chapter, teaching was described as an orchestration of teaching skills selected from the pedagogy tool box of successful teachers. Effective planning is an integral part of this orchestration—the part of teaching that determines what will be taught in the lessons, the units, year to year. Planning is to teaching as writing music is to a symphonic performance. It's analogous to the notes, the scales, the written plan that the musicians follow. Without the written music, a symphony orchestra would be reduced to nothing more than discordant noise with no connection or purpose. Without a plan that focuses on what children are expected to learn (not just do) in that lesson a teacher is simply keeping youngsters "busy, happy, and good" (Placek, 1984). Effective teachers develop goals and objectives, plan lessons to accomplish those goals, and then assess to determine if the goals and objectives have been met (chapter 13). This is referred to as instructional alignment (Petersen & Cruz, 2004), which is also called "designing down and teaching up"—that is, determining the goals and then teaching to accomplish these goals.

## After reading and understanding this chapter, the teacher will be able to

- ▶ analyze the important link between planning and teaching,
- ▶ describe the tendencies to avoid extensive planning and ways these tendencies can be avoided,
- ▶ explain why planning is so important to a successful program of physical education for children,
- ▶ describe the concept of and need for personalized planning,
- ▶ analyze the use of objectives as a guide for creating lessons, and
- ▶ compare and contrast the important reasons for connecting long-term and daily planning.

This chapter discusses many of the important features of planning. It begins by describing the need for planning and follows with a straightforward analysis of why there are tendencies to avoid planning in physical education. Realistic ideas about planning for busy people are presented in the third section, and long- and short-term planning are discussed in the final part of the chapter.

## I Think I'll Skip This Chapter . . .

When I envision you reading this book, I wonder if you will be tempted to skip to the later chapters—"the good stuff." If you do, I hope you will return to this chapter at some point. This chapter is designed to provide realistic and candid thoughts not only on the importance of planning but also about ways that planning can be done in the real world of teaching.

## THE NEED FOR PLANNING

In theory, teachers spend an hour or two each day at their desks planning. In fact, teachers plan in the shower, on the drive to work, at meetings, and as they are falling asleep at night—as well as at their desks (Graham, Hopple, Manross, & Sitzman, 1993; Placek, 1984).

Few question the importance of planning (Byra & Coulon, 1994; Coulon & Reif, 1994; Hastie & Vlaisavljevic, 1999). The question is, How much planning is necessary? We know that in the beginning of our careers we need to spend a lot more time planning than we do after we have gained experience. This is no different from taking a trip for the first time—we need to study maps and landmarks to know exactly where to go. After we have made the trip several times, we can spend far less time reviewing maps.

We also know that the amount of planning necessary is related to the type of program a teacher decides to provide for children. Teachers who "roll out the ball" probably spend 5 to 10 minutes a week thinking about what they will do (Placek, 1984). In contrast, teachers who have truly educational programs spend considerable amounts of time poring over books and notes in order to design lessons that fulfill the needs of children. My assumption is that your goal is to become a subject-matter expert who wants to develop a high level of teaching expertise (Hastie & Vlaisavljevic, 1999) and that you are a teacher who sincerely wants to develop the best program of physical education for children that you can; you therefore recognize the need to plan extensively.

# Limited Actual Teaching Time

The minimal amount of time allotted for physical education in many schools is one of the major reasons effective planning is so crucial. Thirty-minute classes that meet twice a week, for example, have approximately 32.4 hours a year of available time (tables 2.1 and 2.2). Realistically, however, there is even less time for actual practice. In fact, Kelly (1989) estimated that the actual instruction time in a twice-a-week program is 16.2 hours a year.

His estimate for a five-day-a-week program is slightly over 40 hours (Kelly, 1989) for the school year. Forty hours seems like a lot, yet when we consider how long it takes to

Table 2.1 Annual Time Available in Physical Education by Number of Days of Instruction Per Week for a 36-Week School Year

| DAYS OF INSTRUCTION PER WEEK | 1 | 2 | 3 | 4 | 5 |
|---|---|---|---|---|---|
| Total instruction days available per year | 36 | 72 | 108 | 144 | 180 |
| Minutes per class | 30 | 30 | 30 | 30 | 30 |
| Total time scheduled per year in minutes | 1,080 | 2,160 | 3,240 | 4,320 | 5,400 |
| Uncontrolled lost instruction time | 108 | 216 | 324 | 432 | 540 |
| Available instruction time per year in minutes | 972 | 1,944 | 2,916 | 3,888 | 4,860 |
| Available instruction time per year in hours | 16.2 | 32.4 | 48.6 | 64.8 | 81.0 |
| Actual learning time per year in hours assuming 50 percent active learning time | 8.1 | 16.2 | 24.3 | 32.3 | 40.5 |

Reprinted, by permission, from L.E. Kelly, 1989, "Instructional time: The overlooked factor in PE curriculum development," *Journal of Physical Education, Recreation and Dance* 60: 29-32.

Table 2.2 Method for Calculating Amount of Available Instruction Time and the Number of Objectives That Can Be Addressed

**A = Number of weeks of school per year: 36**

**B = Number of days of instruction per week: 2**

**C = Length of instruction period in minutes: 30**

**D = Instruction time available per year: 36 × 2 × 30 = 2,160 minutes**

**E = Adjustment for lost instruction days: 2,160) × .9 = 1,944 minutes**

**F = Estimated on-task time percentage: 50 percent (.5)**

**G = Actual instruction/learning time available: 1,944 × .5 = 972 minutes**

**H = Time converted from minutes to hours: 972 / 60 = 16.2 hours**

**I = Number of objectives to be taught in a given year: 25**

**J = Average time available to teach each objective: 16.2 / 25 = .65 hours or 39 minutes**

Reprinted, by permission, from L.E. Kelly, 1989, "Instructional time: The overlooked factor in PE curriculum development," *Journal of Physical Education, Recreation and Dance* 60: 29-32.

learn to hit a golf ball in a straight direction or stand on a pair of ice skates, it's obvious that we don't have much time—even if we were to teach only two skills a year.

## Teaching Environment

In addition to the limited amount of time, we also need to plan carefully because of the variables that influence our lessons. Class sizes, equipment, and facilities all dictate what can be taught successfully. So does the climate. Teachers in Florida and southern California can teach outside comfortably much of the year; in Anchorage the tennis courts used in warm weather become ice hockey rinks in cold weather.

Physical education class sizes of 50 or 60 are still all too common. Many teachers use cafeterias and multipurpose rooms during the winter months and on rainy days. Equipment for physical education has improved since the days when a teacher started the program with three red rubber playground balls that wouldn't hold air past lunch and two dozen wooden bats and softballs. All of these contextual factors require teachers to plan carefully and adjust lessons, depending on their environments. Fortunately, these limitations don't prevent teachers from developing quality programs of physical education, but developing quality programs does require creative and thoughtful planning.

## Pedagogical Content Knowledge

Our experience in and out of school also influences our need to plan. When we don't know something very well (dance or rhythms, for example), we need to spend a lot more time planning and developing the expertise to teach these activities to children effectively.

This teacher expertise is often referred to as "pedagogical content knowledge" (PCK) (McCaughtry & Rovegno, 2003). PCK includes knowing about teaching in general (pedagogical knowledge), knowing about the content in general (content knowledge), and knowing about students and how they learn, and then combining the three kinds of knowing into an integrated whole (McCaughtry & Rovegno, 2003). We all recognize such expert professionals when we see them at work: "She could teach a broomstick to polka!" This book focuses on the first of the three characteristics of PCK, the pedagogical knowledge. It explains and provides examples of some of the pedagogical tools used by expert teachers so that you can include them in your pedagogy tool box.

Some teachers enrich their content backgrounds through reading or using the Internet (see chapter 14). Others attend conferences and workshops. Some ask other teachers for help. In recent years teachers have started to exchange videos of successful lessons. Some districts also organize monthly sharing meetings that focus on a topic of interest to the teachers in the district.

The elementary school physical education teacher is expected to be an expert in virtually every subject taught in physical education—similar to what is expected of the classroom teacher. This means that we often need to find ways to learn about new activities or ones that were neglected in our teacher preparation programs so that we can offer children a complete and well-rounded program. This is also a part of planning.

## Children's Background

A fourth reason we need to plan carefully, in addition to gaining the content knowledge, is that not all children are alike. One fifth grade is different from another. Schools are different also. Should the skills of basketball be taught in an inner city where many of the children play basketball continually at recess, after school, and on weekends? Should the skills of soccer be taught in a suburban school where most of the children have opportunities to join a soccer team when they're five years old?

Obviously the yearly plan for a teacher whose children have daily PE will be different from that for a teacher whose children have physical education only twice a week. If the program is effective, when the children reach fourth or fifth grade, the children with daily PE will have different needs from those of their twice-a-week counterparts.

## Pro or Con?

Imagine that you teach in a community where basketball, soccer, or softball is popular. Would you devote a lot of time to those skills as a teacher or would you assume that the children can learn them outside of your program? Discuss your response with a friend or colleague. You probably won't have to search far to find someone who has a viewpoint different from yours.

## Follow-Up by Classroom Teachers

A fifth reason physical education teachers need to plan has to do with the classroom teachers in a school (Faucette & Hillidge, 1989; Cone, Werner, Cone, & Woods, 1998; Wolf & Dodd, 1993). Does the PE teacher have to write weekly plans for the classroom teachers to follow? Do classroom teachers actually follow them?

Some PE specialists work with classroom teachers who organize lessons designed to follow up the lesson taught on Tuesday, for example. Other classroom teachers view physical education as a "break" for both them and the children, and physical education times are considered as recess; thus children in their classes receive no instruction designed to reinforce the lessons taught by the PE teacher.

Obviously the school principal plays a pivotal role in the way physical education is taught by classroom teachers. When the PE specialist has effectively "educated" the principal, the classroom teachers are required to supplement the lessons of the specialist; when the principal neither understands nor values physical education for children, classroom teachers rarely reinforce the lessons taught by the PE teacher.

All of these factors (the time available, the teaching conditions, the pedagogical content knowledge of the teachers, the background of the children, and the support of the classroom teachers) suggest that, because conditions and situations are so different, the planning needs of each teacher are quite different. Planning is necessary, but it's not necessarily the most enjoyable part of teaching. Consequently, many teachers naturally tend to avoid planning.

# TENDENCIES TO AVOID PLANNING

Because the content of physical education is so enjoyable to children, it's relatively easy to avoid a lot of planning. Every PE teacher has a bag of tricks to pick from to provide 30 minutes of enjoyment. Because of this, teachers might avoid careful planning.

Another reason to avoid planning is that there is no universally agreed-upon purpose for physical education in elementary schools. Some teachers see physical fitness as the major purpose; others emphasize motor skill learning; some focus on cognitive understanding, learning lead-up games and sports, or learning to cooperate with others as the major purpose of a physical education program for children. There is no single recognized goal. In contrast, math or reading teachers seem to agree on a generally accepted and recognized purpose for their programs. The *National Standards for K-12 Physical Education* (NASPE, 2004) provide an excellent starting point for physical education teachers and program coordinators to reach a consensus on the most important goals of physical education for the youngsters in their schools or districts.

In addition to a historical lack of consensus about the goals of physical education, another reason some physical education teachers avoid planning has to do with the perceived value of physical education in a school. When a content area such as physical education, art, or music is undervalued, it's hard for teachers to remain convinced that their work is important (Graham, et al., 2002). When this is the case, it's harder to put the time and energy into planning a truly educational program.

Many administrators and parents do not understand educational physical education. As long as children appear happy and there are no serious injuries or complaints, they are delighted with the program. Thus little accountability is placed on the physical education teachers. This is in marked contrast to reading, for example, in which children are tested throughout the year and expected to improve their abilities.

# PERSONALIZED PLANNING

If all teaching situations were identical, there wouldn't be a need to plan individually. Teachers in a district could design a single plan and use it throughout the district. Because situations are different, however, planning should be personalized to match the needs and interests of the children at each school. It's easy to create "ideal" prepackaged plans; it's much harder to develop plans given the equipment, facilities, and scheduling and background limitations typical of children's physical education programs. Above all, planning must be realistic. If it is going to be of any value, it needs to be designed with a specific school in mind. We want to do so much for the children, but typically there isn't time to accomplish as much as we hope to.

Let me illustrate with an example. One state guide, since revised (table 2.3), suggested 25 objectives to be accomplished in third grade (Kelly, 1989). Based on this analysis, children in a twice-a-week program have about 40 minutes to learn each objective (table

Table 2.3 Number of Objectives Targeted for Instruction by Grade and Goal Area in the State of Virginia Standards of Learning for Physical Education

| GRADE | FIT | M/E | R/D | S/T/G | G/S | I/S | T/S | TOTAL |
|---|---|---|---|---|---|---|---|---|
| K | 3 | 8 | 3 | 5 | 4 | | | 23 |
| 1 | 3 | 7 | 3 | 4 | 6 | | | 23 |
| 2 | 4 | 3 | 4 | 7 | 6 | | | 24 |
| 3 | 4 | 3 | 3 | 9 | 6 | | | 25 |
| 4 | 5 | | 6 | 8 | 10 | | | 29 |
| 5 | 5 | | 5 | 5 | 9 | | | 24 |
| 6 | 4 | | 6 | 4 | 9 | | | 23 |
| 7 | 4 | | | 4 | 5 | 9 | | 22 |
| 8 | 2 | | | 4 | 5 | | 5 | 9 | 25 |
| 9 | 3 | | | 3 | 2 | | 7 | 4 | 19 |
| 10 | 3 | | | 3 | 3 | | 9 | 2 | 20 |
| 11-12 | 3 | | | 1 | 1 | | 4 | 2 | 11 |
| **Totals:** | **43** | **21** | **45** | **58** | **59** | **25** | **17** | **268** |

Fit = physical fitness; M/E = movement education; R/D = rhythm and dance; S/T/G = stunts, tumbling, and gymnastics; G/S = games and sports; I/S = individual sports; T/S = team sports.

Reprinted, by permission, from L.E. Kelly, 1989, "Instructional time: The overlooked factor in PE curriculum development," *Journal of Physical Education, Recreation and Dance* 60: 29-32.

2.2). Children in a program of daily physical education would have about 100 minutes to learn each objective. Although 100 minutes per objective is certainly better than 40 minutes, one wonders how realistic it is to think that children can learn to kick a ball efficiently or do a forward roll in that amount of time. Is there enough time for children to develop a functional understanding of the skill so they can use it successfully in a game or routine?

## *How Can I Do It All?*

Make a list of the motor skills and concepts you believe children should learn by the time they leave elementary school. How many are in your list? My list totals 18. In a twice-a-week program that means, using the figures from tables 2.1 and 2.2, I would have approximately 55 minutes to devote to each of the 18 skills. Of course, there are many other areas (fitness and wellness concepts, for example) I want to include as part of the program. Realistically, then, I have substantially fewer than 55 minutes to spend on each of the motor skills. As a teacher, should I be satisfied with simply exposing children to these skills? Or should I eliminate some of the skills? If so, which ones?

As specialists we have two ways to solve this perplexing problem. One way—perhaps the easier—is simply to expose children to the various motor skills, concepts, and experiences that comprise physical education. The second alternative—to me the harder one—is to teach only skills that can truly be learned in the short amount of time provided, which means making difficult decisions about what to exclude.

Beginning teachers are faced with the dilemma of not knowing how long it takes children to learn a particular concept or skill. Experienced teachers typically have a much better understanding of this, although there is hardly a consensus. This is one of the reasons that experienced teachers and beginning teachers typically use different formats for planning.

## How Long Will It Take to Learn?

Here is a list of skills and concepts we might typically see taught in an elementary school program of physical education. Estimate how many lessons (or minutes, if you prefer) you think it will take for children to learn the skill described. Compare your notes with those of other teachers; expect to find differences based on both the estimates of time and also your expectations for when a skill or concept has been learned (i.e., your operational definition of when children have truly acquired a skill or concept). If you are a beginning teacher, try to compare notes with an experienced teacher. How many lessons (minutes) do

- **second graders need to show the difference between symmetrical and asymmetrical balances;**
- **third graders need to be able to catch a gently thrown yarn or rag ball from a distance of 50 feet; and**
- **fifth graders need to be able to cooperate, without arguing or fighting, when they work in groups of six?**

# PLANNING FORMATS AND COMPONENTS

Now that I have described the need for planning and explained why one plan doesn't suit all teachers in all schools, I want to focus on formats for planning. If I had written this book 10 years ago, I would have suggested a single format for planning. Today I realize that teachers have many ways of planning. There simply isn't a single approach to planning that can be expected to be successful for every teacher. Both research (Byra & Coulon, 1994; Graham, Hopple, Manross, & Sitzman, 1993; Housner & Griffey, 1985; Placek, 1984) and my own experience tell me that we also plan differently as we gain in experience. In this section a discussion of ideas and thoughts about planning is divided into three sections: program (the entire five or six years), yearly, and daily planning.

## Program (Exit) Goals

What do you want your first graders to know (to be able to do) in five years when they move on to middle school? This is a hard question to answer. I know of few teachers who have these exit goals written out, although many of them are able to describe the goals in general terms. Increasingly I have come to realize that this is a valuable exercise, although answers might change for a variety of good reasons. Table 2.4 provides one example of how a district defined its goals for a program (Kelly, 1988).

Table 2.4 Sample Kindergarten Through Fifth Grade Program Plan

| | | K-5 PROGRAM PLAN | | | | | |
|---|---|---|---|---|---|---|---|
| | | K | 1 | 2 | 3 | 4 | 5 |
| Locomotor patterns | 1.1 Run | XX | | | | | |
| | 1.2 Gallop | XX | | | | | |
| | 1.3 Horizontal jump | | | XX | | | |
| | 1.4 Vertical jump | | | XX | | | |
| | 1.5 Hop (right-left) | | XX | | | | |
| | 1.6 Slide | | XX | | | | |
| | 1.7 Skip | | | | XX | | |
| | 1.8 Leap | | | | | XX | |
| Object control | 2.1 Underhand roll | XX | | | | | |
| | 2.2 Bounce/dribble | | | XX | | | |
| | 2.3 Underhand throw | | XX | | | | |
| | 2.4 Overhand throw | | | | | XX | |
| | 2.5 Kick | | | | XX | | |
| | 2.6 Punt | | | | | | XX |
| | 2.7 Two-hand sidearm strike (baseball) | | | | XX | | |
| | 2.8 Catch/field | | | | | | XX |
| | 2.9 Underhand strike (volleyball serve) | | | | XX | | |
| | 2.10 Chest pass (basketball) | | | XX | | | |
| | 2.11 Bounce pass (basketball) | | | | XX | | |
| Physical fitness | 3.1 Knowledge | | | | | | XX |
| | 3.2 Training concepts | | | | | | XX |
| | 3.3 Terminology | | | | | XX | |
| | 3.4 Leg strength | | | XX | | | |
| | 3.5 Flexibility | | | XX | | | |
| | 3.6 Abdominal strength | | | | XX | | |
| | 3.7 Endurance | | | | | XX | |
| | 3.8 Arm and shoulder strength | | | | | | XX |
| | 3.9 Agility | | | | | XX | |
| | 3.10 Speed | | | | | | XX |
| Social | 4.1 Self-discipline (control) | | XX | | | | |
| | 4.2 Cooperation | | XX | | | | |
| | 4.3 Good sportsmanship | | | | XX | | |
| | 4.4 Handling winning and losing | | | XX | | | |
| | 4.5 Respect equipment and property | XX | | | | | |
| Body management | 5.1 Nonlocomotor | XX | | | | | |
| | 5.2 Body awareness | XX | | | | | |
| | 5.3 Spatial awareness | XX | | | | | |
| | 5.4 Use of space | | | XX | | | |
| | 5.5 Quality of movement | | | XX | | | |
| | 5.6 Relation of body to other objects | | | | XX | | |
| | 5.7 Basic dance patterns | | | | | XX | |
| | 5.8 Forward roll | | | | | | XX |
| | 5.9 Rope jumping | | | | XX | | |
| Game and sport skills | 6.1 Follow directions | XX | | | | | |
| | 6.2 Knowledge of safety and rules | | XX | | | | |
| | 6.3 Member of team | | | | | XX | |
| | 6.4 Participate in games and sports | | | | | | XX |

XX indicates when the objective is to be mastered. This does not mean that the objective is only worked on during this year. Many objectives will be worked on during all the years preceding mastery and even after mastery has been achieved for retention.

Reprinted, by permission, from L.E. Kelly, 1988, "Curriculum design model," *Journal of Physical Education, Recreation and Dance* 59(6): 29.

## *Exit Goals*

List the five or six most important goals that you think students should have reached when they leave a program. Have all of the current fifth or sixth graders in a program accomplished them? Will your current first graders be able to do so? Are the goals realistic? Probably the most important time to measure a program's success is when children leave a program after five or six years. What can they do? How do they feel about physical activity? What do they know?

If we're not careful, our exit goals become lists of what we will cover in the program; they will not be statements of what we want children actually to learn. State or national physical education standards (NASPE, 2004) serve as a good resource for beginning to think about exit goals that children can accomplish by the time they leave your program.

Ideally, the long-term goals for a program are consistent with the goals of the middle (junior high) school and also the high school. This assumes that teachers representing K-12 meet from time to time and discuss the goals for the various grade levels. Unfortunately, this is rare in education. The elementary school program may or may not dovetail with the middle school program. This explains, at least in part, why middle and high school teachers often wonder aloud, "What do they teach in the elementary school?" An exchange day, when teachers move up or down to a different school for a day, has a way of quickly answering this question. "I didn't realize . . ." and "No wonder . . ." preface many of the comments teachers make after an exchange day.

Because the content of physical education is somewhat less understood than many of the other content areas taught in the schools, this communication between grade levels is especially important. It makes little sense, for example, for an elementary specialist to teach the rules for playing various sports when the students will spend several days learning them again in sixth or seventh grade. It also doesn't make much sense for students to be taught how to grip a bat or throw a ball in tenth grade when they have learned to do so in fourth grade.

# When Should _____ Be Taught?

With several other physical educators (ideally, elementary through secondary teachers), discuss these questions:

- **At what level (elementary, middle, or high school) should the rules for team sports be taught?**
- **What basic motor skills can children be expected to learn by the time they leave elementary school?**
- **At what level should a major emphasis be placed on learning the important concepts of physical fitness?**
- **Should folk and square dance be taught at the elementary, middle, or high school level? Should the same dances be taught, or different ones?**
- **Basketball dribbling lessons, at all levels, often begin with the basic cues about using the finger pads, looking over the ball, and so forth. By what grade should children have learned these refinements so it is no longer necessary to start with them?**

Obviously, as the discussion progresses, you will think of many more questions that will be helpful in establishing exit goals for all levels of physical education programs.

## Planning for the Year

It's hard to know what can be accomplished in five or six years. It's somewhat easier to figure out what can be achieved in a single year. Some teachers accomplish this task using a calendar. They list the days and weeks of the school year and then write in the topics for various days. Some teachers believe that children learn best when lessons are massed together in a series of lessons on the same topic (units—e.g., gymnastics or ball-handling units). Others believe that topics should be distributed throughout the year and organize their year around various themes (e.g., balancing, kicking, striking) (Graham, Holt/Hale, & Parker, 2007).

In either case, successful teachers make realistic assessments of what the children are going to learn that year. These types of plans also serve as a guide for the year's lessons. When this isn't done, there seems to be a tendency for teachers to plan the year more by how they feel on a given day than by a systematic plan that leads in a desired direction.

WELL, WE SPENT 30 WEEKS ON GAMES, SO NOW WE'LL HAVE TO TRY AND SQUEEZE DANCE AND GYMNASTICS INTO THE LAST TWO WEEKS OF THE YEAR.

The physical education teacher who doesn't stick to a plan for the year is no different from the history teacher who announces one day in April, "We need to cover the second half of the book in the final six weeks of the year." Time spent on unrelated topics or unfocused discussions in the beginning of the year detracts from the overall direction.

What I have written up to this point might suggest that effective teachers stick to a plan regardless of the progress made by the children. I don't think so. If children aren't grasping a concept, teachers spend more time on it than allotted on the yearly calendar. They readjust while remaining sensitive to the overall plan for the year, however, and attempt to stay on schedule if possible. In fact, some teachers even post the calendar for the year with the various units and themes listed so that children have an idea of what they will be learning and when. This has an added benefit. It avoids the ever-present question asked by children of virtually every teacher: "What are we going to do today?"

# How Many Days in a Row?

Refer to table 2.3 in this chapter. Look at the fourth-grade objectives in games and sports (G/S). As you might assume, the 10 objectives include skills such as throwing, catching, and volleying. Assume that you have a daily program of physical education and have approximately 81 hours for the year (table 2.1). These 10 objectives represent roughly 35 percent of the objectives for the year, about 28 hours (or roughly 56 lessons). Use a calendar and decide how you will organize the G/S objectives for the year.

- **Will you spend 56 lessons in a row (roughly 11 weeks) on these objectives?**
- **Will you spread them out in eight consecutive lessons at seven different times during the year, separated, for example, by sequences focused on fitness and dance?**
- **Or do you think it might be more effective to teach four lessons in a row focused on the G/S skill objectives at 14 times during the year?**

Obviously there is no single right answer to the question of how to sequence content for the year. However, we know that it makes sense to distribute lessons on various topics throughout the year rather than massing them together in relatively long units (Schmidt, 1991). This allows a teacher to review important ideas to promote retention and understanding. When this isn't done, children seem to forget from one year to the next key concepts that were emphasized 10 or 11 months earlier. For example, when children are reminded three or four times a year, several months apart, to turn their side toward the target when striking with a racket, the potential for remembering that important cue is far higher than if they heard it for one week in October and then not again until the next fall (Graham, Holt/Hale, & Parker, 2007).

In concluding this section, it is important, as with the five- or six-year goals, that the yearly plan be realistic if it is going to be of any value. For example, I have seen lists of motor skills that children were going to learn (not simply do) in a twice-a-week program. My hunch is that these lists must have been written to appease a superintendent or coordinator or state department because they were virtually impossible to accomplish—even for a "super teacher." There was just not enough time in the year for the teacher to do anything but expose children to these skills because there were so many. In that sense the yearly plan is similar to a budget or a diet plan—easy to write, but quite hard to stick with when it's unrealistic.

## Daily Planning

As with yearly planning, there is no single, correct way to plan individual lessons. Some beginning teachers, for example, spend many hours writing out detailed plans. They consult notes and various texts and reflect on their own experiences to develop interesting lessons. Because elementary school physical education specialists typically teach 7 to 11 classes a day, they often group the classes (e.g., first and second, third and fourth). Some plan for each grade level; others use different clusters.

## *Where's the Perfect Reference?*

I remember how I planned my lessons during my first years of teaching. I would get to school early, start the coffee, and then go to my desk. I always wanted to find the "perfect" plans for the day in a single book. Before long, however, I had six or seven books spread over my desk as I tried to discover the best way to accomplish my objectives for that day. Interestingly, I still plan many of my lessons that way. No single book seems to have all the ideas I want for a single lesson—even ones I've coauthored!

Experienced teachers who have developed a schema for the content typically write less on paper than beginning teachers do because their planning takes the form of mental processing (Byra & Coulon, 1994; Graham, Hopple, Manross, & Sitzman, 1993). Nevertheless, because of their years of experience and insights, effective teachers seem to have an acute and obvious sense of the purpose of the lesson and its place within the overall plan for the year. It is also clear to the children and to the occasional observer that the lesson has a specific purpose.

Figures 2.1 and 2.2 are the lesson plans of a student teacher and an experienced teacher. The plans were written for a dribbling lesson taught to the same class of children. It's easy to see that the plan of the beginning teacher was far more detailed than that of the experienced teacher. At the beginning of his career, the experienced teacher also wrote extensive and detailed plans (Graham, Hopple, Manross, & Sitzman, 1993). With experience, however, he found it no longer necessary to outline the lessons in such detail.

## Lesson: Dribbling

I. Student objective

Control in general space while moving and dribbling a ball.

II. Teacher objective

Use student names (6)

III. Equipment: Jump ropes, red rubber playground balls

IV. Warm-up: Jump rope (blue handle)

Introduction: Today we are going to dribble while moving in general space.

Q Can you dribble beside your body?

Q What part of your fingers do you use?

Q Can you dribble with the other hand?

Q Can you dribble around one leg?

Q Can you dribble around the other leg?

Q Can you dribble in and out around both legs?

Q Can you move down to the ground and back up, keeping the ball going?

Q How many times can you go up and down without losing control of the ball?

Q Can you dribble beside your body and travel forward?

Q Can you dribble backward?

Q Can you dribble to the right?

Q Can you dribble to the left?

Q Can you dribble 5 times with one hand and switch to the other hand while moving forward?

Q Can you walk forward 5 steps, stop your feet, but keep the ball going for 5 bounces, then walk 5 more steps?

Q Can you do the same thing again (walk 5 steps, dribble 5 times) but after you dribble 5 times, switch hands?

Q What can you do with your legs to help control the ball while you move?

Q Can you walk forward and dribble 5 times with one hand and then 5 times with the other hand?

Q Can you walk backward 5 times dribbling with one hand then switch to the other hand?

Q Can you move to the right and dribble 5 times and then dribble 5 times to the left?

Q Can you dribble right and left again, but not go in a straight line?

V. Closure:

- What skill did you work on today?
- What part of your hand do you use?

**Figure 2.1**  Example of a lesson plan written by a beginning teacher focusing on teaching children to maintain control of a ball while dribbling and traveling.

Monday and Tuesday—Dribble: The kids are to warm up by jumping rope. Ask them to work on changing direction. The lesson focuses on dribbling and traveling. The refinement is to be in control of the ball while moving. I will begin with the children in personal space and move into general space if possible.

**Figure 2.2**  Example of a lesson plan written by an experienced teacher focusing on teaching children to maintain control of a ball while dribbling and traveling.

As with program planning and yearly planning, one of the challenges for a teacher is to determine what is realistic for a given amount of time. In my work with beginning teachers, for example, I find that they will list the purpose of a lesson for third graders as "learning to strike a ball repeatedly with a paddle." When I ask them if that is possible in 25 minutes, they quickly realize it's not. As we work through the process, however, I help them realize that learning to stand with one's side toward the target is an objective that can be accomplished in a single lesson.

## Learnable Pieces

Interestingly, my experience suggests that when we designate an achievable objective for a 20- or 30-minute lesson as a learnable piece ("side to the target"), we teach differently than when the objective is simply unrealistic for a particular lesson. We seem to improvise more to develop experiences that really help children learn to "stand with their side toward the target." When our objective is unrealistic, our lessons seem to consist of simply presenting a series of activities for children without modification or adaptation (Griffin, Chandler, & Sariscany, 1993).

When—if—we write objectives (i.e., realistically define a learnable piece for that time period), it is helpful to be as specific as possible. Otherwise our objectives are general and hard to evaluate. For example, the statement "The children will learn to volley a ball" is not only general but unrealistic for 30-minute lessons. "The children will learn to bend their knees as they receive and volley a ball" is a specific direction or focus for the teacher and, as we will see in subsequent chapters, becomes the focus of the entire lesson. Although some advocate using behavioral objectives as a guide for planning, my experience indicates that the exact format recommended in behavioral objectives might be unnecessary. Specificity is important, however. Here are some helpful questions to ask about the way you write your objectives:

▶ Is this truly a learnable piece for the 30 minutes I teach the children?

▶ Can I actually see if I have accomplished these goals when I observe my children?

▶ Could someone else see if I have accomplished these goals?

▶ Are my objectives helpful in letting me know how successful my program has been?

▶ Am I thinking about my objectives when I am actually teaching, or are the objectives just statements on paper?

▶ Does an assessment verify that the youngsters have actually grasped the concepts or critical components that are the learnable pieces for the lessons? (chapter 13).

## Additional Lesson Components

In addition to one or two objectives for the lesson, most plans include the following components:

▶ A format for indicating the topic of the lesson, the grade level, the date, and other information helpful for keeping track of which class has been taught which lesson. This is especially important for those who teach 20 or more different classes of children in the same week—especially when they are at different schools.

▶ An introduction to the lesson that is quickly organized and stimulating to the children. This "instant activity" may or may not be related to the remainder of the lesson (chapter 5).

▶ A brief introduction to the purpose of the lesson, which is intended to provoke interest in the lesson. This is often called a set induction or anticipatory set. This portion of the lesson frequently relates to other lessons that have already been taught (chapters 3 and 11 provide additional information about this component).

▶ A brief description (in many instances a list) of the tasks or activities that will be developed in that lesson (also see box 9.1 on page 133). This progression clearly relates to the objectives of the teacher. It is not simply a list of things to keep the children busy; rather, there is a clear progression of tasks that logically lead to the desired outcomes for the lesson. One of the reasons that beginning teachers, especially, list a number of tasks (figure 2.1) is so that they can make a lesson flow smoothly from one task to the next in a logical and orderly progression. When this isn't done, there is a tendency in the beginning to skip around and lose sight of the focus.

## *I Remember*

I remember watching a student teacher whose lesson was focused on jumping and landing. She decided to use hoops as a prop for the children to jump over. About halfway through the lesson, some of the children began picking up their hoops and tried to "hula" with them. Others quickly followed. The lesson ended with the teacher trying to show the children how to hula-hoop—hardly the focus she had started with 20 minutes before.

Teachers often write down the cues, prompts, refinements, or questions they will emphasize during the lesson. These are the secrets or shortcuts that help children learn the learnable piece more quickly and efficiently. Chapters 6, 8, 9, 10, and 11 include discussions of these segments of the lesson.

Many teachers use sketches or diagrams to outline the formations and arrangements they will use in the lesson. This is especially helpful early in the teaching career because it virtually forces the teacher to visualize how the transition from one activity to another will be made.

Finally, a closure is often included as a way of slowing down the end of the lesson and reminding children of the important features of the lesson (chapter 13). Often this is a question or two related to the objectives of the lesson. Some teachers also use this time to assign "PE homework."

These are some of the segments of daily lesson plans typically used by PE teachers. Some teachers write this information in planning books, others use three-ring binders, and some organize their plans on a computer. In time, teachers typically write less as they develop the schemata of various sequences of lessons. This economy comes from teaching 10 or 20 classes a week on the same topic. This isn't meant to suggest, however, that experienced teachers don't plan. They do. But the format they use is different.

## Fun

Before we conclude this chapter, it seems important to discuss fun as a purpose for physical education lessons. Clearly no one is against youngsters having fun in any class—math, science, or physical education (Griffin, Chandler, & Sariscsany, 1993). When teachers are able to make learning enjoyable, it seems better for both the children and the teacher. Because of the nature of the content we teach, it is not terribly difficult to make physical education fun—at least for many of the children in a class. Problems occur when fun becomes the sole purpose of physical education (Griffin, Chandler, & Sariscsany, 1993).

If physical education class is nothing more than a time to have fun, a break from the classroom, then it becomes increasingly difficult to justify its inclusion in a school curriculum. This is especially true as pressure increases for youngsters to pass standards in subjects like reading, social studies, and science. Few question the value and importance of physical education as expressed in the national standards (NASPE, 2004). Fun, however, is not a standard! It is a byproduct of an effective program that is developmentally appropriate for youngsters. When physical educators are forced to defend the existence of a physical education program to a school board, fun is never used as the sole reason why physical education should not be eliminated or reduced. Increasingly, administrators and parents want to be convinced that youngsters are learning in school—no matter what the subject. Physical education has valid and important goals for youngsters. When these goals are achieved in enjoyable ways, few would suggest it should be otherwise. When a program's goal is all fun, with no obvious learning taking place, most would suggest that physical education can be replaced by recess or play after school.

Unfortunately, many consider art, music, and physical education to be curricular frills—thus it is becoming increasingly important to be accountable for what youngsters are learning in those subjects (chapter 13). In contrast, subjects like reading and math are considered "core" subjects that every youngster needs to learn. Thus, the teacher who just creates fun reading or math classes, with little or no student learning, is also apt to find herself under scrutiny from parents and the principal. School is meant to be enjoyable, but learning is expected and standards are to be met, and teachers are increasingly being held accountable for doing so.

## SUMMARY

The interesting problem faced by physical education teachers is that there just isn't enough time to do all that we would like to do for children. In fact, many teachers who see their children only once or twice a week face a real dilemma: "What can I effectively teach in such a small amount of time?" This assumes, of course, that a teacher is truly focusing on children actually learning important concepts and skills.

If a teacher's program consists of simply teaching some fun games, neat stunts, and a few dances that children enjoy, then planning is far less difficult. In that case, it is simply a matter of choosing activities with little thought to progression and sequencing.

In fact, planning for this type of teaching can be done relatively quickly at the beginning of the year.

When a teacher is truly focusing on what and whether children are learning, however, planning is more involved. Lessons are carefully designed and sequenced to be certain they provide maximum opportunities for children to learn. Each lesson is based on the teacher's observations and reflections from previous lessons. What does this class need? Have they learned to change directions quickly yet? Are they placing their hands in the appropriate position? Do they understand the difference between symmetrical and asymmetrical shapes? How is Ms. Dean's third-grade class different from Ms. Patterson's third-grade class?

When teachers are truly focusing on helping children to learn, planning is crucial. Without it, lessons become haphazard and random. The children have fun, but they don't learn as a result of a sequential progression that the teacher designs to help them learn. Without effective planning, a program can easily become simply a fun time for children, unfortunately, with little long-term benefit to the children.

# QUESTIONS FOR REFLECTION

1. What are the consequences of teachers not planning? Can you think of any examples from your past that might have been a consequence of either limited or superior planning?

2. Why do you think teachers tend to avoid planning? Do you think it has any connection to the universal distaste for homework?

3. In this chapter I used two analogies to planning: consulting maps before taking a trip and the music (notes) followed by a symphony orchestra. Create your own analogy to express the relation between planning and teaching.

4. Think about your elementary school. What contextual factors would a teacher have to consider in planning at that school? (For example, my elementary school had no grass, only blacktop.)

5. All teachers, beginning through advanced, have a tendency to describe their goals and objectives in general or overly optimistic terms. Why do you think this is true?

6. The objectives for each lesson are theoretically tied to a yearly plan, which is based on a number of exit goals. Describe one exit goal you think is important for children to have accomplished by the time they leave elementary school. How would this goal be reflected differently in each yearly plan? In actual lesson plans?

7. The chapter describes "learnable pieces" as parts of goals or objectives that can be learned in a single lesson. Pick a motor skill, such as batting, dribbling, or rolling. Describe, specifically, five learnable pieces for that skill that youngsters might realistically learn in three 30-minute lessons.

8. The final section in the chapter describes features that many teachers incorporate into their lesson plans. Why do you think I didn't provide a single guide for you to follow? Figures 2.1 and 2.2 provide some interesting insights for your reflection.

9. If you are a beginning teacher, reflect on the features typically contained in lesson plans and develop a format that you think will be helpful. If you are an experienced teacher, consider the way you plan now. Which features do you typically include and exclude? Why?

# REFERENCES

Byra, M., & Coulon, S.C. (1994). The effect of planning on the instructional behaviors of preservice teachers. *Journal of Teaching in Physical Education, 13,* 123–139.

Cone, T.P., Werner, P.H., Cone, S.L., & Woods, A. (1998). *Interdisciplinary teaching through physical education.* Champaign, IL: Human Kinetics.

Coulon, S.C., & Reif, G. (1994). The effect of physical education curriculum development on the instructional behaviors of classroom teachers. *The Physical Educator,* (Early Winter 1994), 179–187.

Faucette, N., & Hillidge, S.B. (1989). Research findings—PE specialists and classroom teachers. *Journal of Physical Education, Recreation and Dance, 60*(7), 51–54.

Graham, G., Holt/Hale, S., & Parker, M. (2007). *Children moving.* 7th ed. New York: McGraw Hill.

Graham, G., Hopple, C., Manross, M., & Sitzman, T. (1993). Novice and expert children's physical education teachers: Insights into their situational decision-making. *Journal of Teaching in Physical Education, 12,* 197–217.

Graham, G., Wilkins, J.M., Westfall, S., Parker, S., Fraser, R., & Tembo, M. (2002). The effects of high-stakes testing on elementary school art, music and physical education. *Journal of Physical Education, Recreation and Dance, 73*(8), 51–54.

Griffin, L.L., Chandler, T.J.L., & Sariscany, M.J. (1993). What does "fun" mean in physical education? *Journal of Physical Education, Recreation and Dance, 64*(9), 63–66.

Hastie, P.A., & Vlaisavljevic, N.C. (1999). The relationship between subject-matter expertise and accountability in instructional tasks. *Journal of Teaching in Physical Education, 19,* 22–33.

Housner, L., & Griffey, D. (1985). Teacher cognition: Differences in planning and interactive decision making between experienced and inexperienced teachers. *Research Quarterly for Exercise and Sport, 56,* 45–53.

Kelly, L.E. (1988). Curriculum design model. *Journal of Physical Education, Recreation and Dance, 59*(6), 26–32.

Kelly, L.E. (1989). Instructional time: The overlooked factor in PE curriculum development. *Journal of Physical Education, Recreation and Dance, 60,* 29–32.

Locke, L.F. (1975, Spring). *The ecology of the gymnasium: What the tourist never sees.* Paper presented at the meeting of the Southern Association for Physical Education for College Women, Gatlinburg, TN.

McCaughtry, N., & Rovegno, I. (2003). Development of pedagogical content knowledge: Moving from blaming students to predicting skillfulness, recognizing motor development, and understanding emotion. *Journal of Teaching in Physical Education, 22,* 355–368.

National Association for Sport and Physical Education (NASPE). (2004). *Moving into the future: National standards for physical education.* 2nd ed. Reston, VA: NASPE.

Petersen, S., & Cruz, L. (2004). What did we learn today? The importance of instructional alignment. *Strategies,* May/June, 33–36.

Placek, J. (1984). A multicase study of teacher planning in physical education. *Journal of Teaching in Physical Education, 4,* 39–49.

Schmidt, R.A. (1991). *Motor learning and performance.* Champaign, IL: Human Kinetics.

Wolf, D.W., & Dodd, D.K. (1993). Comparison of the impact on fifth grade students of physical education programs taught by specialist vs. non-specialist. *Illinois Journal* (Spring 1993), 53–57.

# Chapter 3

# Creating a Positive Learning Environment

*I was teaching a volleying lesson and had just finished showing my students how to use their forearms (for the bump). One of my second-grade girls interrupted and said, "I don't have four arms, I only have two." Needless to say, I was speechless.*

**Crystal Coffman, Ladd Elementary, Waynesboro, Virginia**
Reprinted with permission from PE Central (www.pecentral.org).

How do you prefer to teach? Are you loud and excitable? Or do you prefer an atmosphere that is relatively quiet and calm? Do you stop children by blowing a whistle, hollering, giving a hand signal, or beating on a drum? Are you loud when you talk to children, or do you talk in a conversational tone? Do you play music during your class? What are the characteristics of a pleasant physical education atmosphere that also encourages children to become involved in activity?

Obviously there is no single definition of a pleasant atmosphere. We all have our preferred approaches to working with children in a physical education setting. The significance of these questions, however, is that they are decisions made by the teacher, not the children. As teachers we decide the characteristics of the environment for which we have control—and then we teach the children to function within that environment.

The atmosphere we create is an important one. After all, this is our job! We spend many hours in schools, and it makes sense to make the atmosphere as pleasant as we possibly can—given the obvious limitations. An elementary school gymnasium or multi-purpose room is not a luxury hotel. There are many things teachers do, however, to build a pleasant, positive atmosphere. In this chapter we look at ways that teachers go about creating a positive environment for lessons that both the teacher and the children enjoy—and that encourages youngsters to want to come to physical education class.

## After reading and understanding this chapter, the teacher will be able to

▶ **analyze the concept of teacher expectancy and its importance in creating a pleasant atmosphere in physical education,**

▶ **describe teacher stereotypes of children and how they can be avoided,**

▶ **describe management protocols that teachers develop with children,**

▶ **relate the important difference between explaining and teaching management protocols, and**

▶ **describe the characteristics of teachers who create positive environments in physical education.**

Why place the chapter on creating the learning environment so early in the book? Most books that devote a chapter or section to this topic place it at the end or near the middle, not at the beginning. I did this for three reasons.

The first reason is that, especially for beginning teachers, the question "Will I be able to 'control' the children?" is very important. It's a genuine concern that deserves some attention. There's an honest fear that the children may run wild and never stop and listen—hardly a pleasant atmosphere in which to work every day. So why put off a discussion of how to achieve order in physical education classes when it is foremost in the minds of many novice teachers?

## Rachel's Fear

This excerpt is from Dolly Lambdin's dissertation, for which she interviewed elementary school teachers about their lives. Rachel describes a fear that most teachers have had at one time or another in their careers:

**I remember when we had double first grade classes. I sat down one time and I just looked at that long line of kids and I thought, if they got organized they could tie me up, take out all the equipment, have a wonderful time, because there were 60 of them. And there would not be anything I could do. (Lambdin, 1992, p. 13)**

The second reason is that teachers who design and implement effective and positive learning environments are successful because they begin to develop an environment for learning at the beginning of school. In fact, they start the process on the first day of the school year (Carter & Doyle, 1989; Fink & Siedentop, 1989). Recognizing this fact, it seemed logical, albeit unorthodox, to place this chapter near the start of the book—partly because it deals with frequently asked questions for which solutions require early and carefully planned and implemented strategies.

The third reason is the most important: If a teacher is unable to create a positive, effective learning environment, then most of what is written in the subsequent chapters of this book will be of little value. Youngsters won't listen to the teacher. They will bicker with one another and argue over equipment, who pushed whom in line, and whose turn it is. The teacher will find himself continually nagging the children to listen, stop playing with the equipment when he is talking, and keep their hands to themselves. What could be a positive physical education experience for both the teacher and the children will at best be unpleasant, and all too often negative. The best made plans will rarely work as intended—and thus all too many physical education classes will end up being frustrating and unpleasant for all involved.

# TEACHER EXPECTANCY

It is up to teachers to design and then build the atmosphere for their classes. Teachers, sometimes in conjunction with the children, decide how they want their classes to operate. Beginning teachers often find this attitude, known as teacher expectancy, difficult to develop (Martinek, 1983). There is a feeling that children "are a certain way" and that we have to adjust to the children—not true. Children can learn to stop, for example, when they see the teacher raise her hand or when they hear a hand clap. The type of signal doesn't really matter (as long as it can be heard or seen); what matters is that children learn to understand and follow the directions of the teacher. The teacher expects certain things of children—for example, not to push and shove—and then insists that they follow these rules in physical education class. Interestingly, the difficult part for many teachers is to learn to expect children to operate within the framework that the teacher wants to establish for the gymnasium or playground. Perhaps an example will help illustrate this point.

In church we expect people to behave a certain way. There are times when it's unacceptable to speak out loud. Many churches also have dress codes. We teach our children these protocols for operating in church as soon as we can. Gradually they learn to function in concert with the protocols of the church we attend. It doesn't happen simply because we tell them not to talk in church, for example. We have to work at it together—often over a period of weeks or even months.

In many ways the same is true in physical education classes. The protocols are obviously different, but the process of learning them takes time and practice. And just as parents insist that their children learn how to behave in church, the effective physical education teacher insists that his children behave in physical education. The challenge for the physical education teacher, however, is to simultaneously teach 25 or 30 children the protocols of behavior.

For most teachers, I suspect, this is one of the least enjoyable parts of teaching. There's not much satisfaction in teaching children how to put away equipment or choose a partner. Consequently, there is a temptation to devote less time to these protocols than might be necessary. Nevertheless, it's important, if we are going to be satisfied in our teaching, that children learn the customs of our gymnasium or playground. When they do, our teaching lives are far more enjoyable.

# TEACHER STEREOTYPES

Another extremely important characteristic that effective teachers develop is the avoidance of stereotypes. This characteristic is every bit as difficult to develop as teacher expectancy, often because it is more subtle and covert. As teachers we need to be aware of our personal stereotypes related to ethnic origins, socioeconomic statuses, genders, handicaps, religions, abilities, and physical appearances (Colvin, 1998; Hutchinson, 1995; Lyter-Mickleberg & Conner-Kuntz, 1995; Williamson, 1993).

Several stereotypes are associated with physical activity. Here are some of the more common ones:

> Boys are better throwers than girls.
>
> African Americans are fast runners.
>
> Girls like gymnastics, dance, and jumping rope.
>
> Boys like football.
>
> Youngsters with mental retardation are poorly coordinated.
>
> Hispanics are good soccer players.
>
> Boys don't mind being hollered at.
>
> Girls cry when you holler at them.

These are just a few of the stereotypes. As physical educators, we have to be especially sensitive to these stereotypes because they can quickly become self-fulfilling prophecies for youngsters if we promote them as inevitable truths (Williamson, 1993). How can we avoid these stereotypes?

An important first step is to become aware of our stereotypes. Do you agree with any of the listed statements? If so, you are stereotyping youngsters. Although any of these statements may be true for some youngsters, they are not true for all children. For example, some girls throw better than some boys; some boys like dance more than some girls; some African Americans are slow runners; some Hispanics are poor soccer players; some mentally retarded youngsters are excellent athletes. The important point is that we cannot accurately generalize to any race or gender or physical characteristic. If we do, we make it extremely difficult for youngsters, who might not fit the stereotype, to avoid the self-fulfilling prophecy. If, for example, gymnastics was offered only for girls, then a boy who had Olympic potential might never have the opportunity to uncover his talent.

In addition to our internal stereotypes, we also need to be sensitive to our behaviors as teachers. For example, do we interact differently with girls than with boys? Do we spend more time with attractive youngsters as compared to unattractive ones? Do we kid around more with athletes than with nonathletes? Do we provide more feedback to poorly skilled children? One good way to become aware of these enacted stereotypes can be revealed by videoing a class and then watching the video with another teacher, or a trusted friend, and asking them if they notice any obvious differences in the ways you interact with youngsters.

Finally, it is important to avoid the trap of thinking, *These are just kids. They don't notice!* Oh, but they do! And the covert messages you send as a physical educator are exceedingly important to youngsters at such an impressionable age as they make decisions about the sports and physical activities they will do for the rest of their lives. When physical educators send messages (usually inadvertently) that youngsters cannot do something because of race or gender or abilities, we might be cutting children off from a sport or physical activity in which they might excel as adults. What if a physical educator convinced Theresa Edwards, the two-time Olympic gold medalist and professional basketball player, that basketball was a boys' sport? What if a teacher was somehow able to convince Tiger Woods that golf was only for white kids? Physical education classes should be a positive place for learning about physical activities, and a teacher's attitudes—both expectancy and stereotypes—are vitally important parts of creating this positive environment.

# CREATING AN EMOTIONALLY SAFE ENVIRONMENT

Teacher expectancy and teacher stereotypes clearly affect the way we interact with youngsters. As we become sensitive to these attitudes, there are several things we can do to create supportive and emotionally positive physical education classes. Here are some guidelines related to creating an emotionally safe environment for children (Helion, 1996).

**1. People are not for hurting.** This refers to physical harm but also to behaviors such as name calling, belittling, intimidating, and making fun of others.

**2. Never use sarcasm.** A comment from a teacher like "nice throw" to a child who throws the ball well over the head of his partner is not only painful to the child who threw the ball but also signals to other youngsters that sarcasm is acceptable in that teacher's class.

**3. There are no stupid questions.** When we teach 8 to 10 classes a day we often hear the same question in every class. It is easy for us to lose patience as a teacher—but we need to remember that it is the first time this child has asked the question. We also need to develop a protocol so that youngsters are encouraged to ask questions, but that the question and answer session does not take away from "activity time," as can often happen with a class of young children who enjoy being recognized by the teacher.

**4. Physical education is for everyone.** Team games are often dominated by a few highly skilled youngsters. This is not physical education for every child, as the less-skilled often become competent bystanders rather than active participants in the game. Small-sided games with two to three children on a team are one way to heighten the chance that every child is an active participant (Graham et al., 1992).

**5. Walk your talk.** Children are keen observers. They learn from what they see us do—perhaps more than from what we say. Whether we want to be or not, we are role models for youngsters.

# DETERMINING MANAGEMENT PROTOCOLS FOR YOUR CLASSES

Technically, the word protocol refers to established forms or courtesies that have been predetermined and used, for example, in official dealings among heads of state. Most children's physical education classes that I see and teach are far from ceremonial or official, however. Nevertheless, there are predetermined ways we want the children to function in our classes. There are also courtesies we want the children to extend to us and to one another. These are really protocols or routines that we expect our children to be guided by in our classes. The summary of these protocols is expressed in the rules we post on the gym wall. Typically we have protocols for the following aspects of our classes: entering and leaving the playground or gym; starting and stopping at a signal from the teacher; gathering up equipment when the stop signal is given; getting out and putting away equipment; and selecting partners, teams, and groups.

**See Establishing Protocols**

The DVD that accompanies this text provides an explanation and example of one teacher's protocols.

## Entering and Leaving the Playground or Gym

Whenever possible, it's preferable to have the classroom teacher bring the children to physical education. This allows the PE teacher to teach longer classes—when we have only a few minutes, every one is important. In the beginning of the year, however, many teachers prefer to go to the room and talk with the children about the protocols for entering and leaving the gym as well as the signals for stopping and starting. (I prefer the classroom teacher to be present on the first day of class when I explain the protocols to the children so that she understands my expectations for the youngsters.)

Most principals insist that children walk to and from physical education in quiet, orderly formations—typically in lines. In schools in which it is the PE teacher's responsibility to bring the children from the classroom, it is important to practice the protocol for walking to and from physical education. Because children are often excited about our classes, this can be somewhat problematic because they are in a hurry to get to us and eager to begin.

What seems to work best is to have children actually practice moving from the classroom to the playground in a quiet and orderly manner. In fact, this is an important part of the first day's lesson. Once children get to the playground, they are expected to do one of several things. For example, some teachers have children line up in squads; some have them sit quietly on a circle or line; some write directions on a white board or posterboard telling children what to do that day. Regardless of the way we begin the class, that routine needs to be practiced. In a few cases this means that the children will have to return to their classroom—because they ran noisily through the hallways—so that they can practice the routine again. The important point for the children to realize is that this is a protocol: It's the routine used at that school for getting to and from the gym. It's not just a nice idea. It's a routine to be followed (even if it means returning to the room several times) every time they come to physical education class throughout the year.

## How Children Define Walking

Children have interesting definitions of walking. For many it means that as long as you don't bend your knees it's acceptable to travel as fast as you can and have it still be considered walking. We can see those children—stiff upper bodies, head erect, wildly swinging arms, rushing to be first—who, when reprimanded, reply in unison, "We were walking!" Perhaps we shouldn't define the mode of traveling, but rather the speed: If you get to the gym in 45 seconds or less, you will be given a speeding ticket. The penalty is to return to the classroom and try again.

## Starting and Stopping Signals

Once children have entered the gym according to our protocol, we need to have stop and start signals. The type of signals we use doesn't really matter as long as the children can hear or see it. Inside, most teachers use their voices. Some use a hand clap or a beat on the drum. Others use music with a remote control to stop and start songs. A few teachers use a whistle, but, especially inside, many prefer to create a more pleasant, businesslike atmosphere as opposed to a loud and rowdy recess environment. For this reason the voice or hand clap seems to be preferred because it is less harsh and piercing than a whistle, and the children need to keep their talking to a level that permits the teacher to be heard.

As with entering and leaving the gym, stops and starts also need to be practiced. It's reasonable to expect all children to be stopped two or three seconds after the signal is given. And the signal is given once, not four or five times.

## Teaching Stopping and Starting

Several activities are excellent for helping children learn to listen while they move. "Numbers" is one example. Children are asked to walk, hop, or skip in a defined area. When the teacher calls out a number, children quickly form groups totaling that number. For example, four children group up when the teacher says, "Four." The key is for the teacher to say, rather than shout, the number so that children have to listen carefully. A variation of this game is "Colors." The teacher calls out different colors marked on the floor or pavement. As quickly as they can, the children hop or skip to that color. Another version is "Body Parts." When the teacher calls out various body parts, the children touch those parts to the ground or floor (e.g., hands and feet, seat, back, elbows and knees).

The starting signal most teachers use is "Go." This is important because children typically don't want to stop and listen for long; once they think they understand the teacher's directions, they want to begin immediately. Often, however, the teacher has another item or two to add; thus, it's important for children to wait until the teacher is finished talking before they start. As with the stop signal, this needs to be practiced. When children start before the signal, they are called back and reminded to wait for the "go" signal. To keep children's attention, some teachers vary the word that means "go" to encourage children to listen carefully (e.g., "hopscotch," "Friday," "Nintendo").

Typically, the words "stop" or "freeze" signal the class to stop moving and be silent. Sometimes a drum is necessary, such as when children are dribbling balls and it is hard to hear the teacher over the noise made by the balls hitting the floor. Some teachers also use a whistle when they're outside.

Once the stop signal has been given, most teachers insist that the children listen, without talking, to the teacher and to other children who might be responding to a question by the teacher, for example. This needs to be practiced. Probably the most frequently used approach to practicing listening is for the teacher to start over if she thinks the children are inattentive and to repeat the comments. Another tactic that helps children listen more effectively is for the teacher to practice talking as briefly as possible without repeating comments (chapter 6). This takes time to learn, but it does help children listen more intently. When a teacher falls into the trap of repeating comments two or three times, it's no wonder children don't bother to listen to every word. My experience suggests that teachers probably talk far more than is necessary for children to understand directions, especially when a demonstration accompanies the instructions.

# What Do Children Hear?

In recent years an increasing number of children in our schools do not speak English as their native language. As an observer I am always fascinated to see how quickly they are able to follow the teacher's directions even though they were unable to understand what the teacher said. I also see this with children who talk the entire time the teacher is talking, yet are able to begin a task quickly. Obviously these children have learned to rely on observing their peers and not on listening to the teacher talk.

# Equipment Protocols

Often instructions are related to equipment used in a lesson. There are typically three protocols to be established in relation to equipment: how to get it out, what to do with it when the teacher is talking, and how to put it away.

## Getting the Equipment

As always, the children can't wait to get started, so all 25 want to rush up and get their equipment so they can begin. Teachers typically use two approaches to distribute equipment quickly and efficiently. One—the quicker way—is to spread equipment throughout the area in small piles. This prevents the overcrowding that results when everyone in the class tries to get a ball from the same basket at the same time.

Another approach is to call on a few children at a time to get their equipment. Some teachers will tap children on the shoulder as a signal to get their equipment. Sometimes teachers will call out birth months; color of shirts, hair, or eyes; or type of shoes to signal different groups to get their equipment.

Once children get the equipment, they need to know what to do with it. Some teachers ask children to get equipment and then hold on to it. Many teachers find it more effective to provide a task for children to begin working on once they get their equipment (e.g., "After you get your hoop, find a self-space and warm up by jumping over your hoop."). I find it seems particularly difficult for children to stand still and hold a ball; it's as if they were given a chocolate ice cream cone and asked to hold on to it without taking a lick until everyone in the class has a cone.

# I Want the Blue One . . .

Distributing equipment is easier when types and colors of equipment are either identical or very different. When all balls but two are yellow, some children will compete to get one of the two differently colored balls. The same is true for ropes, hoops, and so on. For this reason many teachers try to purchase equipment of either the same color or a variety of colors. To an adult this seems like a trivial matter, but it's not to children.

## Holding on to Equipment

The difficulty of holding a ball without playing with it is one of the reasons that many teachers have a protocol for what needs to be done with equipment after the stop signal is given. Some teachers require children to place the ball immediately on the ground. Others require them to hold the ball next to their belly buttons. When teachers fail to teach this protocol to children, it is inevitable that teachers will constantly be repeating, "Remember not to play with the ball when I'm talking."

# Keeping the Air in Balls

I used to think that it makes sense for children to sit on their ball when the teacher is talking. Sitting on the ball is comfortable and keeps the ball out of the way. Early on, however, I was told that sitting on a ball causes it to lose air quickly. Since then I have always taught my classes not to sit on a ball. I wonder, though, if balls really do lose air more quickly when they are sat on. I wonder, too, if it is excessively harmful for volleyballs to be dribbled or kicked. I have learned that pulling a patch from a ball is fascinating to children; unfortunately, patch pulling results in flat balls. So, too, does plucking foam balls. These are two more good reasons for requiring children to put a ball down or hold it a certain way when instructions are given—and for making instructions as brief as possible.

## Putting Equipment Away

Children can't wait to get equipment, and once they get it, they don't want to put it away. This, too, needs to be practiced.

Some teachers use the same technique as for getting equipment—it's done in groups or individually. Others prefer to have children simultaneously replace the equipment where they got it. One of the greatest temptations, of course, is to throw a ball from 30 feet away and try to land it in the equipment cart. This is why the technique of placing, not throwing, equipment is taught. One technique that some teachers use is to ask one or two children to show the remainder of the class how the equipment is to be placed, not thrown, when putting it away. As with the other protocols discussed in this section, this protocol is taught—and practiced until learned—at the beginning of the school year.

## Protocols for Selecting Partners, Teams, and Groups

Throughout the year we are constantly asking children to work with a partner or in a group. This is an especially important time to be careful not to damage a child's self-concept. In the old days we used to assign captains to pick teams. Today there are far too many adults who suffered through the emotional pain of being picked last class after class and who continue to be against physical education, largely because of the embarrassment of repeatedly being chosen last (NASPE, 2008).

Fortunately we know better today. One of the techniques that many teachers use is simply to ask children to find a partner or form a group of five, for example. The advantage of this approach is that it is relatively quick, and children tend to select partners or groups of about the same ability level. The game of "Numbers" can also be used as a quick way to form groups. Call out a number and, as quickly as possible, children gather into groups made up of that number. As the game progresses, and you call out various numbers, it is fun to call out, "One," and watch children scramble to find others until they realize that for this number they don't need to find a partner or a group. The last number you call identifies the number of children you would like in a group. So, if your task needs children in groups of three, you would call out, "Three," and they would be ready to go once you explain the task. Whenever you play numbers with children, you (the teacher) always represent "lost and found." When a child doesn't have a partner or group, instruct the student to quickly come to you and then you can help the child find a partner or group. There are times when teachers will want to form groups or teams themselves to accomplish a specific purpose.

# Boys Do This, Girls Do That

Some teachers use gender as a way to group children—"the boys here, the girls there." This tends to perpetuate the boy–girl stereotype emphasizing differences rather than similarities. It also seems to discourage the idea of boys and girls cooperating and working together, especially in the upper grades. For this reason many teachers discourage grouping children by gender. It has always struck me as interesting that fifth-grade boys and girls, for example, will work together on a project in the classroom but somehow expect not to work together on the playground. I hope that, in a few years, grouping by gender will be as rare as captains picking teams.

There are many ways to organize children into groups. The protocol that children need to practice is how to do this quickly and without hurting the feelings of others. Many teachers emphasize that it's not OK to say no to classmates when they ask you to be their partner or in their group. As with every protocol, however, there are exceptions. I am reminded of the few children we teach who, for whatever reason, are very difficult to work with as partners or in a group. For these children, exceptions need to be made because it is unfair for them to continually ask the same child to be their partner. This is the art of teaching: How do we take care of the children's feelings and still remain fair to all children involved?

# Shuffling the Deck

Lambdin (1989) has developed a variety of ways to organize and group children by using a deck of playing cards. As they enter the gym, children are each given a card and asked to memorize it. Then, to form partners, she asks them to find a partner who

- **has the same color and number;**
- **has the same number;**
- **has the same color;**
- **has the same suit;**
- **has the same suit and pairs 1 and 2, 3 and 4, 5 and 6; or**
- **has an even number if their number is even, odd if their number is odd.**

In addition, she has devised ways to organize a class into two or four groups based on the cards the students were given at the beginning of class (table 3.1).

Table 3.1 Shuffling the Deck

| FOUR GROUPS | TWO GROUPS |
| --- | --- |
| Clubs, spades, diamonds, hearts | Reds and blacks |
| Even black, odd black, even red, odd red | Odd and even numbers |
| Black 1-3, red 1-3, black 4-6, red 4-6 | Clubs and hearts and diamonds with spades |
| | Ace-3 and 4-6 |

Reprinted, by permission, from D. Lambdin, 1989, "Shuffling the deck: A flexible system of classroom organization," *Journal of Physical Education, Recreation and Dance* 60(3): 25-28.

## Other Protocols

These are some of the protocols that children's physical education teachers regularly use in their programs. It goes without saying that there are others that I haven't discussed—as well as variations in the way teachers implement the ones I have described (Bell, 1998; Todorovich & Curtner-Smith, 1998). Some other important protocols include what the children do

▶ during a fire drill or a tornado drill,

▶ when an accident or injury occurs during class,

▶ about drinking water during physical education class,

▶ when they need to go to the bathroom during class, or

▶ when they bring valuables to class, such as jewelry or money.

In addition to these examples, there are even more protocols that a teacher must be aware of and which will no doubt be needed during a school year. Good teachers prepare for them in advance. For example, the worst time to teach children how to react if a child is injured and bleeding is when an accident occurs (Almquist, 2001). If the protocol is taught and practiced ahead of time, children will understand how to summon assistance and what the teacher needs to do. But, as with any of the protocols mentioned previously, these situations will need to be practiced if they are going to be remembered and used appropriately.

## Decision to Practice Protocols

One of the most important decisions a teacher makes, once the protocols have been thought through, is to spend time practicing them. This is especially difficult in children's physical education because the time is so limited, yet this is exactly why the protocols need to be rehearsed—to save time. When protocols aren't learned, an inordinate amount of time is wasted over the course of a year.

The research on teaching physical education is very clear on this topic; unfortunately, children in physical education classes spend more time listening, managing, and waiting than they do in purposeful physical activity. In fact, it's common for children to spend less than one-third of a class moving. When children learn the behavior protocols at the beginning, more time can be devoted to the content of physical education the rest of the year.

## TEACHING BEHAVIOR PROTOCOLS

Deciding on the management protocols to use in one's classes is a relatively easy task. The challenging part is to teach these protocols to the children.

As with any teaching process, there is no single approach that works for all teachers. Teachers who create pleasant atmospheres seem to display certain attributes as they work on building the environment for children. Teachers who effectively teach the behavior protocols often display two characteristics. They are firm but warm while displaying a high degree of "critical demandingness." They also post their rules for children to see and often discuss them so that children feel a certain degree of ownership.

# Firm but Warm

At one time we thought successful teachers threatened children: that is, that they scared them into being good. Today we know better (Doyle, 1986; Fernandez-Balboa, 1990; Kounin, 1970). Successful teachers exhibit a certain degree of firmness: They mean what they say. At the same time, however, they are warm and caring toward the children. They don't want to frighten the children, but they want the children to know they mean business. Children quickly learn to distinguish when a teacher means what he says and when he doesn't. Successful teachers mean what they say, and they exhibit it by not allowing the children to get away with not following the protocols. They don't get excited or hysterical or threaten children, however. In calm, reassuring, firm ways they simply communicate the message that things are going to be done a certain way and that not much else is going to happen until the protocols are learned. This is one of those skills used by effective teachers that is difficult to put into words, yet if we watched 10 teachers we would quickly be able to identify those teachers who were firm but warm.

# Critical Demandingness

We would also be able to quickly recognize critical demandingness when we saw it. In many ways these two teaching skills overlap, yet they are different. The significant aspect of this skill is that the teachers have a built-in knowledge of how they expect children to follow the protocols, and they insist that the protocols be followed. In other words, they know how they want children to enter the gym. When children enter that way, the lesson proceeds as planned. When children don't follow the protocol for entering the gym, the teacher doesn't accept their behavior. She insists (demands) that they go back and enter the gym according to the way they had practiced earlier.

This is especially difficult because, typically, we as teachers want to get on with the lesson we have planned. It's hard for us to spend time having children go back and reenter the gym. In the long run, however, teachers who are critically demanding spend less time on these distracting events than those who don't spend the time at the beginning of the year. One advantage for the children who have a critically demanding teacher is that they know exactly what to expect. The teacher is consistent, day after day.

## Rules—Clear, Positive, Posted

Posted rules also help with consistency. Rules are essentially brief reminders of the behavior protocols. Most teachers list five or six rules, state them in positive ways, and post them prominently. Simply writing and posting them, however, is no guarantee they will be followed. They must be practiced.

## *RESPECT Rules*

At Garrison-Jones Elementary School in Palm-Harbor, Florida, the physical education rules spell out **RESPECT** (Hart, 1997; Moone, 1997) to remind children of the protocols for their classes:

**R**ecognition gained properly by raising your hand, listening to the teacher, and following directions.

**E**quipment used on teacher's signal. The equipment is for you; treat it carefully.

**S**tay on task to have a safe and positive class.

**P**ractice skills, as best you can, to become skillful movers.

**E**ncourage each other to do your best and support each other with positive statements.

**C**onsiderate of others' feelings through good sportspersonship.

**T**ogether we will learn and become our best.

One reason for posting the rules, in addition to serving as reminders, is their benefit for children new to the school. This allows the teacher to briefly review the behavior protocols with these children. In recent years, with the easy availability of videos, some teachers are beginning to video classes of children following the various behavior protocols that demonstrate the rules. This video can then be made available to new students for viewing so that they can see exactly what is expected of them in physical education class.

In certain parts of the United States where teachers are continually threatened by malpractice lawsuits, it is suggested that teachers make a video illustrating the behavior protocols. They should then ensure that every new child views the video before participating in physical education. In extreme instances, teachers may actually quiz children (in writing or orally) or ask them to sign a copy of the rules, indicating that they have viewed the video.

Although these suggestions might seem extreme to some, others who have been involved in malpractice lawsuits will quickly recognize the potential benefit to be derived from this procedure. This is especially important for those who teach in schools with high rates of student turnover. And, in fact, this is an effective approach for teaching new children the protocols of behavior that will save time in the long run.

Other teachers send letters home to parents at the beginning of the school year outlining policies on dress for physical education (especially footwear), medical notes, and what the children will be learning in the coming year. These letters also typically provide information about contacting the physical educator if questions arise about classes, policies, or other issues (Hopple, 1998).

## Developing Ownership

We know that the rules (behavior protocols) will be followed more closely when children, and parents for that matter, understand why they are necessary and when children develop a certain sense of ownership for them. For this reason many teachers, as part of actually practicing the rules, include discussions with children to help them understand the importance of rules. It's interesting to make a video of children who are intentionally not following the protocols in order to illustrate what happens when the rules are not followed. (You will have no problem recruiting a class who would be thrilled to help you make a videotape demonstrating all of the ways *not* to behave in the gym!) The videotape then becomes an excellent resource for involving children in discussions about why it's important to have and follow selected management protocols.

In addition to sharing the rules with the children, it's also a good practice to provide the principal and classroom teachers with a copy of the rules. This is especially true in schools that do not have a unified discipline plan (e.g., assertive discipline; see chapter 4). In some schools it might also be worthwhile to share the rules with parents, especially when the teacher plans on sending notes to the parents of children who do not follow the established behavior protocols. This will depend, however, on such factors as the philosophy of the school and the policies of the principal and the board of education.

# SUMMARY

Essentially, teachers who develop orderly learning environments with a minimum of disruptions to the system of work perform three different functions (Carter & Doyle, 1989):

▶ They design the system in advance by thinking about how they want the children to function in physical education; at the same time they envision the various management procedures that will be necessary to develop and maintain a smooth, flowing program of action.

▶ They communicate to children the various protocols that combine to form a management system. They do this as they would teach any topic in physical education; that is, they explain it, furnish examples, set up tasks for children to practice the protocols, and provide feedback about how well children are progressing. They begin this process on the first day of school.

▶ They monitor children to be certain that they are following the protocols within reasonable limits. This reduces the need for frequent reprimands because noticing the early signs of potential disruption helps avoid crises.

# QUESTIONS FOR REFLECTION

1. Think of yourself teaching children. Briefly describe five characteristics of a pleasant teaching environment that are important to you. Can you explain why?
2. Why is teacher expectancy such an important aspect of establishing a pleasant learning environment?
3. Why do you think the phrase *management protocols* was used rather than a term such as *rules* or *procedures*?
4. When you think of yourself teaching, which of the protocols is the easiest for you to develop? Which is the hardest? Do you know why?
5. Why is the distinction made between explaining the management protocols and teaching them?

6. You are no doubt aware of teachers who, intentionally or unintentionally, stereotype children. Briefly describe two examples of teachers stereotyping children from your experiences.

7. Reflect on teachers you have had in the past. Recall the teachers you had who were firm but warm or who were critically demanding. Do you think these are natural attributes, or can they be gradually learned?

# REFERENCES

Almquist, S. (2001). The emergency plan. *Strategies,14*(5), 30–32.

Bell, K. (1998). In the big inning. *Teaching Elementary Physical Education, 9*(4), 12–13.

Carter, K., & Doyle, W. (1989). Classroom research as a resource for the graduate preparation of teachers. In E. Woolfolk (Ed.), *Research perspectives on the graduate preparation of teachers,* 51–58. Englewood Cliffs, NJ: Prentice Hall.

Colvin, A.V. (1998). Learning is not a spectator sport: Strategies for teacher-student interaction. *Journal of Physical Education, Recreation and Dance, 69*(2), 61–63.

Doyle, W. (1986). Classroom organization and management. In M.C. Wittrock (Ed.), *Handbook of research on teaching.* 3rd ed., 392–431. New York: Macmillan.

Fernandez-Balboa, J.-M. (1990). Helping novice teachers handle discipline problems. *Journal of Physical Education, Recreation and Dance, 67*(2), 50–54.

Fink, J., & Siedentop, D. (1989). The development of routines, rules, and expectations at the start of the school year. The Effective Elementary Specialist Study [Monograph]. *Journal of Teaching in Physical Education, 8*(3), 198–212.

Graham, G., Casteneda, R., Hopple, C., Manross, M., & Sanders, S. (1992). *Developmentally appropriate physical education for children: A position statement of the Council on Physical Education for Children (COPEC).* Reston, VA: National Association for Sport and Physical Education.

Hart, C. (1997). Effective instruction with large classes. *Teaching Elementary Physical Education, 8*(6), 4–5, 17.

Helion, J.G. (1996). If we build it, they will come: Creating an emotionally safe physical education environment. *Journal of Physical Education, Recreation and Dance, 67*(6), 40–44.

Hopple, C.H. (1998). Happy new year! *Teaching Elementary Physical Education, 9*(4), 4–7.

Hutchinson, G.E. (1995). Gender-fair teaching in physical education. *Journal of Physical Education, Recreation and Dance, 66*(1), 42–47.

Kounin, J.S. (1970). *Discipline and group management in classrooms.* New York: Holt, Rinehart and Winston.

Lambdin, D. (1989). Shuffling the deck: A flexible system of classroom organization. *Journal of Physical Education, Recreation and Dance, 60*(3), 25–28.

Lambdin, D. (1992). *The interaction of elementary school teachers' lives and cares: An interview study of physical education specialists, other specialists and classroom teachers.* Unpublished doctoral dissertation, University of Massachusetts.

Lyter-Mickleberg, P., & Conner-Kuntz, F. (1995). How to stop stereotyping students. *Strategies, 8*(6), 6–21.

Martinek, T. (1983). Creating Golem and Goleta effects during physical education instruction: A social psychological perspective. In T. Templin and J. Olson (Eds.), *Teaching in physical education,* 59–70. Champaign, IL: Human Kinetics.

Moone, T. (1997). Teaching students with respect. *Teaching Elementary Physical Education, 8*(5), 16–18.

National Association for Sport and Physical Education. (2008). *Appropriate practices for elementary physical education.* Reston, VA: AAHPERD.

Todorovich, J., & Curtner-Smith, M. (1998). Creating a positive learning environment in middle school physical education. *Teaching Elementary Physical Education, 9*(4), 10–11.

Williamson, K.E. (1993). Is your inequity showing? *Journal of Physical Education, Recreation and Dance, 4*(8), 15–23.

## Chapter 4

# Minimizing Off-Task Behavior and Discipline Problems

*On my kindergarteners' second day of class I decided it would be a good idea to teach them how to move and work in stations. I set out a handful of stations with brightly colored balls, hula hoops, and other manipulatives. As one of my students came in for class, his eyes got huge and he leaned over to whisper to me, "Oh, Mrs. Michaelis—I just love what you've done with your place!"*

**Kristen Michaelis, Pleasant Street Elementary, Norwalk, Ohio**
Reprinted with permission from PE Central (www.pecentral.org).

Wouldn't it be great if we could just teach? No children misbehaving, no children off task, every child eager to listen and learn. It would be, but that's a dream. Even teachers who develop the management protocols described in the previous chapter still have some children who misbehave. The reality of teaching is that there are always going to be a few children who, for whatever reason, are going to march to the beat of a different drummer. The purpose of this chapter is to describe and analyze some of the ways teachers prevent off-task behavior.

As part of the introduction to this chapter, I want to emphasize that the techniques described here are typically necessary for only a few children in a class. Most children try to please the teacher, follow the rules, and work hard at their tasks. This assumes, of course, that the tasks are appropriate for the skill level of the children and are modified at appropriate times in the lesson. Activities or tasks that are too easy, too hard, or too protracted invite off-task behavior by the children.

My experience suggests that when a class or child who is well-behaved most days becomes off task it is often my teaching that needs to be modified. Perhaps my activity was too hard or too easy, or perhaps something unique is going on in the classroom and the children are overexcited that day. Nevertheless, some children have a difficult time staying on task day in and day out. A recent study asked teachers to classify student misbehavior in physical education (Kulinna, Cothran, & Regualos, 2006). Some of the most common misbehaviors reported by teachers included talking, not sitting still, arguing, not paying attention, interrupting, not following directions, seeking attention, giggling, and laziness. As we well know, the tendency of these misbehaviors may be rooted in situations outside of school; nevertheless, we have the responsibility and the challenge of working with them in our classes.

## After reading and understanding this chapter, the teacher will be able to

▶  describe strategies that teachers use to minimize off-task behavior;

▶  describe the general concepts of two discipline systems used in schools today: Canter's Assertive Discipline and Hellison's Personal and Social Responsibility Model;

▶  analyze the role of parents, principals, and classroom teachers in the effective use of a discipline system; and

▶  describe the feelings and strategies of teachers during discipline confrontations.

# STRATEGIES FOR MINIMIZING OFF-TASK BEHAVIOR

Even teachers who effectively teach the behavior protocols presented in chapter 3 are still going to have incidences of off-task behavior. Therefore, a teacher needs strategies that can minimize the misbehavior of children. Unfortunately, they are just strategies, not guarantees. Some of them succeed with some children some of the time. I wish I knew foolproof strategies that would be successful for all teachers all of the time, but I don't; no one does. Good teachers seem to have a repertoire of strategies that they use—sometimes consciously and sometimes without really thinking about them. They include back-to-the-wall, proximity control, with-it-ness, selective ignoring, overlapping, learning names, and positive pinpointing.

## Back-to-the-Wall

One of the simplest strategies is referred to as back-to-the-wall. By standing on the outside of the boundaries (the wall in the gym or the edge of the playground), a teacher can better see what is going on in a class. When a teacher stands in the middle of a class, automatically about 50 percent of the children will be out of his sight; this means that he might not be able to see the off-task behavior until it has gone on for some time.

**See Back-to-the-Wall**
The DVD that accompanies this text has a brief description of back-to-the-wall followed by a teacher demonstrating the technique.

The ability to detect off-task behavior as soon as it begins appears to be a characteristic of successful teachers. Immediate detection seems to prevent the behavior from escalating. When the behaviors persist for several minutes, several children might become involved. Thus a relatively minor incident can escalate into a major incident, for example, as one child tries to wrestle a ball away from another child. This is known as the ripple effect (Kounin, 1970). When a teacher sees the beginning of such an incident, he can quickly prevent it from escalating because his targeting and timing are appropriate. He identifies the children correctly and quickly, thus preventing a situation from developing into a crisis.

## Proximity Control

One of the techniques the teacher may have used to prevent the ball-taking episode from escalating is proximity control—simply walking in the direction of the off-task child to let him know that she sees him and, by "the look," to let the child know he's off task.

Veteran teachers know what I mean by "the look." It's a certain way a teacher looks at a child to say, "You're off task; now get back to work." Obviously, however, a teacher needs to be close enough to the child so that the child can see the teacher's expressions.

Sometimes the look isn't even necessary. Simply standing by a group of children on the verge of becoming off task is often enough to let them know you see them and expect them to remain focused.

Proximity control implies that a teacher is moving around the gym. Early in our careers we have a tendency to stand in one place. Although standing in one place may be more comfortable for the teacher, it's not as effective. Virtually without exception, good teachers move about the classroom, the gym, and the playground.

## With-It-Ness

The strategies of back-to-the-wall and proximity control provide the impression to children that a teacher has with-it-ness—having eyes in the back of your head (Kounin, 1970). When he began his series of research studies on discipline, Kounin hypothesized that teachers who had classes that were well-behaved and consistently on task would be those who threatened children and, in fact, scared them into behaving. He discovered this wasn't true. The teachers who had the fewest discipline problems communicated to their classes in a calm and reassuring way that they knew what was going on in their classes, they knew the tricks, and students shouldn't even bother to try them. By keeping their backs to the walls and quickly targeting and timing children tending toward off-task behavior, they were effective in convincing children that indeed they were "with it."

## *With It and Without It*

Remembering my days in elementary school, I can recall a sixth-grade teacher who was particularly "with it." She was friendly and warm, yet from the first day we could tell that she wasn't about to let us get away with anything. It was uncanny how she could identify children who were "off-task types" and, with looks and proximity control, keep them from misbehaving much of that year. The next year, however, we had a teacher who was "without it"; the same class of children quickly escalated into a rowdy group who were continually yelled at and threatened, though without much success. I am sure we were difficult to teach that year. We were essentially the same children, but, among other things, the teachers possessed different degrees of with-it-ness.

## Selective Ignoring

Yesterday I watched a first-grade lesson focused on round, narrow, wide, and twisted shapes. At times the children were making shapes in their own space; at other times they were traveling around the gym in their shapes. Whenever the opportunity was given to travel, one of the children, Bryan, ran. My reaction and that of my college students who were also observing was to immediately want to stop Bryan from running. The teacher ignored him, however. As we watched, I realized that Bryan really wasn't bothering other children. In fact, they ignored him also. Another teacher might have considered Bryan's behavior off task; Bryan's teacher didn't. And, after watching the entire lesson, I think she was right. Bryan was one of those high-energy children—some might have labeled him hyperactive. He was doing what the teacher asked but at a fast speed. The teacher obviously saw him but chose to selectively ignore him. It was an effective strategy in that lesson.

Selective ignoring works with many classes because the children in the class have been helped to understand why a child looks or acts a certain way. The ability to understand children who behave in ways outside the "normal" pattern of behavior has been one of the major advantages of mainstreaming in schools. As I observe children in a class who are assigned to work with other youngsters who have special needs, I am always warmed by their ability to understand the situation and their genuine willingness to help. This understanding doesn't happen automatically, however. Good teachers intentionally teach their classes to understand and work with these special children.

## *Nick's Insight*

When my oldest son, Nick, was in fourth grade, I remember talking to him about some of his classmates after I had observed his class. I remember commenting on one boy who was off task constantly and obviously annoying the teacher. I commented to Nick that the boy who was off task seemed to be a distraction to the class and a troublemaker. I expected Nick to agree. He surprised me, however, by providing me with one of those glimpses into how children view the world when he said, "Dad, it's not all his fault. The teacher doesn't understand him. He's really a good guy if you give him a chance. She never really gave him one." I try to remember Nick's insight when a child misbehaves in one of my classes.

## Overlapping

Overlapping is more of a teacher skill that is learned with practice than a strategy that can be easily learned, as is back-to-the-wall. It's the ability to focus on several things that are happening simultaneously and still maintain an intended direction.

Teachers are continually required to deal simultaneously with several children or situations. For example, the teacher nods his head "yes" at the child who has to go to the bathroom; smiles at the child who says, "Watch me"; puts his hand on the shoulder of the child who wants to talk to the teacher, signaling "wait a second"; and continues to observe the whole class as he determines whether to change the task or continue with it for several more minutes. Locke's vignette in chapter 1 is another illustration of how teachers need to develop the ability to overlap.

Overlapping is a pedagogical skill learned through experience. It's a critical skill to have because when we work with 30 or so children there are times when we must overlap if we don't want a lesson to come to a complete stop. Obviously, by establishing routines and protocols we try to minimize the need for overlapping, yet there are times when it is needed.

## Learning Names

Overlapping is a difficult technique to acquire; learning the names of the children is also difficult, but it is possible even for those teachers who have 600 or so children. One of the frustrating aspects of teaching is attempting to get the attention of a child whose name we don't know. As we try to find out, we often halt the flow of the lesson as several children volunteer her name and then stop moving to watch what we have to say to her. When we know a youngster's name, we can often speak it across the gym to let the child know that we see her and offer praise or remind her to get on task.

Some teachers learn names with relative ease. For others it's a struggle. We have all heard of name-learning techniques (e.g., alliteration, using the name several times in conversation, having the children tell you their names when they enter and leave the gym, and taking photos of the children) (Williams, 1995). PE Central (www.pecentral.org) also includes a number of suggestions for learning students' names in the section titled "Tips for the Beginning Teacher." Increasingly, classroom teachers are making name tags for younger children who then wear them to PE until the teacher has time to learn their names. Learning names is even more challenging for teachers who work in schools that have transient populations. Half of the children they teach in September will be gone in May, replaced by a new group. I wish I could suggest a magical, instant solution to this challenge of learning several hundred names, but I can't. I do know, however, that it really helps to know children's names when trying to prevent off-task behavior.

## Positive Pinpointing

When teachers identify one or more children and point them out to the rest of the class as modeling the desired behavior or skill, we call it pinpointing. This is a commonly employed strategy in elementary schools. "I like how Verenda and Tommy are standing quietly" is one example of positive pinpointing. My experience suggests that this technique is more effective with younger children who want to please the teacher. It can be overused, however. Some children seem to ignore it because the teacher is constantly talking about

how well someone is doing something. As with any of these strategies, pinpointing can be effective depending on the children, the way the strategy is used, and the frequency of use. Chapter 6 explains how pinpointing is used when teaching motor skills.

Many of these strategies or techniques seem to be innate characteristics of successful teachers. They are never taught or even discussed, yet they're effectively used by many teachers. But not all teachers use them—especially in the beginning of their careers. It's common, for example, to see a beginning teacher anchored in the same location for a lesson, or fail to see a child misbehave because her back is turned to a child. As with so many of the skills discussed in this book, it's easy to write about them and far more challenging to actually use them when teaching. I hope, however, that both beginning and experienced teachers will reflect on the subtle orchestration of teaching skills and strategies and their value for minimizing off-task behavior. No matter how well we use these strategies, some children will simply refuse to do what we ask. When that happens they're not off task; they have become a discipline problem.

# DISCIPLINE PROBLEMS

All teachers have students with discipline problems. Some of us minimize the problems, however. What strategies do successful teachers use to minimize discipline problems?

To begin with, they spend the first few days of the school year establishing the routines and teaching the management protocols described in chapter 3; they insist that the children learn these routines. They also use many of the strategies previously mentioned for minimizing off-task behavior.

# DISCIPLINE SYSTEMS

In recent years, systems designed to minimize misbehavior have become popular. Canter's Assertive Discipline Model and Hellison's Personal and Social Responsibility Model represent two of the classic systems that have been adapted and adopted in education. These systems are based on the assumption that some children will misbehave and that teachers need ways to deal effectively with misbehavior for the sake of the children who are misbehaving, and also for the other children in the class.

These systems are designed to be taught to children from the beginning of the year and used as needed (Downing, 1996). This is in contrast to the teacher who hopes she doesn't have a child misbehave and, when she does, tries to invent a solution on the spot. As any educator will attest, teachers who can continually invent ways to successfully deter off-task behavior amidst all the goings-on in a class can be found only in the movies and on television (Kulinna, Cothran, & Regualos, 2006). The advantage of having a discipline system in place is that it provides teachers with a structure for making decisions related to discipline—rather than placing them in the unenviable situation of asking, "How can I get this child to stop talking, or interrupting, or not following directions when I have 29 others who need my attention?"

## Assertive Discipline

One of the most helpful trends in elementary schools across the United States has been the inception of schoolwide discipline plans. Assertive discipline is one example of a popular, albeit controversial, schoolwide discipline plan that has been used for years and adapted in many schools (Canter, 1976; Hill, 1990; Moone, 1997; Sander, 1989). Art, music, and physical education teachers find schoolwide plans especially helpful because these instructors teach so many different classes in a day and for relatively short periods of time. When there is a schoolwide program in place, these teachers have a general idea of the expectations and understanding that the children have been taught regarding behavior in other classes. When all the teachers in a school are able to agree on the rules for behavior, and the consequences of misbehavior, it makes the atmosphere more consistent for children and somewhat easier for specialist teachers because, at least in theory, they will need to spend less time teaching children their own discipline systems. The major concepts of Canter's Assertive Discipline Model are outlined in box 4.1.

**Box 4.1**

# Canter's Assertive Discipline Model: Major Concepts

1. All students can behave responsibly.
2. Firm control (not passive or hostile) is fair.
3. Reasonable expectations (rules, appropriate behavior, etc.) should be clearly communicated.
4. Teachers should expect appropriate behavior from students and receive administrative and parental support to stimulate it.
5. Appropriate behavior should be reinforced; inappropriate behavior should be met with logical consequences.
6. Logical consequences for not meeting expectations should be clearly communicated.
7. Consequences should be consistently reinforced without bias.
8. All verbal and nonverbal communication to students should be firm with definite teacher–student eye contact.
9. Teachers should mentally practice expectations and consequences for consistent use with students.

Reprinted, by permission, from A.N. Sander, 1989, "Class management skills," *Strategies* 2(3): 15.

I realize that simply adopting a schoolwide discipline plan doesn't necessarily mean that it will be uniformly enforced. Critical demandingness and teacher expectancy (chapter 3) vary from one teacher to another, as do the children in a class. The concept of schoolwide discipline, however, heightens the chance that teachers in a school will be more consistent with their rules and consequences, thereby providing a more secure environment for the children, who thus know what to expect from different teachers.

In addition to agreeing on how children are expected to function throughout the school, there is also agreement on the consequences for misbehavior. Box 4.2 provides an example of the consequences that are part of an assertive discipline plan (Hill, 1990).

---

**Box 4.2**

# Consequences for Misbehavior

First time a child breaks a rule—child is warned.

Second time a child breaks a rule—5-minute time-out.

Third time a child breaks a rule—10-minute time-out.

Fourth time a child breaks a rule—teacher calls parents.

Fifth time a child breaks a rule—child is sent to principal.

Good behavior all week earns, for example, 10 minutes of free-choice time or a tangible reward (e.g., a smiley face sticker).

---

In some schools the PE teacher will implement his own system of discipline. In other schools, where a schoolwide discipline system is in place, the PE teacher will provide a record of checks for misbehavior to the classroom teacher, who then adds them to her checks for the week. The use of bonus or free time on Friday is widespread, although some teachers, particularly with classes that tend toward misbehavior, use a daily plan rather than a weekly plan, allowing children a few minutes at the end of a class to choose from among several activities. Children who earned checks are not provided with the choice and are required to work on an activity chosen by the teacher.

## Time-Out

Not every teacher and every school uses a formalized discipline system. There are several other strategies teachers use to prevent misbehavior that may or may not be a part of an overall plan. Time-out, part of the assertive discipline system, is probably one of the most commonly used techniques in physical education outside of an actual discipline system. It is especially effective because of our subject matter: Some children might see time away from math or science as a bonus, but they enjoy physical activity, so time-out can be a rather potent technique (Johnson, 1999).

Most teachers provide children with a warning first (Moone, 1997). For example, "If you talk again when I am talking, you will be in time-out." If the undesirable behavior happens again, the child is told to take a time-out. Borrowing from the assertive discipline approach, time-out is most effective when a teacher assumes that some children will be

in time-out at various times during the year. They "teach" time-out at the beginning of the year, almost as one of the management protocols, so that children clearly understand the process. Some teachers place time-out numbers at different locations on the walls or on the playground. The misbehaving child is then told to take a time-out at number 4, for example. This prevents several children from getting together to chat, as often happens when there is no designated time-out location and two or more children are timed out at the same time.

Some teachers use a clock, or a kitchen timer, for a time-out. For example, children are taught that they can return to the lesson after two minutes. Others provide paper and pencil on a clipboard and ask children to write the reason they were placed in time-out (e.g., the rule they violated) before returning to the class. PE Central (www.pecentral. org) has several examples of written activities for youngsters to complete when they are in time-out. Look in the section called "Paper and Pencil Assessments."

Some teachers require children to come to them and verbally explain why they were timed out before returning to class.

If a child receives a second time-out in the same lesson, many teachers simply require them to remain out of the lesson for the rest of the class. This might seem harsh, but the fact is that often these are children who are so disruptive and demanding that the other children in the class, who are on task and trying hard, are often shortchanged.

## Desirable Rewards and Undesirable Consequences

When teachers choose to use a discipline system (such as assertive discipline) based on extrinsic rewards, it is important that the rewards be desirable to the children and the consequences undesirable. Let me illustrate with several examples. Popcorn parties, in some instances, are desirable. I have been in schools, however, where the air is permeated with the smell of popping popcorn on Friday afternoons. My guess is that popcorn every Friday is not a very desirable reward—beyond perhaps the first few Fridays. It is almost taken for granted after a few weeks.

I have also observed teachers who use free time on Friday as a reward. Although this is motivating for some children, it seems to be more of a reward for the teacher than for the children. The children are frequently threatened with a loss of free time, but somehow part of Friday's lesson is always free time. I also wonder how teachers can justify free time when there is much for the children to learn and so little time in which to learn it.

My observations tell me that popcorn and free time are obviously not effective when they are the only rewards. Some teachers create their own awards. The "golden sneaker" award is a favorite—an old sneaker spray-painted gold and mounted on a board.

In creating an award, the key is to give it value through the presentation. Perhaps this requires a bit of acting by the teacher, but for some it is effective. In addition to old sneakers, some teachers cleverly create awards from an old deflated ball, a rusty trophy, a whistle without its pea, a worn-out or knotted jump rope, or other equipment ready for discard. It's the idea of a reward, more than the value of the item, that is important. Some teachers use stickers as a way of saying "Good job"; others use nontoxic stamp pads with messages such as "Awesome" or "Super kid," which can be stamped on the back of a child's hand.

The undesirable consequence that is probably the most effective is loss of time in physical education. One of the most successful ways this is used is when children who have received misbehavior checks are not permitted to participate in an activity they really enjoy. Parachute activities are often used with younger children, and a group game with a cage ball is used for older children—with some of the children not allowed to participate in these activities because of their misbehavior during the day or week.

The important idea here is that if a teacher is going to use a system of extrinsic rewards the rewards must motivate the children for the system to succeed. If children do not care about the rewards, the system will not be successful.

# Personal Social Responsibility Model

Some teachers prefer intrinsic rewards for children (i.e., internally motivated rewards that are derived from working hard and getting along with others). They believe that children naturally want to do well and that extrinsic rewards are, over the long term, counterproductive. These teachers want children to participate in and enjoy physical activity for its own sake, not because they can earn an extrinsic reward for participating.

The most popular "intrinsic motivation" system in physical education was developed by Don Hellison (2003; Hellison & Templin, 1991; Masser, 1990; Compagnone, 1995; Hartinger, 1997). Essentially, the model is designed to help children understand and practice self-responsibility. The motivating factor in his model is the innate desire of children to get along with others and take responsibility for their own behavior, rather than relying on a teacher to reward them for being good. As with other discipline plans, the model is clearly explained to the children, and they are encouraged to accept responsibility for their own behavior and to work with others. The model has five levels:

**Level 0: Irresponsibility.** At this level children are unable to take responsibility for their own behavior and typically interfere with others by belittling, intimidating, or verbally or physically abusing their classmates.

**Level 1: Self-control.** This is a level of minimal involvement. Children will do what the teacher asks without interfering with others. This is done with minimal prompting from the teacher, although in most instances children at this level appear to be simply going through the motions.

**Level 2: Involvement.** Children at this level become actively involved in the lessons. They try hard, avoid disturbing others, and genuinely take an interest in learning and improving.

**Level 3: Self-responsibility.** This level is the point at which children are encouraged to begin to take responsibility for their own learning. This implies that they need not work under direct supervision from the teacher and that they are able to make decisions independently about what they need to learn and how they might go about learning it. At this level, children are often asked to design their own games, sequences, or dances in small groups. When children are not at this level, however, the challenge of working in groups to create their own versions of an activity is typically doomed to failure, as they spend more time arguing than moving.

**Level 4: Caring.** Children at this level go beyond simply working with others—they genuinely want to support and help others in the class. For example, children at this level are the ones who will volunteer to be a partner for a day with a child in the class who is unpopular, without being asked to do so by the teacher.

Figure 4.1 provides examples of the five levels (Masser, 1990). The different levels are exemplified at home, on the playground, in the classroom, and in physical education class.

Needless to say, this model requires more than simply explaining it to a class of children and then expecting that they will all want to work at level 4. As with the assertive discipline system, the levels are explained to children at the beginning of the year and then used throughout as a way to encourage them to cooperate with the teacher and other children. Some examples follow.

▶ Children are asked to select equipment. The teacher asks how level 0 persons would get their equipment. How about level 1? Level 2? Level 3? Level 4? The children are then asked to walk over and get their equipment, showing the teacher the level they think they can work at (Masser, 1990).

▶ When children are learning a new skill, the teacher asks how children at the various levels might practice. They are then encouraged to work at the upper levels and are complimented for doing so as a group, or they are pinpointed (Masser, 1990).

▶ A misbehaving student is asked to sit out for a few minutes (time-out) and is told why the misbehavior is level 0. The child is invited to return to the class when he is able to tell the teacher what a level 1 behavior, or higher, would be like—and when he assures the teacher that he can participate at that level (Masser, 1990).

▶ A student complains about another student. The student with the complaint is asked to identify the level the other student is functioning at and is then asked for ways to deal with others functioning at that level (Masser, 1990).

▶ If two students are fighting over equipment or use of space (level 0), they can be sent to the talking bench. They sit on the bench until they are ready to explain their solution to the teacher. Assuming the lesson is interesting, most of the time students will want to return quickly, so they will be eager to find a solution to their conflict (Hartinger, 1997).

▶ Fourth- and fifth-grade children are asked to work in groups. Before beginning, they discuss how children at level 4 would work in a group setting. The focus is on how to work with children who might display level 0 or 1 behavior (Masser, 1990).

## What's your level?

Level 0: Irresponsibility
Home: Blaming brothers or sisters for problems
Playground: Calling other students names
Classroom: Talking to friends when teacher is giving instructions
Physical education: Pushing and shoving others when selecting equipment

Level 1: Self-control
Home: Keeping self from hitting brother even though really mad at him
Playground: Standing and watching others play
Classroom: Waiting until appropriate time to talk with friends
Physical education: Practicing, but not all the time

Level 2: Involvement
Home: Helping to clean up supper dishes
Playground: Playing with others
Classroom: Listening and doing class work
Physical education: Trying new things without complaining and saying I can't

Level 3: Self-responsibility
Home: Cleaning room without being asked
Playground: Returning equipment during recess
Classroom: Doing a science project not a part of any assignment
Physical education: Undertaking to learn a new skill through resources outside the physical education class

Level 4: Caring
Home: Helping take care of a pet or younger child
Playground: Asking others (not just friends) to join them in play
Classroom: Helping another student with a math problem
Physical education: Willingly working with anyone in the class

**Figure 4.1**   What's your level?

Reprinted, by permission, from L.S. Masser, 1990, "Teaching for affective learning in elementary physical education," *Journal of Physical Education, Recreation and Dance* 61(7): 19.

# CHARACTERISTICS OF EFFECTIVE DISCIPLINE SYSTEMS

Whether a teacher chooses to adopt or adapt a discipline system based on extrinsic motivation (assertive discipline) or intrinsic motivation (levels of affective development), three important factors apparently contribute to the ultimate success of the discipline system. First, the discipline system should be carefully explained to children at the beginning of the year; second, the teacher should consistently adhere to the criteria; and third, the principal, classroom teachers, and parents must be supportive.

## Developing a Clear Understanding

When a discipline plan works, one of the reasons it works is that children clearly understand its operation and the reasons for its existence. Typically, the system is introduced at the beginning of the year; it is explained thoroughly with examples and then practiced. Some teachers use a class meeting format to introduce the discipline system. During this meeting, children are invited to ask questions and helped to understand why such a plan might be necessary. In either type of system, it helps to involve the children in the implementation of the plan so they truly understand why it is important and how it will be used.

In contrast, when a plan isn't set in place from the beginning, misbehavior is a judgment call for the teacher: What should I do? How severe should I make the penalty for misbehavior? Can I explain level 0 in 30 seconds so the child will understand?

Think of the discipline system as similar to the system set up to deal with automobile parking violations. Decisions are made regarding the length of time one is permitted to park at a meter and the places where cars can and cannot be parked. Once these rules are established, consequences for noncompliance are determined.

▶ In the assertive discipline model, the children are helped to understand clearly the consequences for misbehaving (box 4.2).

▶ In the personal social responsibility model, the levels are explained along with examples (figure 4.1).

When a discipline plan is set in place and explained at the beginning of the year, children can understand exactly what to expect—the violations and the consequences are spelled out. Many believe this helps prevent misbehavior.

## Consistency by the Teacher

A second characteristic of a successful discipline plan is consistency. Once protocols and rules have been established, teachers need to use the same standards from one day to the next. This is easy to say, yet so hard to do. Nevertheless, it's important for children to understand exactly what is expected.

There is a tendency in teaching toward slippage. We start off consistently enforcing the protocol, for example, that when the teacher says, "Stop," equipment is placed on the floor. After a few lessons, however, there is a tendency to slack up. One child doesn't put the ball down, and we ignore it. Gradually, however, it becomes two or three children, then six. Slippage has crept in. Effective teachers prevent slippage through consistency. Children quickly understand that the teacher is really going to enforce the rules as discussed at the beginning of the year.

## *65 MPH? Or Is It Really 72 MPH?*

As I write this section on slippage, I am reminded of the 65-mph speed limit. Drivers seem to understand that the limit isn't really 65 mph. The conventional wisdom in this part of the United States is that it's really 72 mph. So that's where we set our cruise control—until our radar detector sounds. Then we slow down to 65 mph. Children see their parents drive this way. The message is clear: There are rules, but they aren't really what they say; they can be stretched. The same is true in our classes. We establish rules and then allow them to be stretched; that is, we allow slippage. It seems that the rule we post on the wall is meant to be negotiated (Tousignant & Siedentop, 1983). As teachers, we determine whether and how much our rules can be stretched.

## Role of the Principal and Classroom Teacher

Occasionally we find children who are unwilling, perhaps even unable, to sit out for a few minutes without disrupting others in the class. The time-out doesn't work; rewards and consequences aren't effective either. In these instances teachers have little choice but to remove the child from the class. When this happens, the child's classroom teacher, the principal, or a guidance counselor can be helpful in two ways. First, they might be aware of the reason the child misbehaves and provide effective strategies. They might also be helpful in creating a location in the school where the child can go when he is unable to function in a class without disrupting others.

Clearly we prefer to have these children in physical education classes. The reality, however, is that there are days and times when they are simply unable to work in a group setting. Teachers have no choice but to remove them from the gym or playground. When this happens the cooperation of others in the school is vital.

## Role of the Parents

In some schools, parents can be counted on to help when their children are misbehaving. In these schools, phone calls or letters home are very effective.

## *Post-It Technique*

When he was teaching in Dublin, Virginia, John Bowler had children write their name, phone number, their misbehavior, and the date on a yellow Post-it note, and then he put the note by the phone in his office for one week. If the child behaved for one week, he threw the note away. If the child misbehaved again, John called the parent (Watson & Lounsbery, 2000). Having the child fill out the note provided a clear warning of what would happen if the misbehavior reoccurred. This technique was highly effective for John and his students.

Some teachers make it a weekly practice to telephone the parents of several hardworking children and tell them how well their children are doing in physical education. These teachers also call the parents of misbehaving children. When possible, however, they try to call the parent again as soon as possible with "good news"—that is, that their child's behavior has improved. This is a potent combination.

Whether a teacher decides to write letters or make telephone calls, it seems to be more effective when the teacher can be specific about the behavior of the child, citing specific protocols or rules that have been followed or broken. This is particularly true for the "bad news" phone calls (Watson & Lounsbery, 2000).

Unfortunately, involving parents is not effective in every school setting. In some schools, the principal and teacher are forced to rely on the types of things they can do for a child during the school day because a parent cannot be counted on to work with a child in desirable ways. When parents can become involved in situations in which a child is chronically misbehaving, however, this can be very effective.

# THE DISCIPLINE CONFRONTATION

The strategies discussed so far are designed to minimize and prevent discipline problems. Nevertheless, most teachers, even in ideal situations, will occasionally find themselves confronting a child who has misbehaved. At times, this can be upsetting for a teacher. Several strategies can make the discipline confrontation less unsettling and ultimately beneficial for both the teacher and the child (Cothran, 1998).

Try to remember that the child's misbehavior is not personal. Try not to be upset. In fact, at times it's wise to catch your breath, become centered, and then deal with the child.

These confrontations are often most successful when done in relative privacy. It's not a good idea to yell across the gym at a child. Instead, walk over, call the child to the side, and then conduct a brief interaction. I prefer to give the other children a task so that they are active instead of standing and watching the confrontation. This makes it easier on the child being confronted, especially when this child is older and more concerned with what his peers will think.

The most effective strategy is to calmly and quietly use the child's name, explain the rule (protocol) she violated, and then pause. At times it might be wise to ask for student input. When we do ask the child if she has anything to say, it's important to listen with respect and try to understand her view of the situation. With some children, however, it might be counterproductive to ask for their version of what happened. When to ask and when not to ask for input can be determined only as a teacher gets to know his students. In either case, when the interaction is finished, the teacher concludes by telling the child the predetermined consequence of her behavior—a check, a time-out, a loss of free time.

Disciplining seems to be more effective when a teacher has thought through the confrontation process ahead of time. Often, when we are upset or excited, anger enters into the confrontation, which makes it ultimately less productive than it might be under calmer circumstances. I don't mean to suggest that successful teachers never get angry. They do from time to time, but calm interactions seem to be far more effective than angry ones. Although a child has misbehaved, we still want to preserve his dignity. Once the child's feelings of hurt, anger, or frustration have somewhat dissipated, we want the child to understand that what he did was a violation of the rules, but that he is OK as a person.

## *Assertive Communication*

Communicating effectively is always a challenge. This is especially true when we are angry or upset. Fernandez-Balboa (1990) suggests strategies that beginning teachers can use to assist them in communicating assertively to children when they misbehave:

1. Describe the behavior in a nonjudgmental way—"Austin, you are taking Carter's equipment away from him."
2. Express your feelings as a teacher—"I am annoyed because you haven't been listening."
3. Acknowledge the feelings of the child—"Are you . . . (frustrated, sad, angry)?"
4. Explain the effect the described behavior is having on you and the rest of the class—"When you talk when I am talking, it distracts me and the others in the class."
5. State your expectations for future behavior—"I expect you to listen, and not talk, when I am talking." (pp. 51–52)

# SUMMARY

Teachers who minimize off-task behavior and discipline problems do so largely because they have thought through a number of strategies that are effective for preventing problems from escalating into major confrontations. As they teach, they are constantly aware of off-task behavior and attempt to minimize it by employing teaching strategies that help keep children focused and on task. In addition, they typically have implemented a discipline system that the children understand: the teacher's expectations, the consequences of misbehavior, and the benefits of cooperating with the teacher and other children. Some discipline systems are based primarily on extrinsic motivation (e.g., Canter's Assertive Discipline Model), and others are designed to emphasize the development of intrinsic motivation (e.g., Hellison's Personal and Social Responsibility Model). Regardless of the type of discipline system that a teacher chooses, it is imperative that she be consistent and rigorous in the implementation of the system while respecting the dignity and feelings of the children in the class.

# QUESTIONS FOR REFLECTION

1. This chapter describes several teaching strategies that teachers use to minimize off-task behavior and discipline problems. Think about your own teaching. List three strategies that are most natural to you. List one or two that are less comfortable to use. Can you explain why?
2. Two discipline systems were selected as representative examples. Which of the two is more appealing to you? Why?
3. Remembering teachers you had as a student or teachers you know, describe aspects of either of these systems used by these teachers. Analyze how effective they were.
4. Think about the use of intrinsic and extrinsic rewards for children and the reason that some teachers might favor one over the other. Select a typical misbehavior that occurs in elementary school physical education. Describe how teachers using an extrinsic discipline system would handle the misbehavior.

Then describe how a teacher using an intrinsic discipline system would handle the same misbehavior.

5. If you have a video of yourself teaching a lesson, analyze the use of the following teaching skills: back-to-the-wall, proximity control, with-it-ness, selective ignoring, overlapping, and positive pinpointing. Reflect on the use of these skills and how they might help to minimize discipline problems if used differently.

6. From time to time teachers do get angry at a child or a class. Can you understand and explain the reasons for this? How do teachers avoid becoming angry at certain misbehaviors?

7. What are the consequences of believing that children today are harder to teach than they were in the past? How might that belief be reflected in the way we deal with children who are off task?

# REFERENCES

Canter, L. (1976). *Assertive discipline: A take-charge approach for today's educator.* Santa Monica, CA: L. Canter and Associates.

Compagnone, N. (1995). Teaching responsibility to rural elementary youth. *Journal of Physical Education, Recreation and Dance, 66*(6), 58–63.

Cothran, D.J. (1998). Anger management in the gym. *Strategies, 12*(2), 16–18.

Downing, J.H. (1996). Establishing a discipline plan in elementary physical education. *Journal of Physical Education, Recreation and Dance, 67*(6), 25–30.

Fernandez-Balboa, J.M. (1990). Helping novice teachers handle discipline problems. *Journal of Physical Education, Recreation and Dance, 67*(2), 50–54.

Hartinger, K. (1997). Teaching responsibility. *Teaching Secondary Physical Education, 3*(5), 15–17.

Hellison, D.R. (2003). *Teaching responsibility through physical education.* 2nd ed. Champaign, IL: Human Kinetics.

Hellison, D.R., & Templin, T.J. (1991). *A reflective approach to teaching physical education.* Champaign, IL: Human Kinetics.

Hill, D. (1990). Order in the classroom. *Teacher.* April, pp. 70–77.

Johnson, R. (1999). Time-out: Can it control misbehavior? *Journal of Physical Education, Recreation and Dance, 70*(8), 32–34, 42.

Kounin, J.S. (1970). *Discipline and group management in classrooms.* New York: Holt, Rinehart and Winston.

Kulinna, P.H., Cothran, D.J., & Regualos, R. (2006). Teachers' reports of student misbehavior in physical education. *Research Quarterly for Exercise and Sport, 77*(1), 32–40.

Masser, L.S. (1990). Teaching for affective learning in elementary physical education. *Journal of Physical Education, Recreation and Dance, 61*(7), 18–19.

Moone, T. (1997). Teaching students with respect. *Teaching Elementary Physical Education, 8*(5), 16–18.

Sander, A.N. (1989). Class management skills. *Strategies, 2*(3), 14–18.

Tousignant, M., & Siedentop, D. (1983). A qualitative analysis of task structures in required secondary physical education classes. *Journal of Teaching in Physical Education, 3*(1), 47–57.

Watson, D., & Lounsbery, M.F. (2000). D.A.P.S.I.S.: Strategies for phoning home. *Strategies.* July/August, 16–18.

Williams, E.W. (1995). Learn student names in a flash. *Strategies, 8*(5), 25–29.

## Chapter 5

# Getting the Lesson Started

*I meet my students for class at the place of learning, which in this case was the track. I saw a student who was not dressed out for PE but who was running the track. I called him over and asked him why he wasn't dressed out. He said, "It's OK, I'm excused, I have a note from my mother that I can't do PE today." I replied, "I've just seen you running around. What's wrong with you?" The student replied, "I don't know. I can't read my mom's writing."*

**Dave Phillips, Florida State University School, Tallahassee**
Reprinted with permission from PE Central (www.pecentral.org).

The children are in their classroom. Eyes glance at the clock. It's 10:25 a.m. PE begins at 10:30. Then they'll have 30 minutes to move, play, and escape the confines of the classroom. Hearts beat faster as they move toward the gym. Some feel as if they are going to burst with excitement as they anticipate exploding into movement.

These feelings are characteristic of some children (we hope the majority) immediately before physical education class. The way the teacher begins the lesson will determine how the children feel in a few minutes. The purpose of this chapter is to describe successful ways of beginning physical education classes.

**After reading and understanding this chapter, the teacher will be able to**

▶ describe techniques for involving children in activity as soon as they enter the gym or playground,

▶ analyze the pros and cons of instant activity for children,

▶ explain the purpose of and techniques related to set induction and lesson scaffolding, and

▶ analyze the roles of calisthenics and lap running as introductory activities.

# INSTANT ACTIVITY

Children come to physical education class ready to move. They want to be active, not to listen to the teacher talk. Thus many teachers provide an instant activity for their students. As soon as they arrive at the gym door or the edge of the playground, children are encouraged to begin moving. This is one of the protocols taught at the beginning of the year (chapter 3). Teachers use posters, bulletin boards, verbal reminders, and music as ways of involving children in activity as quickly as possible.

## Posters and Bulletin Boards

Depending on the physical setting, some teachers have bulletin boards inside the gym that tell children how to begin (e.g., get a rope and work on your jump rope routine). Others use posters, such as these, posted outside the gym:

▶ If your last name begins with the letters A to L, practice your partner sequence on the mats.

▶ If your last name begins with M to Z, find a ball and practice a dribbling routine.

▶ When the music stops, put equipment away and sit on the center circle.

Written instructions work well for many teachers. One of the advantages of providing different tasks (rather than the same task for the entire class) is that it encourages children to read the poster or bulletin board rather than simply checking to see what the first few students to arrive are doing.

**See Instant Activity**

The DVD that accompanies this text provides a brief description of instant activity along with an example of how one teacher uses a poster to direct youngsters to a fitness station to begin the class.

## Verbal Reminders

Of course many younger children are not yet reading. In this case, teachers might tell them how the next class will begin at the end of the current class. "Next class the scoops and the balls will be against the wall. As soon as you come in, find a scoop and a ball and start throwing and catching to yourself." Depending on the number of days between classes, some children will forget. But there are always a few who will remember, and they quickly remind the others. This is one of the routines practiced at the beginning of the year, so children gradually learn to listen carefully so they can remember how the next class will start.

## Music

Some teachers start their classes with music. The music is on when children arrive, and they start traveling as instructed by the teacher (jogging, hopping, log rolling, skipping backward, dribbling and jogging, roller-skating like an elephant, and so on). An advantage to using music is that it provides a relatively consistent guide for the length of an introductory activity. Most songs range from two to three minutes, which is adequate time to allow children to move before beginning the formal part of the lesson.

PE Central, a Web site (www.pecentral.org) for K–12 physical educators, contains a variety of instant activity suggestions.

## *The Content of the Introductory Activity*

The actual content of the introductory activity may be related to that day's lesson, or it may be a review of something done in the past. Some teachers use the intro activity to provide practice on skills or routines that are best practiced for relatively short spurts (e.g., jumping rope). The activity can also serve as a warm-up for the content of the day's lesson.

# WHY INSTANT ACTIVITY?

Some children's physical education teachers express a concern that children will be out of control if they don't enter the gym and sit down quietly before moving. As I watch teachers who begin their classes with instant activity, I rarely find this to be true. After a few minutes of vigorous activity, children seem far more ready to listen to instruction. It's important to remember, however, that the teacher taught the children how to begin each lesson as part of the protocols practiced during the first few days of the school year (chapter 3).

In contrast, I have observed teachers require children to enter the gym and sit quietly on a line before any activity can begin. It often seems that several minutes are wasted because children are so eager to begin moving that their squirming and fidgeting leads to talking and pushing, which means they have to try to sit quietly even longer.

Another advantage of instant activity is that it allows children to talk to the teacher without disrupting the entire class. As any elementary teacher will attest, especially at the primary grades, there is always a child or two who wants to tell you about something that happened at home since the last class: the new TV, the lost tooth, the baby sister, the puppies, the accident down the street, the game over the weekend, their new WebKinz pet, and so on. The few minutes of activity at the beginning of the class allow these children to share a few moments with you privately while the rest of the children are moving.

# COMMUNICATING THE PURPOSE OF THE LESSON

After a few minutes the introductory activity ends. Children then gather around the teacher and listen quietly for instruction about the day's lesson. As part of their protocol for beginning a class, some teachers have children sit in a circle with them. Some use squads. Some teachers simply ask children to come over and stand or sit by them. It is during this time that the teacher explains the purpose of the day's lesson (Dyson & Pine, 1996).

Set induction and scaffolding aid children in understanding how lessons interconnect and how they relate to their lives today—and still will in 20 years. These strategies shouldn't take much time but are most helpful in answering the important questions "What is the purpose of physical education? Why are we doing this stuff?"

## Set Induction

Successful teachers do more than simply tell children what they will be doing, however. They find ways to provoke children's interest and enthusiasm so that they are eager to become involved in lessons. The technical term for this teaching strategy is set induction (also called cognitive set or anticipatory set).

**See Set Induction**
The DVD that accompanies this text provides a brief description of set induction and an example of how one teacher introduces the technique of using "quick feet" when children are attempting to dodge moving objects.

The purpose of set induction is to motivate children so they become interested in the lesson and understand its purpose, thereby encouraging them to practice efficiently and eagerly. Set induction has the advantage of helping them understand why they will be doing certain activities or tasks during a lesson. In some ways it is also a preview to the lesson (Dyson & Pine, 1996). Others suggest it is a way of "marketing" the lesson to a class (Weiller, 1992).

The following are examples of set induction that teachers have used in an attempt to heighten children's interest in a lesson:

▶ "When you jump, how quietly can you land? Can you land as quietly as a cat? A feather? Today I want to help you practice quiet landings."

▶ "Do you remember which test we did last week? Right. The pull-up test to assess upper-body strength. The purpose of today's lesson is to find ways we can improve our upper-body strength when we're at home watching TV."

▶ "When you play a basketball game, does anyone ever steal the ball from you? In today's lesson we are going to practice two 'secrets' to help you keep others from stealing the ball."

▶ The teacher stands 10 feet from a wall and hits a ball to the wall with a racket 10 times without a miss. Then she says, "In today's lesson I want to show you two cues that helped me become a good tennis player."

▶ "Do you ever get mad at your friends when you're playing a game? Do you ever say mean things to one another? The purpose of today's lesson is to understand why we say mean things to others and to find some ways to avoid making our friends feel badly."

All too often teachers know the purpose of the lesson, but the children don't. It's obvious to us, not to them. This is often demonstrated at the end of a lesson during closure (chapter 13) when we sit and talk with the children. We then discover that they didn't really understand the purpose of the lesson and they can't recall the key points of the objectives.

## Forehand or Backhand?

Yesterday I watched one of our undergraduates teach a lesson on the tennis backhand to his peers. Because he wasn't clear, two of his students spent the entire 10-minute lesson practicing the forehand. He realized the problem later when he watched a video of his lesson.

Effective set induction might be harder for specialists because we teach so many classes a day, often on the same topic. After teaching four or five balancing lessons in a row, we are ready to get on with the lesson rather than attempting to stimulate the interest of the children. We need to remember that the lesson is new for the children, no matter how many times we have done it.

## I Wonder What's Going on Here?

Watch the first five minutes of a video or an actual lesson. Try to enter the world of the children and view the beginning of the lesson from their eyes. Would the purpose of the lesson be clear? Would you know what is going on? Would you be excited about the lesson?

## Scaffolding

Have you ever been in a class and wondered, "What are we doing? I have no idea what the purpose of this lesson is and what point the teacher is trying to make"? Along with set induction, scaffolding is designed to communicate the purpose of a lesson and its relation to past and future lessons. Scaffolding links a series of lessons in a unit or skill theme or, in some instances, the year. It is often difficult for children to realize that our lessons are designed sequentially to help them improve their understanding of skills or concepts (i.e., to realize that one lesson is related to another). When we relate a lesson to past experiences, we help students understand a lesson and place it in perspective.

This is especially important for children because they live so much in the present. It's hard for children to understand that practicing striking a ball with a racket might some day lead to easier, faster progress in tennis, badminton, or racquetball. When we are able to show them the interconnectedness of these activities, however, much as a scaffold is erected outside a building at the beginning of construction, we help them develop a schema (a mental outline) of the overall purpose of the series of lessons on a particular topic. Because we have the advantage of teaching many of our children over several years, we can gradually fill in this scaffolding as we revisit lessons and units from year to year.

**See Scaffolding**
The DVD that accompanies this text contains an example of scaffolding related to the "quick feet" example used in set induction along with a brief description of this teaching technique.

## Post the Yearly Plan

Teachers can erect a physical education scaffolding for children in several ways. Some teachers, typically those who have taught at the same school for several years, post the yearly outline (curriculum scope and sequence; chapter 2) on a bulletin board. This allows children to see the entire sequence of lessons and, if guided by the teacher, how they connect over the year. It also minimizes one of the most often-asked questions of physical education teachers as they interact with children in the halls and cafeteria, "What are we going to do today in PE?" As youngsters enter the gym, a quick glance at the topic for the day tells them quickly what will be happening.

Although the idea of posting a yearly schedule is logical, beginning teachers or teachers new to a school might find it difficult to know exactly how long they will spend in various activities throughout the year. When they develop a yearly plan (chapter 2), they often revise it frequently because the children and settings at schools are so different.

After several years at the same school, however, a teacher begins to develop a reasonably accurate portrait of the time needed to develop a particular theme or unit.

## Physical Education Vocabulary

Another technique that helps children understand scaffolding for physical education is to display the program vocabulary on the wall of a gym or on a bulletin board designated for physical education. This permits the teacher not only to verbally tell the children about the lesson but also to show them the written terms. This is especially helpful when referring later on to terms that were studied months earlier. It is also valuable for classes that are just learning to read. Many teachers share this vocabulary with classroom teachers to assist them in integrating physical education into the classroom.

## Notebooks

A technique that some teachers use is to have the upper grades keep PE notebooks or logs. These notebooks have a variety of uses, but one is that they can help children link different lessons (units) together by using the same terminology and concepts over a number of lessons.

Notebooks are useful for storing and referring to

- written descriptions of child-designed games, sequences, or dances that can be recalled in future lessons;
- completed worksheets on various topics studied throughout the year—for example, names of muscles and bones;
- individual skill and fitness test scores that can be used as a benchmark for measuring individual improvement;
- individual entries recording how children feel about themselves and physical activity at various times; and
- records of activity performed at home—for example, minutes of physical activity versus minutes of watching television or playing video games.

Obviously notebooks can be used at various times and in various ways. Their advantage is that they help children to better understand and link activities practiced over the year. Notebooks are an aid to understanding the scaffolding of the overall physical education program and, in turn, the entire curriculum.

# TRADITIONAL WAYS TO START A LESSON

In concluding this chapter, I want to comment on how teachers have traditionally started lessons—with calisthenics and laps—and explain why some believe we have better ways to begin physical education classes for children.

## Calisthenics

Research in recent years has caused many to question the value of calisthenics as they were done in the past (i.e., the same calisthenics done as a warm-up routine to every class) (Branner, 1989; Graham et al., 1992). We know today that there are many different ways to warm up the body and that, ideally, calisthenics or stretches are designed to prepare children's bodies to participate in a certain type of activity (Anderson, 1980).

We also know that some calisthenics, as done in the past, are simply bad practice, no matter when they're done. Straight-legged toe touches, straight-legged sit-ups, and sit-ups with hands clasped behind the head are potentially harmful to children, and adults, for that matter (Anderson, 1980; Branner, 1989). Also, many experts today recommend that stretching be performed as a cool-down to a lesson rather than as a warm-up.

As a result of this research, and also the limited amount of time available for physical education in many schools, some teachers simply skip calisthenics. Their instant activity serves as the warm-up for the lesson. Rather than simply doing calisthenics because they have traditionally been done at the beginning of physical education lessons, many teachers use calisthenics only when they think necessary. They are trying to teach children the correct way to use calisthenics as well as the reasons to use (or not use) them.

At times, before a gymnastics lesson, teachers have children do gentle stretches after a total body warm-up in an instant activity. This time can be used to teach children the recent innovations in stretching (e.g., long, slow stretches as opposed to the "bouncing" stretches we used to do). Some teachers have children stretch at the end of a lesson, such as calf and hamstring stretches after they have done a lot of running.

## Laps

Some teachers also question the value of running laps as a way to start physical education lessons. Three to five minutes of jogging (as in running laps), while perhaps beneficial as a warm-up, does not lead to improved cardiorespiratory fitness—that would take at least 15 minutes. Obviously, then, the purpose of running laps is not to improve cardio-respiratory endurance.

Thus some teachers use instant activity, described at the beginning of this chapter, as an alternative to running laps. This allows children to obtain much-needed practice while also warming up. Examples are tag games, listening games (chapter 3), running and dribbling a ball with hands or feet, jumping rope, and practicing leaping with a partner.

To these teachers, simply running is not only boring to children but is also wasted time because children aren't really learning anything.

When these teachers do have children run laps, they are often trying to teach them to pace themselves so that they can run or jog the entire time. As anyone who has ever tested children on a distance run will recall, children who haven't learned about pacing will quickly run the first lap or so, only to end up walking the last half of the distance. If teachers focus on pacing, running laps is valuable to children to help them understand the concept of running slowly at the beginning to avoid having to walk at the end.

Increasingly, elementary schools are providing opportunities for children to jog or walk vigorously at the beginning of the school day. Rather than children arriving at school to sit for 15 or 20 minutes, teachers have outlined a course for children to walk or jog, and they are encouraged to do so. Programs like these allow physical education teachers to focus on the important skills, knowledge, dispositions, and behaviors that children need to learn. Parents, classroom teachers, and paraprofessionals are quite capable of supervising these before-school walk-jog programs.

## SUMMARY

The first few minutes of a physical education lesson are important. When children come to our class and their curiosity and understanding are stimulated immediately, the odds are increased that they will not only be eager participants but also that they will learn from our lesson. In contrast, when a child is greeted with the same old calisthenics and laps, lesson after lesson, a message is sent that perhaps these classes are to be endured rather than enjoyed. The ways we involve children in our lessons, provoke their curiosity and intellect, and stimulate them to learn and practice go a long way toward setting the tone for the entire lesson—and the entire program.

The examples and discussion in this chapter represent only a sample of the ways a teacher might begin a lesson and provoke the children's interest and involvement. I do not mean to suggest that there is one right way to begin a physical education lesson. There are many ways. The essence of this chapter is that the beginning of a lesson is important and that successful teachers devote time and energy to ensure that the opening relates to that day's lesson, lessons from the past, and future lessons. Teachers are able to provoke the children's eagerness for that day's lesson while also helping them understand how the lesson connects with what they did in past lessons and where the lesson will lead in the future.

# QUESTIONS FOR REFLECTION

1. Try to recall how you felt as a child when you had been in a classroom for several hours and it was finally time to go outside or to the gym. Describe your feelings and how you would react to instant activity as compared to having to sit and listen for the first few minutes.

2. Some teachers feel uncomfortable with having children enter a gym and begin activity immediately without first talking to them. Why do you think this is true? How would teachers who ask their children to begin activity immediately differ in their feelings?

3. Set induction is commonly found in many aspects of our lives, including movies, books, and lectures. Can you think of several examples that were motivating to you?

4. Think about the concept of set induction and how it might be used to stimulate children's interest in a lesson. What types of things do teachers say and do that different ages of children find interesting and exciting?

5. The strategy of providing children with a scaffold to help them understand the overall curriculum is something that effective teachers do. Can you recall teachers who were adept at providing effective scaffolds? And those who weren't? Describe and analyze the differences for you as a learner.

6. What is your view of calisthenics and laps as ways to start a physical education lesson? Try to find someone with a contrasting view and discuss your reasons for beginning lessons in a certain way.

# REFERENCES

Anderson, B. (1980). *Stretching*. Bolinas, CA: Shelter.

Branner, T.T. (1989). *The safe exercise handbook*. Dubuque, IA: Kendall/Hunt.

Dyson, B., & Pine, S. (1996). Start and end class right. *Strategies, 9*(6), 5–9.

Graham, G., Castenada, R., Hopple, C., Manross, M., & Sanders, S. (1992). *Developmentally appropriate physical education for children: A position statement of the Council on Physical Education for Children (COPEC)*. Reston, VA: National Association for Sport and Physical Education.

Weiller, K.H. (1992). Successful learning = clear objectives. *Strategies, 5*(5), 5–8.

## Chapter 6

# Instructing and Demonstrating

*During a physical education class my first-grade students were paired up. After observing a pair working together and noticing they looked very much alike I asked the students if they were related. One replied, "I think so, we are in the same kindergarten class."*

**Rachel Henning, Duffield Elementary, Ronkonkoma, New York**
Reprinted with permission from PE Central (www.pecentral.org).

The lesson is four minutes old. As soon as the second graders arrived at the playground, they were challenged to run and find different ways to jump over the carpet squares spread over the blacktop. The torrent of energy stored up after three hours in the classroom has erupted. Bursts of running interspersed with leaps, hops, giggles, and jumps demonstrate the children's exuberance at being outside in a space where movement is not only allowed but encouraged. To be able to move—unrestricted, free, emancipated for a few minutes from the confines imposed by walls, tables, and chairs—creates genuine joy.

The song that has been playing on the tape player, "Jump" by Van Halen, ends. The children know this is the signal to stop and assemble around the teacher. They do so quickly, realizing that the teacher will not talk long and that they will be able to move shortly thereafter. Set induction is followed by a brief period of instruction and demonstration designed to help the children understand exactly what and how to practice. The children have no questions. On the signal "go," they quickly gather their equipment and begin the first task. This chapter focuses on two of the teaching skills used by the teacher in this vignette: instructing and demonstrating.

## After reading and understanding this chapter, the teacher will be able to

▶ **explain the differences between the two types of instructing: organizational and informational,**

▶ **describe the guidelines for effective informational instruction,**

▶ **describe the characteristics of effective demonstrations by the teacher and by the children,**

▶ **analyze the way children spend their time in a lesson,**

▶ **explain the use of pinpointing and the ways it can be used effectively,**

▶ **describe the technique of checking for understanding and its role in instructing and demonstrating,**

▶ **analyze the role of play-teach-play as part of the instruction and demonstration process, and**

▶ **explain the way videos and other audiovisuals can heighten the interest and understanding of children in physical education settings.**

The ideas presented in the two previous chapters, when implemented effectively, allow successful teachers to arrive at the point in a lesson where they can provide effective instruction and demonstration. As one quickly realizes, however, when a group of children doesn't listen or stop when requested, the quality of instruction is virtually irrelevant—the children simply don't hear it.

We need to recognize that before instruction and demonstration can be successful, no matter how adept a teacher might be at this part of the teaching process, the children must have learned to pay attention to the teacher—and they must be ready to do so. Once the groundwork has been laid (chapter 3), the children are then ready to benefit from the information and demonstrations provided by the teacher.

## INSTRUCTING

Instructing is the process of providing information to the students primarily, but not exclusively, through talking. Over the years, many studies have analyzed physical education lessons. These studies, individually and collectively, present a clear picture: Many PE teachers spend a lot of time talking; many students spend a lot of time listening, waiting, and getting organized (Metzler, 1985; Siedentop & Tannehill, 2000). Teachers need to talk, but in physical education classes children need to move. The purpose of this chapter is to discuss ways teachers can communicate to children so that they understand and learn without subtracting a lot of time from their opportunities to move.

For purposes of discussion, I have artificially divided instruction into two categories: organizational and informational. This is an oversimplification and also a false division, as the two are often intertwined. I hope, however, that this division will be helpful in clarifying the process teachers use to provide information to children.

# Organizational Instructing

One of the challenges of teaching physical education is organizing large groups of children in undefined spaces. Classrooms have chairs and desks—obvious places to sit. In contrast, playgrounds and gyms have lines and walls; grassy fields have a few trees and perhaps a backstop. What are the boundaries in a gym or on a playground or field? Where do children go for instruction? How do they avoid running into one another?

One type of instruction, organizational instructing, tells students what to do, with whom, where, and with what equipment. This is necessary at the beginning of most lessons and typically occurs after an introductory activity. When it is done with clarity, students understand and can proceed quickly to activity (this assumes that students have learned the management protocols—see chapter 3).

Organizational instruction doesn't tell children anything about how to throw a ball or perform a static stretch. It does tell them how activities can be done without interruption in a safe and enjoyable environment. Effective organizational instruction answers the following questions:

▶ Where will I do the activity? What are the boundaries?

▶ Will I do it alone or with others? How will my group be formed?

▶ Do I need any equipment? Where will I find it?

▶ When will I start? Stop? What do I do if I finish early?

▶ What if I have a question?

Obviously this is a lot of information for children—especially young children or ones who are new to a program. One technique that many successful teachers use to enhance the clarity of their organizational instruction is to ask one or more children (depending on the activity) to show other children how the task is done. For example, after telling children they will need to choose a partner, a ball, two cones, and a space away from others to begin their game, a teacher calls on two children and talks them through the actual beginning of the task:

> Ferman, would you please show us how to begin? Right. First he picks a partner—Mark. Now he and Mark pick a ball from the pile, get two cones, and find a spot by themselves. Now they're ready to begin their game. Thank you for showing us how to get organized for the game. When I walk by and tap you on the shoulder, please select your partner and begin.

Asking children to walk through the organization might sound like a waste of time. In fact, it often saves time because the children can visualize how their activity is to be organized. This has the advantage of providing information both verbally (teacher talk) and visually (student demonstration) which is especially helpful to young children (Valenti, 2004; Weiss, Ebbeck, & Rose, 1992; Wiese-Bjornstal, 1993).

The decision on whether to provide a student demonstration while the teacher is talking depends on the task and the particular class. If the class has done the task before and if they are good listeners, it might be unnecessary to demonstrate.

In general, however, the clarity of instruction about organization is aided by demonstration. In time, children will learn the shortcuts. The other day, for example, at the end of the lesson I was observing, the teacher said, "Now I need you in two seated lines." I wondered which of the many lines in the gym he meant. The children knew exactly. They quickly sat on two red lines by the door ready to move into the hallway.

# Into the Great Beyond

One of the things we learn in our educational psychology classes is that young children have yet to develop adult concepts of space awareness. I am always reminded of this when I watch a teacher describe a rather poorly marked general space. Typically, after the explanation, the teacher asks the children, "Do you understand where the boundaries are?" Twenty-nine six-year-old heads all bob "uh-huh" in unison. The teacher says, "Go." Ten seconds later, seven children are happily traveling beyond the boundaries without realizing they are out of bounds.

# Informational Instructing

The organizational instruction tells children what they are going to be doing. It doesn't tell them how to do the activity successfully, however. Instruction about how to land from a jump, make a symmetrical shape, pace a distance run, and form a group, I have classified as informational instruction. It has also been termed lesson presentation (Mustain, 1990).

# Teaching Is More Than Instructing

Instructing is one aspect of teaching. It is the single aspect, however, that the general public considers to be the total process of teaching. A teacher who is clever and witty is often considered to be effective. What experienced teachers know is that the real measure of success as a teacher is what the children are doing—and how they feel about what they are doing—and that this is what makes the difference. Motivating children to work hard and continue to practice requires much more than simply providing a clever set of instructions. If teaching and instructing were synonymous, this might be a book with one chapter!

Successful teachers follow four guidelines in providing skill (informational) instruction.

## 1. One Idea at a Time

One guideline is to keep it simple. For a novice, an explanation of how to grip a racket, how to move to the ball and prepare to swing, and then how to actually swing—in the same minilecture—is information overload, even for an adult learner (Schmidt & Wrisberg, 2008). Students simply can't remember all of that information. By explaining and demonstrating one idea at a time (e.g., "level swing"), learners can better remember the concept and begin to incorporate it into their schema. When several concepts are explained simultaneously, it is difficult for children to know which one they should think about as they practice. Instruction about one idea at a time is especially effective when the teacher then provides feedback to the children about the way they are (or are not) swinging in an appropriate plane (i.e., feedback that is congruent with the instruction; see chapter 10).

Obviously in some instances more than one idea can be successfully explained, especially when one is a review of past lessons. Too often, however, we provide children with far more information than they can process—even if they want to remember it all. The critical point here is that the teacher is not demonstrating an entire skill, but

rather a specific aspect or component of the skill (Oslin, Stroot, & Siedentop, 1997; Parson, 1998). This is not to say, however, that successful teachers teach only one idea or concept in a lesson—they may teach several in a lesson—but they do so one at a time and, based on progress, move to another concept based on observations of their students (chapter 8).

## 2. Keep It Brief

Another advantage of explaining one idea at a time is that the instruction can be brief. Children are far more willing to listen when they know an explanation will be quick and they can return to activity.

In keeping with this guideline, it is important to avoid falling into the habit of repeating the same explanation two or three times. Beginning teachers are particularly prone to this habit as they try to find words to enhance their explanation. This is because, in many instances, they haven't talked about the ideas they are attempting to teach—the content is new to them as teachers (Brown & Brown, 1996). Consequently, some children tend to hear the first explanation and not bother to listen to the next one; conversely, some might prefer to wait until the second or third explanation because they know the idea will be explained more than once.

## Uhs . . . , Ums . . . , OKs, and You Knows

It's common for teachers, especially early in their careers when they are unaccustomed to public speaking and are presenting information for the first time, to use certain phrases or filler words that are distracting to listeners. The most common are "uh . . . ," "um . . . ," "OK," and "you know," but others also creep into our vocabularies. There is a reason for using these words—they allow us to stall for time as we think about what we want to say next. It's natural. It's also distracting. One of the quickest ways to discover these habits is to record a lesson to determine if any of these habits have crept into our instruction. If they have, simply becoming aware of them is often enough to eliminate them from our speech. In some cases, however, a habit has become so ingrained that it won't go away. Fortunately, there is an effective technique for eliminating these habits: Select a class you work well with. Ask them to help you eliminate your habit. They will already be aware of it. Ask them to repeat the distracting phrase to you every time you say it. For example, every time you say, "OK," ask them all to say "OK?" back to you. Although the lesson you are instructing might not be very good, you will quickly stop using that word. It works—and children really enjoy helping you change the habit.

## 3. Reminder Word or Phrase

Our explanations, of necessity, require a number of words. When we can provide the children with a reminder word or phrase, it helps them recall the idea more easily (Buchanan & Briggs, 1998; Dillard, 2003; Melville, 1988; Parson, 1998). It presents them with an easily remembered "mind picture." For example, the cue often used with beginners when striking a ball with a racket is that the side of the body (as opposed to the front of the body) is facing the target when the ball is struck. Designating the word "side" as the reminder word serves as a shortcut to remembering this concept (Dillard, 2003). This also makes it easier for the teacher to provide feedback because she can simply say, "Side" as a reminder to try to turn the side toward the target. Although this might not seem important at the beginning of the day, after seven or eight classes, a shortcut like this can be very helpful (table 6.1).

At times these reminder words are not easy to create. Often children can help identify a word or phrase to serve as a reminder. For example, the refinement of bending the knees, hips, and ankles when landing from a jump was identified by children as "squashing" the landing.

Table 6.1   Sample Verbal Cues for Motor Skills

| MOTOR SKILLS | VERBAL CUES |
|---|---|
| **RUNNING** | |
| • Elbows bent, arms close to body, not flying out to the sides | "Steam engines" |
| • Feet straight, avoiding flat-footed landing | "Heel-toe, straight we go" |
| **JUMPING** | |
| • Horizontal jump using a preparatory movement that includes flexion of both knees and arms extended behind the body | "Make a low table" |
| • Horizontal jump in which arms are forcefully extended forward and upward reaching full extension above the head | "Swing for the sky" |
| **BALL HANDLING** | |
| • Dribbling by pushing with the fingers, not slapping | "Pet the kitty" |
| • Catching with eyes on the ball, arms extended in preparation, and elbows bending to absorb force | "Look, reach, give" |
| • Fielding a ground ball by getting in front of the ball with hands down | "Tunnel with bars" |
| • Catching self-tossed balls on the finger tips (not the palms) | "Spiders playing catch" |

Reprinted, by permission, from S. Melville, 1988, "Thinking and moving," *Strategies* 2(1): 18-20.

## *The Knuckle of the Big Toe*

A soccer player was trying to help another student with a soccer-style kick for distance. The player didn't want the other student to use his toe, but she didn't want him to use the inside of his foot either. In attempting to describe that location on the foot between the toes and the inside, middle of the foot (actually the joint of the first metatarsal), she came up with the term "the knuckle of your big toe." Perhaps not quite accurate, but easy to remember.

## 4. Based on Observation

As explained previously, some classes will have needs different from those of others. Effective teachers have the ability to observe a class, reflect on the students' movements, and then select the appropriate cue from their repertoire of understanding about that skill and how it is learned to determine the content of the instruction that will be most beneficial to children at that skill level. In teaching dribbling with the hands, for example, the following cues (chapter 8) might be helpful:

- Use the finger pads.
- Push the ball—don't slap it.
- Look away from the ball.
- Dribble low.
- Keep the ball on the side away from the opponent (NASPE, 1995).

If children are beginners, the first two or three cues might be emphasized one at a time. A class of more skillful children would benefit from the latter two cues. The decision on which cue or refinement to emphasize (chapter 9) is based on the teacher's observation, however, not on a preset notion of what "all third graders need" (chapter 8). That information is then combined with his knowledge of what cues children will find most beneficial. In some instances cues will have already been taught, albeit with a different skill and the teacher will need to spend less time explaining and demonstrating that cue because it has already been introduced. For example, the overhand throwing motion is in the same family of skills as the overhand volleyball serve, the tennis serve, and the badminton overhead clear (Wilkinson, 2000).

The ability to observe a class and make these decisions is not a skill that comes easily. As with many of the tools in the pedagogy tool box, it takes time and practice. In the beginning it is helpful to have several cues in mind and then scan the class to determine which of the critical elements will be most beneficial to this class. If the majority of students are gripping their rackets correctly, then it is of little use to explain the grip to the entire class. This can be done individually. In contrast, if most children are swinging their rackets in uneven pathways, causing them to miss or mis-hit the ball, then time needs to be spent on their swing pathways. This is a decision best made through observation.

# DEMONSTRATING

Demonstrating is typically part of instruction—the part where we show a movement rather than only talking about it. Demonstration is especially important for young children, who might have difficulty understanding verbal explanations of the concepts (Valenti, 2004). Demonstration is also crucial in many schools that have classes with non-English-speaking or hearing impaired children.

Much of our teaching involves using words to describe how to perform motor skills. Words are helpful but are not as efficient as actually demonstrating a skill. The same is true for music or art. Words are helpful, but listening to a symphony or seeing a portrait in an art gallery is far more instructive than trying to create a verbal explanation of a particular work of art or piece of music. Words are obviously effective in focusing our attention on particular aspects, phases, or sequences of a movement—and even more effective when combined with a demonstration. As with instruction, several components come together to compose a successful demonstration (Adams, 1993; Darden, 1997; Rink & Werner, 1987; Wiese-Bjornstal, 1993).

## Location for Demonstrating

The first component is common sense. Stand in a location in which all children can see you easily. If you're outside, stand so the sun isn't in the children's eyes. Also be sure that you can see all your students. This is obvious yet from time to time forgotten. There's really not much more one can write about this aspect—it's simply a matter of trying to be aware of students and what they are seeing and hearing.

## Whole or Part?

Generally the first demonstration should be the entire movement. This allows children to form a complete mental picture of the skill (Darden, 1997; Housner & Griffey, 1994; Rink & Werner, 1987). If the skill is kicking, the teacher (or a skilled student) demonstrates the actual kick. The next phase of the demonstration focuses on the part (e.g., showing the placement of the nonkicking foot next to the ball). This may or may not be followed by another whole demonstration. It's important to verbally highlight the critical component or cue before the demonstration so that children know what to pay attention to as they are watching the demonstration (Valenti, 2004). If this is not done, children might focus more on the outcome of the movement rather than the cue you are trying to emphasize.

**See Demonstrating**

The DVD that accompanies this text contains a brief explanation of the process of demonstrating and two examples of effective demonstrations.

## Normal or Slow?

Sometimes children need to see a skill at normal speed; other times it helps to slow it down, often when the cue is demonstrated. If the demonstration isn't slowed down, many children will be unable to see the movement that is demonstrated. The movement will simply be a blur. This is especially true for higher-skilled students when a teacher is attempting to refine a complex sports skill (e.g., a certain sequencing of movements of body parts, such as when swinging a golf club or racket or when throwing). The focus may be on how the hips, arms, and shoulders move in relation to one another.

## Verbal Focus by the Teacher

If children are going to benefit from a demonstration, the teacher will need to tell them where to look before the demonstration: "Watch the 'plant' foot; notice that it is placed alongside the ball." This helps direct the children's attention. If this isn't done, as the ball is kicked many children will watch the flight of the ball, "oohing" and "aahing" as the ball sails away, and forgetting to notice where the plant foot was placed.

## *What if I Can't Do the Skill to Be Demonstrated?*

A question often raised by beginning teachers is "What do you do when you aren't skilled enough to demonstrate?" My answer is "Don't." Most of the time you will know a child or two in the class who can demonstrate the whole skill. That same child can then demonstrate the part of the skill you want to emphasize, often in slow motion. There is also some evidence that peer modeling is more motivating to youngsters because the movement appears more like their own than that of an adult or expert does (Darden, 1997). Although some might be uncomfortable with the fact that a teacher is not highly skilled in everything she teaches, I don't think the children find it especially troublesome if the teacher is honest about it. I think such situations are excellent times to point out how long it takes to become proficient at a skill and how few individuals are proficient at every skill. In fact, one of the aspects of teaching I enjoy most is when children attempt to teach me a skill that I am not very good at. The sharing, the compassion, and the support they provide as they try to teach me to do a handstand or twirl a hoop around one leg helps create an environment that says, "It's OK not to know everything; it's fun to learn and to try; this is a place where you can feel comfortable when you try and fail—because failure is a part of learning."

# CHECKING FOR UNDERSTANDING

At the culmination of an instruction–demonstration episode, one technique that effective teachers use is to quickly test students to be sure they understand the instruction and the demonstration. This is called *checking for understanding*. Teachers use a variety of techniques to ascertain if students have grasped the concept they are attempting to convey (Wiese-Bjornstal, 1993). The decision on which technique to use depends largely on the developmental level of the students, the time available, and the content being taught. Five checking-for-understanding techniques include recognition, verbal, comprehension, performance checks, and closure.

## Recognition Check

One of the quickest ways to check for understanding is to demonstrate a movement and then ask children to raise their hands, give a thumbs-up sign, or some other form of recognition to indicate that the movement was performed correctly or incorrectly. For example, "Thumbs up if my elbow is in middle level; thumbs down if it is not in middle level." The problem with this technique, of course, is that children often check with each other rather than providing their own responses.

## Verbal Check

Another way to check for understanding is to ask children to tell you the cue or concept that you are teaching. This allows you to determine if children are recalling the concept you have emphasized. Ideally, several children at a time can be asked to tell you, for example, three cues they have learned for catching a ball. Although you could ask the whole class at the same time, when 25 youngsters are all talking at once it is virtually impossible to know which of the children have really grasped the concept. Another technique some teachers use is to ask youngsters to explain (in their own words) a concept taught during the lesson as they exit the gym or playground. This allows teachers to quickly interact with each child in the class while assessing their overall understanding.

**See Checking for Understanding**
The DVD that accompanies this text illustrates a teacher asking children to provide another word or phrase for the concept of *flow* in movement sequences.

## Performance Check

"Show me how to squash a landing after a jump" or "Show me where not to put your arms when you do a crunch" are examples of performance checks. They ask the children to actually demonstrate their understanding. This technique works especially well in physical education because we are teaching movement, and a teacher can quickly scan youngsters to see if their demonstrations indicate they have understood the concept being taught.

Checking for understanding provides a way of evaluating children's comprehension of the functional use of a cue. Given the number of classes typically taught by elementary school physical education specialists and the difficulty of evaluating 300 to 600 children, this technique can be helpful for assessing the progress children are making. It is relatively easy and quick to scan the children to see how many have understood the instruction and the demonstration. It also shows teachers whether children are just memorizing concepts or if they are truly understanding why a cue or concept is important. Of the five techniques this is probably the most effective because it allows teachers to quickly scan each child to determine if they are able to demonstrate their understanding of the cue or concept.

## Closure

Another place in a lesson that teachers normally check for understanding is during closure. This provides teachers with a quick, informal assessment of how well children have learned a concept emphasized in the lesson. Closure occurs at the end of the lesson and is typically brief—ideally two or three minutes. Many teachers bring their students close to them and have them sit down; then one or more things occur:

1. The key points of the lesson are quickly reviewed—usually the critical elements or concepts that were emphasized. This review may be a verbal summary by the teacher, but more often children are asked questions about the lesson using one of the four checking-for-understanding techniques described earlier.
2. The children complete a quick written assessment related to the lesson (chapter 13).
3. The teacher comments on the behavior of the children during the lesson. This typically occurs more in the beginning of the school year when protocols are being established. Many teachers, however, use this as a time to compliment the entire class when they have worked hard and appropriately during the lesson.
4. Homework can be assigned during closure. For example, children can be asked to
   ✓ practice dribbling a ball for at least 10 minutes before the next class,
   ✓ stretch (do crunches, push-ups) during at least three television commercials before the next class, or
   ✓ locate (identify) at least one place in the community where they might go to practice their racket skills (e.g., tennis or racquetball courts, badminton net in a neighbor's backyard).
5. Children are reminded about the instant activity (chapter 5) for next class—such as "On Wednesday when you come out to the playground, find a ball and practice your dribbling or a jump rope and practice jumping. As soon as the music stops, put your equipment away and come stand by me. Who thinks they can remember? OK, we'll see."

Closure also serves as a brief break from the physical activity that was occurring and allows them to wind down before returning to the classroom. Educational psychologists tell us that this is a valuable learning time because children are more likely to recall what happens at the end—and beginning—of the lesson. Closure doesn't need to be lengthy, just two to three minutes, but is an important part of a lesson.

**See Closure**
The DVD that accompanies this text contains an example of closure.

# STUDENTS' USE OF TIME

As I review the sections on instructing, demonstrating, and checking for understanding, I realize that it might appear a substantial part of a lesson is devoted to these activities. I hope not. In fact, as we work with our undergraduates we encourage them to do all three (instruct-demonstrate-check for understanding) in less than 60 seconds. This is obviously an arbitrary limit, but it does reinforce the point that the entire cycle can be completed in one minute or less for many skills—and be easily understood by students.

One way we help our undergraduates understand how children spend time in their classes is through time analysis. This provides them with helpful, relatively objective insights about how long children spend listening to them talk, for example, as compared to how long children actually spend in activity. The following sections explain time analysis as it can be used in your classes.

# DEFINITION OF CATEGORIES

Time analysis is also referred to as duration recording (Siedentop & Tannehill, 2000). The form shown in figure 6.1 is frequently used for time analysis, though it provides a rough rather than precise estimate. You can use this form to categorize how much time children spend in a class into four categories:

▶ Managing—time spent getting out and putting away equipment, organizing into groups, and the like

▶ Activity—time spent moving as they do activities consistent with the purpose of the lesson

▶ Instruction—time spent listening to instruction, watching a demonstration, answering questions verbally, listening to another child talk

▶ Waiting—time spent waiting for a turn or to get the ball in a game, waiting for the teacher to get out the equipment or find the right song on a CD, and so on

## Coding the Time Children Spend in a Lesson

To record the time spent in a lesson, the observer uses a stopwatch and a reproduction of figure 6.1. (A blank copy of the time analysis form is in the appendix.) Start the stopwatch when children enter the playground or gym. Each slash mark represents 15 seconds, and each number represents one minute. This form allows you to code a 30-minute lesson. Focus only on the children. In doing this analysis, the recorder focuses on what the majority (51 percent) of the children in the class are actually doing. In the beginning, novices often focus on the teacher, not the students. For example, if the teacher is talking but the students are moving, the coder would record that time as "Activity," not "Instruction." Record what 51 percent of children are doing at any given time by making a slash mark and then indicating what the children spent the previous seconds doing. Refer to figure 6.1 for the following example:

▶ If they spent the first 30 seconds of the class getting a piece of equipment, the observer would make a slash mark and then place an *M* to indicate that children had spent that time managing.

▶ If children then spent the next 180 seconds (three minutes) in activity, the observer would place an *A* over that section.

▶ If the next 30 seconds were spent listening to the teacher talk, the observer would place an *I* over that section.

Obviously the time when the children change categories is not always exactly at a 15-second slash mark, so we make the best estimate of where the category changed and put our slash there.

Actual lessons or videos can be analyzed to determine how children spend their time. If it is a videoed lesson, the observer will have to make judgments about 51 percent of the children, based on the children who are "on the screen" at any given time. PE Central (www.pecentral.org) has a variety of videos excellent for this purpose because a time bar is embedded into the videos. They are listed under the American Master Teacher Program.

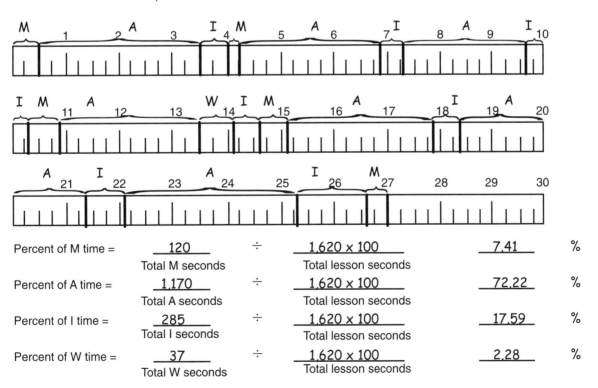

Figure 6.1 Sample form for coding students' use of time.

## Analyzing Students' Use of Time

When a lesson has ended or observation has ceased, the first step is to total the number of seconds for the entire lesson. In the example provided (figure 6.1), the lesson was 27 minutes long (1,620 seconds). All calculations are done in seconds, so the denominator for each of the four categories is 1,620. The number of seconds children spent in each of the four categories is then totaled and placed on the appropriate place on the form. Divide the number of seconds for each category by the total length of the lesson (in seconds) and multiply by 100 to determine the percentage for each of the four categories. In this lesson, for example, children spent 1,170 seconds in activity, which amounted to 72.22 percent of the lesson. Less than 3 percent of this lesson was spent in waiting.

## Interpreting the Form

Obviously there are many ways to interpret the time children spend in a lesson. Some lessons require more instruction than others, for example. Thus the form must always be interpreted in terms of the lesson content, the class taught, the grade level, and so on. Generally, however, we encourage our undergraduate students to try to design and teach their lessons so that children are active at least 60 percent of the lesson. We also encourage our students to aim for no waiting time at all. We assume that in virtually every lesson there will be some instruction and some management time.

# PINPOINTING

Once instruction and demonstration have been completed and the teacher has checked to be sure children have correctly understood, children are ready to begin the task. Typically teachers use pinpointing after a skill has been explained and demonstrated and either some students are having a hard time understanding or are focusing more on the outcome than on the cue being taught. Coded as "Instruction" on the time analysis form (figure 6.1), pinpointing should be relatively brief, ideally taking less than 60 seconds.

To pinpoint, a teacher selects two or more children who are correctly using the component currently being emphasized and asks them to demonstrate for their classmates. For example, "Stop. Now I want you to watch Starla and Todd. Notice how their arms are fully stretched to help them keep their balance as they walk along the beam." Starla and Todd might not be the most skilled students in the class, but they are able to show the correct use of the critical component (in this instance, "fully stretched arms").

Pinpointing is an effective technique because it reinforces instruction and demonstration and tells children that you are more interested in *how* they are balancing (the technique) rather than in whether or not they are falling off the beam (Darden, 1997).

It seems to work best to pinpoint two or more children at once. Children often don't like to perform solo in front of the class. Fear of embarrassment is reduced when several children are moving at the same time. I suggest that teachers try to avoid always pinpointing the highly skilled children—even less-skilled children, who might not have the best balance, can demonstrate how to stretch their arms to maintain their balance. This has an obvious benefit because it indirectly says to the children, "Even though you might not be highly skilled, you can learn to do this part, and I am more interested in

how you do the skill than in the results." It also allows the teacher to reinforce those children who are trying hard but have yet to put it all together (chapter 12).

Jessica, in a study of students' perspectives on teaching strategies (Cothran & Kulinna, 2006, p. 177), had this insight that is related to the pedagogical skill of pinpointing: "Teenagers sometimes have a tendency to not listen to adults when they actually say it, but if a kid, you know, tells them how they are doing or how better to move they actually listen and try to like the ideas they give them." Nick agreed: "Kids really more listen to other kids than they do to adults." This appears to be especially true for older children and adolescents.

**See Pinpointing**
The DVD that accompanies this text illustrates two examples of pinpointing.

# PLAY-TEACH-PLAY

As you might expect, children don't want to listen to long explanations. They want to be active. This fact is compounded by children's focus on the present (i.e., they rarely see the long-term benefits of practicing a skill). It's hard for them to make the connection between practice today and proficiency several years from now. They want to *play*, not practice. This means that they are often reluctant to pay attention to instruction and demonstration provided by the teacher. In addition to pinpointing and checking for understanding, another effective technique that is part of the instruction and demonstration process is play-teach-play. Although this technique can be used with any age, it is typically used with upper-grade children who are interested in playing a game rather than spending time in practice—although they might need the practice. Play-teach-play has two advantages:

▶ It heightens children's interest because instruction and demonstration can be related to the game (or activity) they have just "played." It's similar to fixing a flat tire. If I decided to include a section on changing a flat tire, you might skip over it. If you had a flat tire on the freeway, however, your interest in my instructing and demonstrating would be much greater. When they know they will be returning to a game and the teacher is describing a way to heighten their success in that game, students are more interested in listening to the idea.

▶ The other advantage of play-teach-play is that children practice tasks in the actual context in which they will be used, so activities are more meaningful for them.

Historically, we have structured units (lessons) so that the practice (drill) occurs first, followed by a game. Children want to play the game rather than practice because the two seem unconnected in their minds. In play-teach-play, connections between practice and play are made clearer by initially playing the game (participating in the complete sequence or combination of skills), which then helps both the children and the teacher understand and decide on the skills or combinations of skills to practice.

In many throwing and catching games, children have difficulty throwing a ball when they are moving. Often the receiver (their intended target) is also moving and perhaps guarded. When children are initially involved in a game that requires moving to throw and catch, and when they are continually unsuccessful, then instruction in this skill (and opportunities to practice) makes much more sense to them. The practice is related to the context of the game, not isolated and unconnected. After an opportunity to practice, the game can be resumed. Children play, practice some more, and then play again.

Obviously, throwing and catching while moving isn't learned in a few minutes of practice, so the game may be stopped frequently to provide more practice. The advantage of this approach is that children can clearly see what and why they need to practice.

This isn't always the case when practice is removed from the context of the game. Let's look at dribbling, for example. When children are practicing on their own with no opponent, they typically dribble the ball waist high and in front of them. As soon as someone tries to steal the ball, however, they dribble lower and often to the side. When the teacher points this out to the children, the dribbling practice seems far more useful. This is especially true when they realize that in a few minutes they will be back in a game in which someone is going to try to steal the ball once again.

The frequency and timing of playing, practicing (instructing and demonstrating), and playing is determined by the teacher. In some instances the playing is rather brief; in others it may be longer. At times the play-teach-play cycle may be repeated several times; other times, the complete cycle might not be used because practice is productive and interesting to students, so there is no need to return to the game. As with so much of teaching, these types of decisions are based on the characteristics of particular classes.

Play-teach-play seems especially helpful when a teacher has a class of children who are accustomed to playing games every day as a major part of the lesson. When the game is played first, the teacher is no longer besieged by the question "When do we get to play the game?" The children can clearly recognize that certain skills need to be practiced if the game is truly going to be a game.

## *Serve-Chase-Serve-Chase*

As I write this section I am reminded of the volleyball games I have observed in which children can neither serve nor volley successfully. How dull the game becomes when it consists of serve, chase the ball, serve, chase the ball, serve, miss a volley, chase the ball, and so on. This kind of pattern is often seen in tennis when played by the unskilled. The advantage of placing the children in the game context initially is that they can immediately see the need for practicing the serve and the techniques for receiving the serve.

Play-teach-play, as with so many of the ideas discussed in the book, is a helpful technique for some classes some of the time. My experience has been that as children become accustomed to instructional physical education (emphasizing learning through practice) rather than recreational physical education (simply playing games with minimal instruction), the technique of play-teach-play is used less frequently, if at all, because children understand that physical education is a time to learn (instruction) rather than a time to play with no instruction (recreation).

## CDS AND DVDS

Another technique used to heighten students' interest in instruction and demonstration is the use of videos and CDs. Today videos are probably the most widely used audiovisual technology in schools. Many teachers have found them quite effective for instructing and demonstrating and for motivating children (Melville, 1993; NASPE, 1995; Weiss, Ebbeck, & Rose, 1992).

Increasingly, commercial companies are developing and marketing DVDs and CDs for use in physical activity instruction (e.g., DVDs of aerobic routines). As with any product, the range of quality is broad, and DVDs designed for adults are rarely appropriate for children.

Recent advances in technology provide opportunities for teachers to make DVDs for use in their own programs. The advantage of DVDs over videotapes is the time saved in finding specific segments on the DVD rather than spending time forwarding and rewinding segments on videotapes. Most teachers who make their own videos find it helpful to purchase a cordless microphone because it produces a higher quality audio signal compared to that from a microphone mounted on the camera. This is especially important when there is music playing or when children are dribbling balls, for example.

Teachers have found a wide range of uses for videos made during physical education classes:

▶ Some record segments of television programs and then show parts of them to their classes to demonstrate aspects of a particular skill, sequence, or game or to motivate children to practice more diligently, as a part of the set induction (chapter 5).

▶ Some teachers make videos of older classes of children to show younger children various movements or routines (Melville, 1993).

▶ Some teachers use videos to provide instruction when they will be absent and a substitute teacher will be responsible for the classes. This allows the sub to simply play the instructions of the regular teacher, thereby minimizing the "games" that children often enjoy playing as the sub tries to tell the children what they are going to do that day.

▶ With the increasing specter of malpractice lawsuits haunting teachers today, some teachers are videoing their management protocols, rules, and expectations as they are explained at the beginning of the year (Adams, 1993). They also require students new to the school to view the video before participating in physical education classes.

▶ In a similar vein, some teachers are making DVDs of their explanations (routines and rules) for certain activities that tend to be classified as "high risk" (e.g., climbing ropes, adventure activities, use of equipment in gymnastics) (Adams, 1993). In this way they have a permanent visual record that can be used to document the instruction that was provided to their classes about the guidelines for participating in these activities (chapter 3).

▶ One of the most interesting uses of video is allowing the children to record their own creations and show them to others (NASPE, 1995). This can be both instructional and motivational for children. It also allows teachers to select the more interesting sequences and creations for future showings.

As with any audiovisual aid to instruction and demonstration, there is a tendency to show more than an audience can grasp in a single sitting. When feasible, brief episodes (five minutes or less) are more effective than longer segments. When audiovisual equipment is placed on a cart it is easier to use the equipment for brief intervals. The cart can be easily wheeled out, and the equipment is ready to go. When substantial time has to be spent setting up and taking down equipment, the equipment is less likely to be used.

Finally, the Internet is being used more and more as a platform to share instructional videos. Some teachers, for example, are putting video clips on their personal Web sites that youngsters can access from home. Obviously these video clips are also useful for parents. As the Internet converts to broad bandwidth and streaming video becomes faster, the opportunities for youngsters to observe expert performance and instruction will become widespread and common. Video clips on the Internet also provide excellent opportunities for teachers to share examples of classes, lessons, and teaching techniques with other teachers.

## SUMMARY

The ability to communicate clearly with children is an important teaching skill. The most common way teachers communicate with children is through talking. Demonstrations by the teacher or the children also help children understand what is intended. One of the techniques for communicating effectively with children is the ability to break down instructions into understandable units. For this reason, teachers are encouraged to make their instructions simple and brief. Pinpointing (asking children to demonstrate) is another technique teachers use to heighten clarity. To determine whether the teacher is clear and the children are comprehending the instruction and demonstrations, successful teachers regularly check for understanding to make sure children have understood. The technique of play-teach-play and the use of CDs and videos are other ways to heighten children's interest in instruction.

# QUESTIONS FOR REFLECTION

1. Why do you think the distinction between organizational and informational instruction is necessary?

2. Physical activity instructors tend to tell children far more than they need to know or are able to comprehend. Why do you think this is the case? Why is it so hard to limit instruction to one cue at a time?

3. It seems that physical education teachers don't demonstrate as often as they might. Can you explain why this might be true?

4. Some lessons might require more instruction or demonstration than others. Think of examples when this might be so—consider time of the year, grade level, and content of the lesson.

5. Pinpointing is another form of demonstration. Provide reasons why it can be an effective supplement to teacher demonstration.

6. Checking for understanding is a useful technique for teachers. Interestingly, it isn't employed as often as we might think—why might this be true?

7. Play-teach-play is a technique with advantages and disadvantages. Describe one of each and suggest when play-teach-play might be effective and when it might not.

8. Pull out your crystal ball and look for ways that video might be used in classes in the future. Don't worry about costs; imagine your budget is unlimited. Don't neglect Internet possibilities.

# REFERENCES

Adams, S.H. (1993). Duty to properly instruct. *Journal of Physical Education, Recreation and Dance, 64*(2), 22–23.

Brown, S.C., & Brown, D.G. (1996). Giving directions: It's how you say it. *Journal of Physical Education, Recreation and Dance, 67*(6), 22–24.

Buchanan, A., & Briggs, J. (1998). Making cues meaningful: A guide for creating your own. *Teaching Elementary Physical Education, 9*(3), 16–18.

Cothran, D.J., & Kulinna, P.H. (2006). Students' perspectives on direct, peer, and inquiry teaching strategies. *Journal of Teaching in Physical Education, 25,* 166–181.

Darden, G. (1997). Demonstrating motor skills: Rethinking that expert demonstration. *Journal of Physical Education, Recreation and Dance, 68*(6), 31–35.

Dillard, K. (2003). Using key words to develop sport skills. *Strategies.* November-December, 32–34.

Housner, L.D., & Griffey, D.C. (1994). Wax on, wax off: Pedagogical content knowledge in motor skill instruction. *Journal of Physical Education, Recreation and Dance 65*(2), 63–68.

Melville, S. (1988). Thinking and moving. *Strategies, 2*(1), 18–20.

Melville, S. (1993). Videotaping: An assist for large classes. *Strategies, 6*(4), 26–28.

Metzler, M. (1985). An overview of academic learning time research in physical education. In C. Vendien & J. Nixon (Eds.), *Physical education teacher education,* 147–152. New York: Wiley.

Mustain, W. (1990). Are you the best teacher you can be? *Journal of Physical Education, Recreation and Dance, 61*(2), 69–73.

National Association for Sport and Physical Education (NASPE). (1995). *Moving into the future: National standards for physical education.* St. Louis: Mosby.

Oslin, J.L., Stroot, S., & Siedentop, D. (1997). Use of component-specific instruction to promote development of the overarm throw. *Journal of Teaching in Physical Education, 16*(3), 340–356.

Parson, M.L. (1998). Focus student attention with verbal cues. *Strategies, 11*(3), 30–33.

Rink, J., & Werner, P. (1987). Student responses as a measure of teacher effectiveness. In G. Barrette, R. Feingold, C. Rees, & M. Pieron (Eds.), *Myths, models and methods in sport pedagogy,* 199–206. Champaign, IL: Human Kinetics.

Schmidt & Wrisberg. (2008). *Motor Learning and Performance.* 4th ed. Champaign, IL: Human Kinetics.

Siedentop, D., & Tannehill, D. (2000). *Developing teaching skills in physical education.* 4th ed. Palo Alto, CA: Mayfield.

Valenti, N. (2004). Visual cues, verbal cues and child development. *Strategies, 17*(3), 21–23.

Weiss, M.R., Ebbeck, V., & Rose, D.J. (1992). Show and tell in the gymnasium revisited: Developmental differences in modeling and verbal rehearsal effects on motor skill learning and performance. *Research Quarterly for Exercise and Sport, 63*(3), 292–301.

Wiese-Bjornstal, D.M. (1993). Giving and evaluating demonstrations. *Strategies, 6*(7), 13–15.

Wilkinson, S. (2000). Transfer of qualitative skill analysis ability to similar sport-specific skills. *Journal of Physical Education, Recreation and Dance. 71*(2), 16–18, 23.

## Chapter 7

# Motivating Children to Practice

*We were showing our classes the recently installed AED (automated external defibrillator) in our school. We simply wanted them to see it and to understand this is not a toy and it could save someone's life. We asked them a few questions about emergency situations including this one: "What should you do if you see someone having a heart attack?" We hoped they would say to call 911 or to find an adult. One student eagerly raised his hand and bounced up and down feeling very confident he had the correct answer. "Harry, what should you do?" Harry responded, "Stop, drop, and roll!" It was all I could do to keep a straight face.*

**Len Wojciechowicz, Spaulding, Gurnee, Illinois**
Reprinted with permission from PE Central (www.pecentral.org).

Parents with only one or two children understand the challenge of motivating children to become and stay involved in productive and worthwhile activities. (Only on rare occasions are television and Play Station or X-Box classified by parents as worthwhile.) Teachers understand how much harder it is to keep 25 or more children eagerly involved in the same activity. This chapter focuses on ideas that teachers use to motivate children to become and remain involved in practice that leads to learning and understanding.

## After reading and understanding this chapter, the teacher will be able to

▶ describe and provide examples of three keys to motivating children to practice;

▶ explain how teaching by invitation can be used to motivate children;

▶ analyze differences between teaching by invitation and intratask variation;

▶ describe how task sheets, learning centers, and peer tutoring can heighten the motivation of children;

▶ analyze the effective use of child-designed activities and videos as ways to involve children; and

▶ explain why helping children to set realistic expectations might be motivating.

## *Mentoring*

I am often struck by the fact that teaching is neither terribly difficult nor mysterious when it is one-on-one tutoring (e.g., a mother and daughter, an older and a younger brother, a grandparent and grandchild). Tasks can easily be changed and accommodated to suit the needs and interests of that child. The challenge in schools is that teachers are responsible for many children, have limited resources, and work in confined spaces—an awesome task that, viewed in perspective, is done remarkably well.

# THREE KEYS TO MOTIVATING CHILDREN

It's common knowledge that children learn by doing. Research on teacher effectiveness also clearly supports this premise. The challenge for a teacher is to involve all children most of the time in activities that are appropriate for their varying skill levels. Successful teachers motivate children by creating learning environments in which the tasks or activities are success oriented, intrinsically motivating, and developmentally appropriate (Block, 1995; Tjeerdsma, 1995).

## Success Oriented

Failure, especially when we have never had much success, makes us want to quit trying. If we have never succeeded, there's no reason to believe that continuing to try, and failing, will eventually lead to improvement. This rationale is quite typical of young children who have yet to make the connection between lots of practice and success (Lee, 2004). If we expect children to be motivated to practice a task, it needs to be one at which they can be successful—highly successful. The research literature, as well as common sense, suggest that when we're learning a new skill, success rates close to 80 percent are appropriate (Brophy & Good, 1986; Pellet & Harrison, 1996; Siedentop & Tannehill, 2000; Tjeerdsma, 1995).

With experience and age, we start to make the connection between practice and expertise (Lee, 2004). For example, an adult might think, *If I want to be a good skater, I will need to practice a lot. It will probably take months or even years.* In contrast a child might think, *I want to be a good skater. I tried it today. I fell down a lot. I can't skate.*

Successful children's physical education teachers are able to create and change tasks so that children are able to succeed at high rates. They also encourage children to modify tasks to make them easier or harder to better match their ability. At the same time, they discourage children from making social comparisons (Lee, 2004). Finally they try to make tasks fun so children enjoy doing them without necessarily realizing that participating in those tasks is leading to improvement. The following three examples, taken from actual classes, show how teachers design tasks so that children can succeed.

## Self-Adjusting Target Throwing

Each child in a class has his or her own beanbag and a cardboard box. The teacher challenges each child to throw the beanbag into the box but doesn't tell the child how far away from the box to stand. Watch how the children adjust the distance based on their ability. The less skilled stand closer; the more skilled stand farther from their boxes. Several successful throws might mean moving farther away; several failures mean the beanbag is thrown from a few steps closer to the box. Notice, too, that the more highly skilled children tolerate a lower rate of success than the less-skilled children (Rogers, Ponish, & Sawyers, 1991).

## *Self-Adjusting Shampoo*

One morning as I was showering, I read the label on the shampoo bottle. It claimed that the shampoo was self-adjusting—it would adjust its cleaning action to the particular needs of each person's hair. I thought, *That's exactly what we need for children—self-adjusting tasks that change based on the abilities and interests of the children in the class!*

## Slanty Rope

Here's another example of ways teachers design tasks to promote success. Set up two ropes on the floor in a slanty-rope design (Mosston, 1981). At one end, the ropes are close together. At the other end, the ropes are much farther apart. Children are challenged to jump over the ropes ("the river") without landing in the "water." Observe how they choose the location at which they jump the ropes to match their ability to jump for distance—the less skilled will jump the river at the narrower end, the better jumpers at the wider end.

## Varied Basketball Goal Heights

A third example of children wanting to be successful can be observed when several basketball goals are set at different heights on a playground. If children have a choice, many will choose to play at the lowest goal, thereby increasing their chances for success. Equipment designers have recognized this and now design and sell adjustable basketball goals.

It's interesting to take any of these three tasks and compare the involvement and interest of the children when they have no choice (i.e., when the distance or height is the same for every child). Typically, practice decreases and off-task behavior increases. The low-skilled child becomes frustrated; the higher-skilled child gets bored.

The purpose of designing and adjusting tasks so that children can be successful is so that they will continue trying. That is true in class and out of class. In math homework, for example, experts recommend that problems assigned to young children allow them to succeed at a 100 percent success rate, thereby increasing the motivation to do the homework. I wish I'd had a teacher who provided math homework assignments at which I could have succeeded. My memories are still vivid of the frustration, leading to exasperation, when I could do only 2 of 10 math homework problems. I wonder how much that contributed to my feelings of incompetence in math today.

Obviously, not every task a teacher designs can be self-adjusting and allow every child to be continually successful. The principle, however, is that success is motivating—and we want children to feel good about their physical abilities. They will have plenty of opportunities to experience failure and frustration—teachers don't need to intentionally create such opportunities for children.

## How Successful Are the Children?

One way to determine the success rate of children in a class is to use a coding form to provide objective evidence (figure 7.1). The form is easy to use. In fact, some children can learn to use it quite well (Wolfe & Sharpe, 1996). It can be used effectively, how-

Analysis of practice opportunities and success rate

Teacher's name_____ Observer's name_____

*Directions:* Select one child (try to make it a highly skilled child) and another child (try to make it a low-skilled child). Each time they attempt the skill presented in the task (kick with the instep, catch a ball, etc.) mark an "S" if the attempt is successful; mark a "U" if the attempt is unsuccessful. Switch your observation from one child to the other every other minute.

Criterion skill _____

| *Child #1* | *Child #2* |
|---|---|
| Total successful_____ | Total successful _____ |
| Total unsuccessful_____ | Total unsuccessful _____ |
| Total attempts _____ | Total attempts _____ |
| Success rate | Success rate |
| (Total successful ÷ Total attempts) _____ | (Total successful ÷ Total attempts) _____ |

**Figure 7.1** Sample form for analyzing practice opportunities and success rates.
From G. Graham, 2008, *Teaching Children Physical Education,* 3rd ed. (Champaign, IL: Human Kinetics).

ever, only with practice attempts that are easily counted. Lessons emphasizing throwing, catching, and kicking are ideal. By counting the successful and unsuccessful tries for a low- and a higher-skilled child in a class, an observer can obtain a reasonably accurate estimate of the number of tries for each child, as well as the success rate.

# Mastery Learning

In addition to creating success-oriented environments, effective teachers find ways to help children develop an intrinsic motivation for improving. This is called mastery learning. In a mastery climate, teachers provide children with

> ▶ a variety of tasks,
> ▶ opportunities to make decisions about the tasks,
> ▶ feedback (private recognition and evaluation),
> ▶ self-paced instruction and choices of tasks, and
> ▶ ways to measure personal improvement and avoid social comparisons.

A mastery learning environment encourages children to develop a high sense of independence or autonomy in their lessons, thereby encouraging intrinsic motivation (Valentini & Rudisill, 2004). Mastery teachers encourage children to practice hard so they can gain the satisfaction of seeing their own improvement rather than improve to please the teacher or to win a contest.

Mastery teachers encourage children to build and sustain an intrinsic motivation by avoiding social comparisons, both with other children in the class and with externally validated norms. In classes taught by those teachers, for example, you won't see contests to determine who can make the most shots, do the most sit-ups, or score the most points. Nor will you see teachers encouraging students to compare their performances with state or national fitness test norms. Teachers do invite students to compare their current and past performances to recognize how they are improving and to show them that practice and hard work eventually pay off (Alderman, Beighle, & Pangrazi, 2006; Lee, 2004; Rink, 2004; Valentini & Rudisill, 2004).

Perhaps the emphasis placed on intrinsic motivation can best be understood when placed in the context of a popular activity such as jogging (Xiang, Chen, & Bruene, 2005). Most adults don't start jogging because they expect to win races or set records. They jog because they feel good about improving their fitness and perhaps losing weight. If they want to, they can chart their personal improvement, which occurs rather rapidly. If they were forced to run races and have their times published in the newspaper, I suspect many would quit jogging. From time to time, however, many choose to enter a race. The important point is that they choose to enter a race for their own reasons. They don't have to. Why shouldn't children have those same choices?

## Ban the Spelling Bee

One of the most blatant violations of the idea that children should be allowed to choose whether they want to compete and have their performances compared with others is the spelling bee. For the few good spellers in a class, it's a marvelous competition. For the remainder of the class, who know they are not good spellers, not only is the spelling bee humiliating, but it also publicly reinforces what they have been thinking all along: They can't spell—and now the whole class knows it (Valentini & Rudisill, 2004). We have been doing spelling bees for years, culminating in a national competition every year in Washington, DC. Has this resulted in a nation of good spellers?

There is no way to prevent children from comparing their performances with one another. They do compare accomplishments, especially the highly skilled children. The difference, however, is that to encourage children to succeed on their own, the mastery teacher downplays the comparisons and avoids creating situations in which children are forced to compare accomplishments with one another.

As with virtually any endeavor, the higher-skilled children will seek extrinsic motivation by seeking out comparisons with others, typically through competition. The successful teacher makes these opportunities available but, again, only for those who choose to compete.

## Developmentally Appropriate

A third characteristic of a learning environment that is motivating to children is one that reflects age-related and physical differences in children. An environment that is developmentally appropriate encourages children to work hard and remain on task (Graham et al., 1992; NASPE, 2008; Stork & Sanders, 1996).

As children develop, they are motivated by different opportunities and experiences. Primary-grade children, for example, are eager to please the teacher and are therefore motivated by teacher praise and encouragement. Observe any kindergarten class and you will hear children saying, "Watch me! Watch me!" all day long. Furthermore, if children haven't learned to remain in one location, teachers will continually be trailed by five-year-olds wanting them to say "Wonderful!" after every attempt they make to jump over a rope or throw a beanbag into a box.

As children grow older, the desire to please the teacher is accompanied (in some cases apparently replaced) by a desire to please their peers. They also refine their ability to distinguish between motor skill ability and effort (how hard they try) (Lee, 2004). Attention and respect from peers are important factors in understanding the motivation of intermediate-grade children. The opportunity to work in groups to design activities or solve problems is often motivating for fifth graders who are so interested in peer interaction. They are motivated by the chance to design a game, dance, or movement sequence and then show it to their classmates (Valentini & Rudisill, 2004).

In addition to these age-related differences in children (Garcia, 1994), skill level influences the type of support that is effective. Poorly skilled children, who can be only minimally successful even when tasks are adjusted for them, need lots of praise and encouragement from the teacher to continue to work hard and to try. They also need to be assisted in learning a motor skill to help them understand that proficiency in motor skills requires much appropriate practice (Rink, 2004).

The highly skilled child, who receives satisfaction from succeeding at various tasks, seems to be motivated by praise focusing on the way a task is done (sometimes the results) rather than by the fact that the child is simply working hard. In fact, when teachers continually praise highly skilled children for succeeding at tasks that are relatively easy for them, they might inadvertently give the impression that PE is really for poorly skilled children. I believe this occurs with many athletes who are not challenged in physical education classes. They receive high amounts of praise for accomplishments that are much better than those of others in the class but that represent a relatively minimal effort on their part.

The Council on Physical Education for Children (COPEC) publishes a consensus statement describing both developmentally appropriate and inappropriate practices in children's physical education. The statement is called *Developmentally Appropriate Physical Education Practices* and can be downloaded for free at www.naspeinfo.org. Steve Stork and Steve Sanders used *Developmentally Appropriate Physical Education Practices* to develop a rating scale to evaluate a program's adherence to criteria suggested in the COPEC document (Stork & Sanders, 1996). Their scale is a helpful way to reflect on how well a program is meeting the developmentally appropriate criteria.

# EIGHT TECHNIQUES FOR MOTIVATING CHILDREN

Teachers use a variety of techniques to motivate children in attempting to create a learning environment that provides for high rates of success, avoids social comparisons among children, and accommodates individual differences. Included among these techniques are teaching by invitation, intratask variation, task sheets, peer tutoring and cooperative learning, stations or learning centers, child-designed activities, videoing, and homework practice.

## Teaching by Invitation

Children like to have choices, especially as they get older (Prusak, Treasure, Darst, & Pangrazi, 2004). One effective technique for children of all ages for adjusting tasks or activities to allow for individual differences is teaching by invitation (Tjeerdsma, 1995). The teacher provides two or more tasks and allows children to decide which task best suits their abilities. Let me provide several examples and then continue the discussion of this technique.

▶ "You might want to strike a balloon, a vinyl ball, or a playground ball."

▶ "If this is easy for you, try turning when you are in the air so that you land facing a different direction."

▶ "When you and your partner can catch the ball 10 times in a row, you might want to move your carpet squares farther apart."

▶ "Now I am going to put on some music. If you and your partner are ready, you can try to match your routine to the music."

▶ "I want you to do at least 25 sit-ups today (the teacher knows that every child can do at least that many). If you want to do more than that, go ahead."

▶ "You might want to work alone or with a partner."

▶ "In your game you might want to keep score or not. You decide."

When teaching by invitation, teachers need to be careful not to make one alternative appear or sound better than the other. Neither is better. It's simply a way of allowing children to adjust the task so they can be successful—and challenged. As teachers begin to use this technique, they find that children automatically begin to adjust the tasks to better match their ability. Actually, some children do this even when a teacher doesn't teach by invitation.

---

**See Teaching by Invitation**
The DVD that accompanies this text contains three examples of teaching by invitation preceded by a brief description of the process.

---

## Striking With Paddles: The Self-Challenge

When I teach children to strike with paddles, I often observe them modifying the task on their own to challenge themselves. For example, if I say, "Strike the ball to yourself and stay on your carpet square," some will strike at high level, some will strike at low level, some will strike with both sides of the paddle, and some will find it challenging to see how high they can strike the object and still remain on their carpet square.

When a teacher uses this technique, it's always interesting to see children decide which invitation they will accept. Some will choose to put down a balloon to work with a foam ball. If they realize they aren't successful, they will quickly return to the balloon; the same is true for the choice between punting a round ball or a foam football (Pease & Lively, 1994).

Older children typically choose to work with a partner or a group if they have a choice—but not always. On a number of occasions I have asked a child who seemed always to choose to work with a partner if he felt all right, as he had chosen to work alone that day. Sometimes the child didn't feel very well; other times he just preferred to be alone. I have days like that, too.

Obviously teaching by invitation is one technique in a teacher's toolbox. There are times when safety concerns, for example, make it inappropriate. In other instances teachers have a reason why all children need to work on the same task at the same time.

## Intratask Variation

Like teaching by invitation, the technique of intratask variation is appropriate for some classes and some lessons. It allows a teacher to modify a task based on the abilities and interests of the children. Intratask variation is different from the previous technique because the teacher makes the decision for the children (i.e., the teacher decides that a task needs to be changed for a child [or a group of children] to make it easier or harder) (Pellet & Harrison, 1996; Tjeerdsma, 1995). Probably this is a more difficult technique because the teacher is required to observe the children and then make a series of individual decisions based on his perceptions. Typically, intratask variation is used to make a task easier for the lower skilled—a different type of ball, landing on two feet instead of one, not turning when they jump—or harder for the higher skilled.

Another effective use of intratask variation is to provide highly skilled children, who don't really need basic skill practice, the opportunity to play a game that they are ready for. An example from my teaching illustrates the use of intratask variation. I was teaching hand dribbling to a class of fifth graders. The majority of children were at the stage at which they were challenged by trying to dribble and travel at the same time. A few of the children were well past this stage because they had been playing basketball on teams for several years. When I had provided the entire class with the task of dribbling slowly in general space, I called six children over who were highly skilled. My instructions were "Go down to the other half of the playground. Get a game going that has dribbling in it. As long as you get along and don't make a lot of noise when I stop the rest of the class to talk to them, you can continue with your game." Several things happened:

▶ As you might imagine, the six decided to play a modified version of basketball. They played the entire time. Several times I provided them with suggestions about how to dribble more effectively.

▶ The remainder of the class continued to practice dribbling and traveling and dribbling and trying to keep the ball away from an opponent.

▶ Some asked why they couldn't play with the other six. I explained that they could when they were able to dribble well enough, and I encouraged them to practice hard—not only at school, but at home, too.

Intratask variation allowed me to better match the task to the skill levels of the children. I find this especially appropriate for the highly skilled children, who frequently want to play a game. The fact is that, in many cases, they are ready to benefit from playing a game. On occasions when intratask variation is used, children become accustomed to it because they realize that it's not always the same children who are chosen to participate in the different activities. This is especially important in order to avoid stereotyping lower-skilled children. I have also found that the less-skilled children are delighted not to always have the highly skilled children with them as they learn new skills.

Most of the time, intratask variation is used with individuals or small groups, and others in the class aren't even aware that a task has been changed. To use the dribbling example again, if I didn't want to set up an actual game for the higher-skilled children, I might challenge them privately as I moved through the class: "Can you dribble it behind your back? Between your legs? Make a figure eight?" At the same time I might make the task easier for the lower-skilled: "Try dribbling the ball more in front of you. It's OK if you use two hands every once in a while." The point is that in every class the range of skill level is varied. Both intratask variation (modified tasks for individuals) and teaching by invitation (modifications suggested to the whole class) acknowledge differences by attempting to match tasks to children's skill levels, thereby attempting to minimize the boredom or frustration that occurs when all 25 children are required to do the same task.

**See Intratask Variation**
The DVD that accompanies this text illustrates how one teacher uses intratask variation in a dribbling lesson.

# Task Sheets

Another approach to provide children with higher rates of success by allowing them to progress at their own pace is to use task sheets. Task sheets are especially helpful for activities that are of a self-testing nature, such as jump rope skills or balance activities, but they can also be used with basketball and other team sport skills (Kozub, 2001). Typically the task sheet lists a progression from simple to complex, and children work at their own pace on the task (see figure 7.2). Task sheets are usually composed of individual skills rather than partner or group skills.

## Striking with paddles—task sheet

*Directions:* This task sheet lists 15 tasks. Some will be easy. Some will be hard. When you get to a task you cannot do, that is the one to spend time practicing on. Don't worry about others in the class. Just try to practice a lot so you can improve. I will help you as you practice. When you can do a task, write your initials beside it. You will need a foam paddle for each task.

| Initials | Task |
|---|---|
| _____ | 1. I can strike a balloon with a paddle 10 times in a row without the balloon hitting the floor. |
| _____ | 2. I can strike a balloon with a paddle 15 times and remain on my carpet square. |
| _____ | 3. I can spell my first and last name by saying a letter each time the ball hits the paddle— without a miss. |
| _____ | 4. I can strike a foam ball 20 times in a row without leaving my carpet square or the ball hitting the floor. |
| _____ | 5. I can dribble the ball 16 times in a row without a miss. |
| _____ | 6. I can strike a foam ball 18 times in a row doing "flip-flops"—one side of the paddle, then the other. |
| _____ | 7. I can spell the entire city I live in by saying one letter each time the paddle strikes the shuttlecock. |
| _____ | 8. I can hit a ball against a wall 13 times in a row without letting the ball bounce twice. |
| _____ | 9. I can hit a ball against a wall nine times in a row without letting the ball hit the floor once. |
| _____ | 10. I can hit a ball against a wall without letting the ball hit the floor once and not leave my carpet square. |
| _____ | 11. My partner and I can hit the ball back and forth nine times in a row without letting the ball bounce twice. |
| _____ | 12. My partner and I can hit the ball back and forth 11 times in a row without letting the ball touch the floor. |
| _____ | 13. I can hit a forehand, backhand, forehand, backhand,...against the wall 14 times without letting the ball bounce twice in a row. |
| _____ | 14. My partner and I can hit the shuttlecock across the net 21 times in a row without a miss. |
| _____ | 15. My partner and I can hit the ball to each other 25 times in a row without having the ball hit the floor. Each time I hit I have to change from a forehand to a backhand to a forehand to a... |

*Remember:* This is not a race! Take your time and try to do each task well. I will be here to help you. We will use this task sheet several more times this year.

**Figure 7.2**   Sample task sheet for striking with paddles.
From G. Graham, 2008, *Teaching Children Physical Education,* 3rd ed. (Champaign, IL: Human Kinetics).

Typically, teachers devise a way to hold children accountable for their progress. Some teachers design their task sheets so that the children can observe each other. If a task is done correctly, the child observing initials the task sheet, indicating the task has been accomplished. Other teachers prefer to have children show them when they are ready to be checked off on a task.

As with virtually every idea mentioned in the book, this approach works better for some classes and teachers than others. Obviously children need to be able to read and to work reasonably well on their own (self-directed) to use task sheets. It is also difficult to focus on the quality of the movement with task sheets—the emphasis is on results rather than on the process, which might lead to inefficient movement habits.

Newsome (2005) suggests that task sheets be designed so that even the lowest-skilled children in a class can accomplish at least a few of the tasks. He also recommends having more skills than anyone in the class can finish in the allocated time while reassuring children that they are not expected to complete the task sheet in one class period. This provides an opportunity for teachers to stress honesty and integrity when completing the tasks (Newsome, 2005).

Task sheets are most effectively used over a period of several months so that they can be revisited from time to time, thereby encouraging children to practice on their own because they know the task sheet will be used again later in the year. It's not very difficult for teachers to store the task sheets in a manila folder for later use.

Another advantage of task sheets is that they represent marvelous assessments of a child's progress that can be shared with parents at the end of the year. Some teachers who work in schools with low turnover rates of children can use the same task sheets for several years.

## Peer Tutors and Cooperative Learning

Peer tutoring and cooperative learning often work well in conjunction with task sheets and are another way to motivate youngsters to practice and work hard (Block, 1995, 1996; Ellery, 1995). A peer tutoring program can be especially helpful and motivating for youngsters with disabilities who are mainstreamed into physical education classes and for low-skilled youngsters. If a teacher plans to institute formal peer tutoring into her program, it is wise to select the tutors carefully (Ellery, 1995) and then teach them how to tutor (Block, 1995, 1996).

Ellery (1995) suggests the following criteria for selecting peer tutors:

▶ Age—they should be the same age or slightly older than the youngsters they will be tutoring.

▶ Maturity level—they should be able to cope with youngsters who learn at slower rates and remain positive and encouraging.

▶ Communication skills—they should have good verbal and nonverbal skills.

▶ Physical skill level—they often need to demonstrate, so they should be skilled enough to provide demonstrations.

▶ Volunteers—they should want to serve in this role.

Once tutors have been selected they need to be taught to tutor. They need to learn what skill components to look for so they will be able to provide helpful feedback to the youngsters they are tutoring (Block, 1995).

A less formalized form of peer tutoring, called cooperative learning, can also be motivating for youngsters (Kraft, Smith, & Buzby, 1997). In this process one child assumes a tutor role and the other a learner role. In this case, however, all youngsters serve as both tutor and student. Cooperative learning is often used with task sheets as youngsters work together to help each other improve. Both peer tutoring and cooperative learning have the potential to be motivating to youngsters. As with any of the concepts suggested in this book, however, success depends on the teacher, the youngsters, and the school environment.

## Stations or Learning Centers

Another frequently used approach that can be motivating for children is the use of learning centers or stations (see box 7.1 and figure 7.3). The teacher designs and organizes a number of activities in the gym or outside. The space for each activity is defined by cones or lines on the floor, a poster describing the activity is often displayed for each station, and the equipment necessary for that activity is provided. Children rotate from one activity to another, spending several minutes at each center. Obviously there is a variety of ways stations are used in children's physical education classes.

**Box 7.1**

# Example of a Station or Learning Center Format

## Directions

**Station 1:** Kick the ball against the wall. Try to catch it on a fly. If you catch three in a row, move your carpet square back five steps.

**Station 2:** Throw and catch the ball with your partner. Every time you catch the ball take one giant step backward. If you miss, both of you move back together again.

**Station 3:** This is a chance to practice striking with rackets. How many times can you and your partner strike the ball back and forth? You may want to make up a game.

**Station 4:** Look at the chart on the wall. Each picture shows you one of the tricks we have learned this year. Practice the ones that are hardest for you.

**Station 5:** When you dribble inside the square formed by the cones, someone else can try to steal your ball. When you dribble outside the square, it is a "safe zone" and no one can try to take your ball away.

**Station 6:** Volley the ball back and forth with your partner. How many times can you volley in a row? You and your partner might want to make up a game.

▶ Some teachers use centers as a review and set up five or six stations revisiting skills practiced over the past few lessons or weeks—rolling, dribbling, striking with paddles.

▶ At times, teachers use stations as a fitness workout and set up 15 or so stations that students visit for short periods because the activity at each one is so intense—bench step-ups, sit-ups, jump rope, jumping into and out of hoops.

**See Instant Activity**

Fitness stations are illustrated in the Instant Activity section of the companion DVD.

▶ Teachers frequently find stations effective when teaching primary grades. Young children often lose interest in an activity quickly because their skill levels are low and there isn't an opportunity for much variety within the same skill. Stations provide them

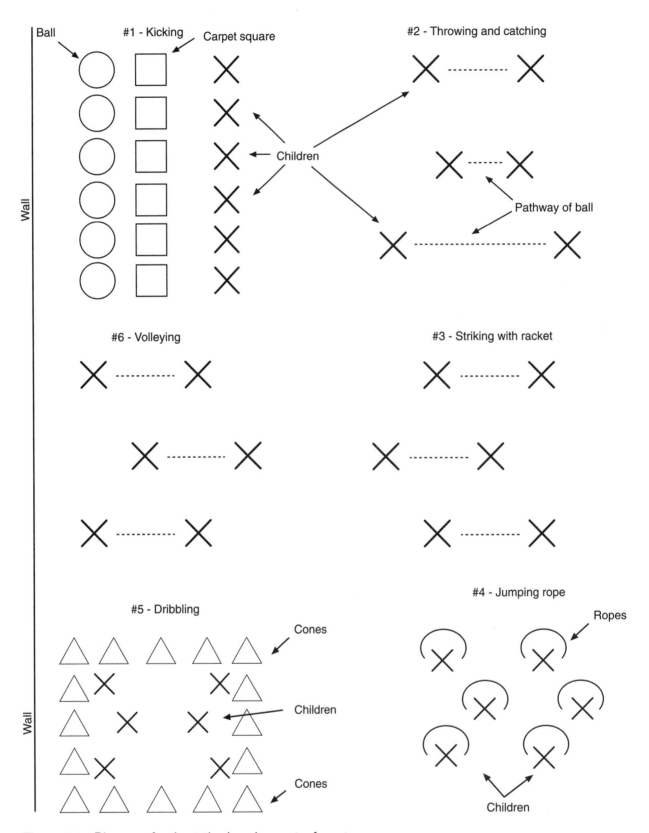

**Figure 7.3** Diagram of a six-station learning center format.

with an opportunity for variety even though all stations might require them to practice the same skill. One station might involve throwing a ball at a square on the wall; another might require throwing beanbags into a box; a third might challenge students to throw tennis balls to knock down bowling pins.

▶ Stations are also helpful when equipment is limited. Waiting for a turn can be eliminated because different equipment can be used at various stations.

As with so many other topics taught in physical education, children initially need to learn the protocol (chapter 3) for using stations. Typically the protocol focuses on

▶ putting equipment where it was before rotating,

▶ learning where to rotate next (from station 1 to station 2) to avoid mass confusion, and

▶ reading the poster at a station before beginning—this is especially important when children have a choice of several activities at the same center based on their ability levels.

## Child-Designed Activities

In a different vein, older children often enjoy the opportunity to work in small groups to design their own games, dances, or gymnastic sequences. This is motivating because children are working with their peers and are also encouraged to use their own creative abilities to solve the problem or meet a challenge presented by the teacher.

Kinetic sculpturing is a good example of a child-designed activity in which children work together to solve a problem. Groups of four to six children are challenged to create a group sculpture that moves. For example, the sculpture can be defined as

▶ symmetrical or asymmetrical,

▶ fast or slow,

▶ interpretive (their version of an escalator, a bicycle, a volcano) or improvisational (simply an interesting movement),

▶ or any number of other characteristics.

No special type of movement is required, so the low- and high-skilled children can work together in the same groups as integral parts of the sculpture.

It's fascinating to assign, rather than have children choose, groups for a challenge like this and watch them accommodate the various ability levels within their sculpture. In a group of five, two higher-skilled youngsters might be in handstands at the ends of the sculpture, supporting their legs on the two children next to them. In the middle we might find the lower-skilled child on his hands and knees, as all five sway slowly back and forth as a single unit. The feelings that emerge from an experience like this, when a solution is eventually achieved, are often positive and motivating for children. They all feel good about their work together.

**See Problem Solving**
An example of children designing their own games is illustrated in the Problem Solving section of the companion DVD.

## Videoing

When children cooperate in groups on a project such as kinetic sculpturing, positive feelings often result, but from a teacher's perspective the movement is often lacking in quality. Children have a hard time working toward a finished product. When children are invited to show one another their creations, it's typical for children to perform a brief dance or sequence that has never been done quite that way because they never do it the same way twice. It's hard to motivate children to really refine their dances or sequences beyond simply combining a few movements.

Video is a valuable tool for aiding this process (NASPE, 1995), because children can see their creations and begin to actually refine their work so that it achieves a certain level of quality—the slows are truly slow, the movements truly synchronous. As children begin to see their work evolve into an interesting design, in synchrony with others, they are often motivated to continue to practice. Without this visual feedback, they might be reluctant to work beyond the initial creation of a sequence to truly develop it into a work of art.

Video is also motivating when children are able to watch their performance of other skills such as batting, kicking, and rolling. It allows them to see how well they are doing and also where they can improve. No topic is more interesting to children than their own performances. Video allows teachers to take advantage of this human characteristic and channel it into a motivational tool in physical education.

## Homework Practice

The last of the eight techniques that can be motivating for some youngsters in some school settings is homework practice (Kraft, Smith, & Buzby, 1997). Children are provided with a homework task card listing a series of tasks for them to work on with a parent. Box 7.2 is an example of a task card for throwing and catching. It also contains a sample letter that a teacher can adapt and then send home with the task card. In some instances teachers might want to lend equipment (e.g., foam rackets, hockey sticks, juggling scarves) to youngsters if they do not have it at home. There is no guarantee that everything will be returned, but it is certainly worth a try if it encourages youngsters to become physically active outside of school.

# HELPING CHILDREN DEVELOP REALISTIC EXPECTATIONS

The approaches to motivating children described so far are techniques that teachers can use when teaching entire classes of children. Obviously there are many variations of each of these techniques that teachers use in their classes. A more long-term approach that doesn't fit neatly into the category of a technique is helping children to create and understand realistic expectations about the length of time and the amount of practice required to learn a skill.

Too often, children expect to learn to throw effectively in a single 30-minute lesson, for example. The teacher provides clear and interesting instruction and a good demonstration followed by a task. She neglects to tell the children, however, that the skill can't be learned in 20 minutes or after 35 throws—it takes much longer than that. When

Box 7.2

# Homework Task Card

Place a check mark next to the correctly completed tasks.

## Tossing

_____ Toss ball straight up in the air and catch it 10 times.

_____ Toss ball to an open space 10 times.

_____ Toss ball against a wall and catch it 10 times.

_____ Toss ball with a friend or parent 10 times.

## Throwing

_____ Throw ball to an open space 10 times.

_____ Hit a target 10 times.

_____ Throw ball against a wall and catch it 10 times.

_____ Throw ball with a friend or parent 10 times.

## Catching

_____ Catch ball on one bounce 10 times.

_____ Catch ball in the air 10 times.

My child, _____ , correctly completed the items checked above.

_____

Parent signature

- - - - - - - - - - - - - - - - - - - - - - - - - - - - - - - - - - - - - - - - - - - - - - - - - -

Dear Parents:

The enclosed ball has been loaned to your child just like a library book. Your child should practice the skills listed on the enclosed task cards and put a check next to the tasks completed. Throwing and catching spot-check lists are also enclosed so that you can make sure your child is doing the tasks correctly.

Please return the task cards and ball by _____ so that other students can benefit from this practice and experience. Thank you for your cooperation!

Reprinted, by permission, from R.E. Kraft, J.A. Smith, and J.H. Buzby, 1997, "Teach throwing and catching to large classes," *Strategies* 10(3): 12-15.

children are continually reminded that it takes a long time to learn a motor skill, they understand better that they're not failing (Rink, 2004; Schmidt & Wrisberg, 2008). It takes a lot of practice to learn a skill. They also understand the need to practice beyond class. There are things, however, that children can learn relatively quickly:

▶ The underhand throw is used for accuracy or when you are close to a target; the overhand throw is used for distance or force.

▶ A wide base of support results in a more stable balance than a narrow one.

▶ A leap means taking off on one foot and landing on the other.

▶ It's harder to take a ball away from someone who is dribbling at a low level.

The idea that it takes a lot of practice and time to be successful at a motor skill is one that apparently many adults don't understand either. Observe a foursome of golfers. If one is less skilled than the other three, watch how the skilled golfers continually provide tips to the poorer golfer. The assumption seems to be that if they could just provide the less skilled golfer with the magic cues, he would instantly become a good golfer.

As physical educators, we know that someone doesn't suddenly become a good golfer when he is told the magic cue. It might be the appropriate cue, but it takes a long time before it is incorporated into a golf swing schema that effectively integrates the cue into a functional motor plan (Schmidt & Wrisberg, 2008).

## *Physical Education Dropouts*

Sometimes I wonder if one of the contributing factors to children dropping out of physical education early might be unrealistic expectations. Others in the class who play on teams or in the neighborhood after school have learned a variety of skills—but not in physical education. If children really expect to become as good as their classmates in relatively few lessons, it's no wonder they become frustrated and conclude early that they're no good at physical activity.

## TEACHER AS CHEERLEADER

In the final section of this chapter on motivating children, I want to comment on the idea that children can be motivated by teachers who are cheerleaders. Cheerleader teachers buzz around the gym shouting things like "Terrific! Outstanding! Fantastic! Awesome!" as they encourage children to continue working and trying. It's an effective technique with some obvious limitations.

The first limitation is that some of us are not cheerleaders. Even if we wanted to be, we couldn't keep it up for 10 classes a day for 30 years. The second limitation is that if children come to expect this type of extrinsic motivation from a teacher, they rely on the teacher rather than on themselves for encouragement and a sense of improvement.

Fortunately, children aren't always taught by teachers who can or want to serve as the total source of motivation for children, even if they could. Given this reality, it is important for children to develop the inner satisfaction that comes from continuing to try and recognizing that, as a result of their effort, they are improving. Teachers can help children recognize that they are getting better, not as quickly as they might like, perhaps, but gradually. Teachers who motivate children this way, it seems to me, make an especially significant contribution to a child's eventual enjoyment of and satisfaction through physical activity. That's not to say that for some children, some classes, and some topics, cheerleading isn't important. It is, but children also need to experience the satisfaction that results from their own desire and motivation to continue working and trying.

# SUMMARY

One of the key challenges faced by any teacher is to motivate children so that they will want to continue learning independently of the teacher. This chapter describes a number of techniques that successful teachers of physical education use to motivate their students. As is true of so much of teaching, one technique alone won't continually motivate children. Effective teachers create an ambiance, an environment, that makes children truly want to learn—not because of the teacher's personality but because the lessons are designed so that children succeed and feel good about their progress.

# QUESTIONS FOR REFLECTION

1. Think about what motivates you to practice—success or failure? Is it different for different sports or activities? Has it changed with experience? With age?

2. Some teachers describe their classes as "no-fault zones." How might this concept apply to the ideas discussed in this chapter?

3. Throughout this chapter, techniques for modifying tasks to increase success are described. Can you think of ways you change tasks (or bend the rules) so that you can be successful?

4. Try to find youngsters (four to eight years old) playing together. Notice how they constantly invent and change the rules of play. Why do you think this is characteristic of the way they play? When do adults modify rules when they play together?

5. Which of the techniques described in this chapter do you feel most comfortable with as a teacher? Least comfortable? Why do you think this is so?

6. Do your students rely on you for their motivation? Do you want them to? Have you found ways to help them develop realistic expectations and intrinsic motivation? Try to understand and explain your answers to these questions.

# REFERENCES

Alderman, B.L., Beighle, A., & Pangrazi, R.P. (2006). Enhancing motivation in physical educa-tion. *Journal of Physical Education, Recreation and Dance, 77*(2), 41–45, 51.

Block, M.E. (1995). Use peer tutors and task sheets. *Strategies, 8*(7), 9–11.

Block, M.E. (1996). Modify instruction: Include all students. *Strategies, 9*(4), 9–12.

Brophy, J., & Good, T.L. (1986). Teacher behavior and student achievement. In C.M. Wittrock (Ed.), *Handbook of research on teaching.* 3rd ed., 328–375. New York: Macmillan.

Ellery, P.J. (1995). Peer tutors work. *Strategies, 8*(7), 12–14.

Garcia, C. (1994). Gender differences in young children's interactions when learning motor skills. *Research Quarterly for Exercise and Sport, 65*(3), 213–225.

Graham, G., Castenada, R., Hopple, C., Manross, M., & Sanders, S. (1992). *Developmentally appropriate physical education for children: A position statement of the Council on Physical Education for Children (COPEC).* Reston, VA: National Association for Sport and Physical Education.

Kozub, F.M. (2001). Using task cards to help beginner basketball players self-assess. *Strategies, 14*(5), 18–22.

Kraft, R.E., Smith, J.A., & Buzby, J.H. (1997). Teach throwing and catching to large classes. *Strategies, 10*(3), 12–15.

Lee, A. M. (2004). Promoting lifelong physical activity through quality physical education. (2004). *Journal of Physical Education, Recreation and Dance, 75*(5), 21–24.

Mosston, M. (1981). *Teaching physical education.* Columbus, OH: Bell & Howell.

National Association for Sport and Physical Education (NASPE). (1995). *Moving into the future: National standards for physical education.* St. Louis: Mosby.

National Association for Physical Education and Sport (NASPE). (2008). *Appropriate practices in elementary school physical education.* Reston, VA: AAHPERD.

Newsome, J.A. (2005). Task sheets and stations: Busy, happy and learning. *Strategies, 18*(6), 22–23, 31.

Pease, D.A., & Lively, M.J.A. (1994). Variation: A tool for teachers. *Strategies, 7*(4), 5–8.

Pellet, T.L., & Harrison, J.M. (1996). Individualize to maximize student success. *Strategies, 9*(7), 20–22.

Prusak, K.A., Treasure, D.C., Darst, P.W. and Pangrazi, R.P. (2004). The effects of choice on the motivation of adolescent girls in physical education. *Journal of Teaching in Physical Education, 23,* 19–29.

Rink, J.E. (2004). It's okay to be a beginner. *Journal of Physical Education, Recreation and Dance, 75*(6), 31–34.

Rogers, C.S., Ponish, K.P., & Sawyers, J.K. (1991). Control of level of challenge: Effects in intrinsic motivation to play. Unpublished manuscript.

Schmidt, R.A., & Wrisberg, C.A. (2008). *Motor learning and performance.* 4th ed. Champaign, IL: Human Kinetics.

Siedentop, D., & Tannehill, D. (2000). *Developing teaching skills in physical education.* 4th ed. Palo Alto, CA: Mayfield.

Stork, S., & Sanders, S. (1996). Developmentally appropriate physical education: A rating scale. *Journal of Physical Education, Recreation & Dance, 67*(6), 52–58.

Tjeerdsma, B.L. (1995). How to motivate students . . . without standing on your head! *Journal of Physical Education, Recreation and Dance, 66*(5), 36–39.

Valentini, N., & Rudisill, M. (2004). Motivational climate, motor-skill development, and perceived competence: Two studies of developmentally delayed kindergarten children. *Journal of Teaching in Physical Education, 23,* 216–234.

Wolfe, P., & Sharpe, T. (1996). Improve your teaching with student coders. *Strategies, 9*(7), 5–9.

Xiang, P., Chen, A., & Bruene, A. (2005). Interactive impact of intrinsic motivators and extrinsic rewards on behavior and motivation outcomes. *Journal of Teaching in Physical Education, 24,* 179–197.

SHOULD I CHANGE THE TASK? OR DO THEY NEED A CUE?

## Chapter 8

# Observing and Analyzing

*After my first graders got done running and leaping around the gym I told them to be sure to get drinks. Quite a few of them came back from the drinking fountain with wet shirts. I said, "Boy, your shirts must have been thirsty too!" Nick replied, "No, but my heart was really thirsty."*

**Carisa Thomason, Pine Ridge Elementary, Bend, Oregon**
Reprinted with permission from PE Central (www.pecentral.org).

Successful teachers provide children with plenty of developmentally appropriate practice. They rely on their ability to observe the children to determine what is appropriate (and inappropriate) for the various classes and children they are teaching. This appears straightforward. Observe the children. Analyze their movement. Make a decision whether to change the task, provide a cue, offer a challenge, or provide individual feedback. Seems easy.

It might be easy if we were teaching only one child. The problem, however, is compounded by the numbers. Some children will stray off task and perhaps become unsafe. Others will be doing the skill inefficiently and will benefit from the teacher providing them with a cue for improvement. Thus, another seemingly easy pedagogical skill is far more complex than it initially appears.

This chapter offers some practical techniques that successful physical education teachers use to observe and analyze both the safety and the quality of children's movement as a basis for making decisions.

## After reading and understanding this chapter, the teacher will be able to

▶ explain the difference between child-centered and subject-centered physical education,

▶ describe techniques for observing the safety and quality of children's movement in physical education classes,

▶ explain the questions a teacher might ask to guide her observation and analysis, and

▶ explain the importance and difficulty of observing and analyzing movement.

# CHILD-CENTERED AND SUBJECT-CENTERED DECISIONS

This chapter is one of the shortest in the book, but don't be misled by its length. It's also one of the most important. For some reason, it is assumed that physical educators are automatically effective observers who can readily detect unsafe behaviors and instantly analyze the critical elements of 25 or more children at a quick glance. Unfortunately, it's not that easy. But this chapter provides some tips and techniques used by successful teachers to heighten their observation skills.

## Child Centered

One of the premises of this book is that successful physical education teachers design their programs specifically for the children they are teaching: The programs are child centered. This means that each lesson is designed for particular classes of children. Lessons aren't rigid and unchanging; they're dynamic and interactive (Hautala, 1989). For example, there isn't one single lesson on dribbling or balancing that will be effective for every second- and third-grade class in a school. Because the skills of one class differ from those of another, teachers vary the way they develop the content of the lessons (chapter 9). Some classes progress more rapidly than others. Some classes are provided with different opportunities than others. In short, the program is child centered—the selection of the tasks and activities and the time spent on them is based on the observations made by the teacher. This is also called reflective teaching (Graham, Holt/Hole, & Parker, 2007).

## Subject Centered

Subject centered is the opposite of child centered. In a subject-centered class, the same lesson might be taught in an identical manner to all second- and third-grade classes in a school. The assumption in a subject-centered curriculum is that all children have the same abilities and can thus be expected to learn at similar rates. In these classes, teacher observation and analysis are not as important because decisions on which activities to teach and how long to teach them are made before the beginning of a class and remain unchanged throughout a lesson.

## Subject-Centered Dribbling for Kindergarten Children

Two examples of subject-centered activities should help make the distinction between child- and subject-centered physical education clear. The first example is from a kindergarten class. The children were partnered up. One in each pair was given a ball. The child with the ball was asked to dribble the ball and catch the partner who was running away—but who didn't have a ball to dribble. The task was interesting. Unfortunately, it was far too hard for virtually every child in the class. They were unable to maintain control of the ball while dribbling and standing still, let alone while running after a partner.

After attempting the task and failing, the children quickly made two adjustments so that they could succeed (chapter 7). Some of the children who were supposed to be dribbling simply tucked the ball under their arms and raced to catch their fleeing partners. Others simply abandoned the ball and chased their partners around the gym. If the purpose of the lesson was to help the children improve their dribbling skills, the activity was ineffective—the children were simply not dribbling. The teacher, however, didn't seem to see (observe) the children, as the activity was continued for several minutes with no change made to the task.

## Subject-Centered Volleyball

Requiring children to play by official, or adult, rules is another example of a subject-centered activity. I will use volleyball as an example. I could just as easily use basketball, soccer, softball, or flag football. Let me tell you what I often see when I observe a class of fourth or fifth graders playing by official volleyball rules. I observe

- some children who are afraid of the ball and who move quickly away from it to allow the more highly skilled children to hit it,
- some children who never hit a successful serve, and
- a lot of chasing after the ball and waiting because there are few successful rallies.

Volleyball is a great game—but only when players have developed sufficient skills to play it. The subject-centered teacher might require a class to play volleyball (official rules) for several days or even weeks in a row, often in a "tournament" format. The child-centered teacher, in contrast, would observe the children, analyze their lack of ability, and then change the game to match the skill level of the children.

Fortunately, we see this happening today in many elementary schools—lowered nets, softer and lighter balls, allowing children to serve as close to the net as they want so they can get the ball over, letting the ball bounce, and opportunities to practice the skills in small groups or play small-sided games with two or three children trying to volley a ball back and forth over a rope tied to chairs or a line on the floor (Graham, Holt/Hale, & Parker, 2007). These teachers are designing their lessons based on observations they make about the skill levels and characteristics of the children in their classes.

## *Subject or Child Centered?*

One of the easiest ways to determine if lessons are subject or child centered is to observe several lessons in a row taught to the same grade level. For instance, if all lessons taught to a third-grade class are virtually identical, the teacher is likely subject centered. If one lesson varies from the next, such as tasks being modified and different cues taught, then the teacher is probably child centered. Another way to assess whether an instructor is child centered or subject centered is to see how many balls are being used in a game. If only one ball is being used, does that assume that every child has the abilities required to play the game successfully and enjoyably? What if virtually all games played during a year use only one ball?

# OBSERVING INDIVIDUALS

In contrast to observing an entire class to make decisions about the appropriateness of an activity, teachers also observe individual children to determine how they can help them perform skills more efficiently. In this case, teachers observe individual children with the intent of helping them improve the quality of their movement and their use of the important components.

Harvey Penick, a famous golf instructor whose students include the well-known golfers Tom Kite and Ben Crenshaw, offered some fascinating insights into the difficulty of analyzing a movement as complex as the golf swing.

> "One of the toughest lessons I ever had to give was to Tom Kite following the 1981 season, when he was the leading money winner. He asked for a putting lesson, and after he left the shop I told one of my members that I dreaded giving Tom this lesson. The man asked why and I told him, 'There are a million things I could suggest to Tommy, and only one or two will help him. The rest could hurt, and I've got to figure out which is the right one or two.'" (Wade, 1989, p. 145)

This lesson was given privately, one on one, to an eager student who no doubt paid diligent attention to the instructor because he was so highly motivated. The situation of teaching entire classes of children, most at beginning skill levels and not all highly motivated, is at the opposite end of the continuum from a private golf lesson. These situations do have one thing in common, though—they both require an ability to analyze movement based on a thorough understanding of how the movement is acquired in developmental stages.

It's not enough simply to understand and analyze a movement, however. An instructor also makes decisions about which cues and feedback the students will benefit from the most (chapters 9 and 10). Again, the thoughts of Harvey Penick are helpful for placing this chapter on observation and analysis in an appropriate perspective:

> "There are six different ways to make a (golf) grip weaker or stronger. You can raise or lower the hands. You can change the ball position, close or open the clubface, or adjust the hands on the club. There's no right answer for everyone" (Wade, 1989, p. 144). And once the instructor has made the decision about the content of the feedback, Mr. Penick offers the sage advice: "You have to make corrections in your game a little bit at a time. It's like medicine: A few aspirin will probably cure what ails you, but the whole bottle might just kill you" (p. 144).

As I ponder Mr. Penick's comments, I can't help but wonder what he would suggest to physical education teachers who are responsible for teaching 25 to 30 children in a single class. I don't know. I do think he would agree that analyzing movement is a difficult task even under ideal circumstances. Clearly the ability to provide feedback (chapter 10) and develop a logical progression of experiences based on observation (chapter 9) is an important one for any physical education teacher. It allows us to provide the shortcuts and the proper foundation for productive practice leading to the eventual enjoyment and satisfaction of physical activity in adulthood.

# TECHNIQUES FOR OBSERVING

In a physical education class a teacher is continually required to observe 25 or more children simultaneously. There are a number of tricks that successful teachers use to effectively observe large groups of children. These tricks help them analyze the appropriateness of the tasks and activities for the children. They also help decide when and what type of feedback and cues will be most helpful. Simply knowing these observation techniques, however, is not enough. As with all of the skills described in this book, they require practice. These skills include back-to-the-wall, scanning, visitor observation, and one component at a time.

## Back-to-the-Wall

One of the most obvious techniques was described in chapter 4—standing with the back to the wall or to the outside of the boundaries. This allows a teacher to see most of what the children are doing. In contrast, when a teacher is in the middle of the action, at any given time half the children are out of sight (Arbogast & Chandler, 2005).

## Scanning

Scanning is another technique used by successful teachers. They have developed the habit of constantly sweeping the teaching area with their eyes, even when they are providing feedback to an individual, so that they are always aware of what students are doing. In the beginning it is a good idea for teachers to consciously scan a class. Most find it easier to scan from side to side, taking 8 or 10 seconds to find out what the children are doing. With practice, this becomes automatic. Although it would be great to have the luxury of observing only one child for a number of trials, similar to the way Harvey Penick taught his golfers, the fact is that as teachers we must constantly be vigilant, watching all children in a class.

## Visitor Observation

Another technique that seems to be valuable is to ask as we scan, "What would a visitor think if she walked into my class right now?" Think of the principal of the school, one

of your university professors, a member of the board of education, or a parent as you scan. This seems to help place observation in perspective and avoid the tunnel vision that sometimes mesmerizes us so that we see only one or two children and fail to see that many of the others have drifted off task.

I am reminded of basketball dribbling lessons I have observed when the teacher focuses on a poorly skilled child, only to look up several moments later to discover that several children have turned the dribbling lesson into a shooting and "slam dunk" contest. Thinking about visitor observation helps some teachers keep in mind the importance of constantly being aware of every child in the class.

## One Component at a Time

Observing a movement to detect errors and provide constructive suggestions is not an easy teaching skill to acquire (Coker, 1998). Some would argue that it is one of the most difficult. One technique that helps teachers become more effective observers is to select only one critical component at a time to observe. Rather than attempting to watch a child perform and pick out errors, the teacher selects an important component to observe. He assigns a task and then watches to see if the children incorporate the cue into their movement patterns. If they do use the cue correctly, then he would focus his observation on a different critical component. If he observed that many of the youngsters would benefit from focusing on the latter cue, then that would become the cue he would emphasize in the lesson. As will be explained in the next two chapters, this critical component is taught as a cue (chapter 9); then the children are provided with specific, congruent feedback (chapter 10) related to their use of that critical component.

For example, in a kicking lesson for first graders, the teacher might focus on using the inside of the foot rather than the toe. In a lesson focusing on striking with hockey sticks for fourth graders, the teacher might focus on keeping the ball close as it is dribbled around the field (Graham, Holt/Hale, & Parker, 2007; NASPE, 2004). The teacher would focus on only these components during observation until she was satisfied that they had been understood and incorporated into their movement, and then she would move on to another critical component.

## *Observing One Component at a Time*

As I watched many beginning teachers, one of the things I realized is how difficult it is for the novice to see all that is going on in a physical education class. For this reason I began to recommend that they observe only one component at a time. Soon after, I began to observe only one component at a time in my own teaching. What a difference it made—and I wasn't a novice! It's not only easier, it's also more effective, and both the teacher and the children are much clearer on exactly what is being taught in that part of the lesson.

# FOUR KEY OBSERVATION QUESTIONS

As I have already said many times, teaching is so complex that it isn't possible to focus on one teaching skill at a time—pedagogical skills are constantly interwoven. The teaching skills of observation and analysis are no different. The teacher is constantly watching students and asking questions. The following schema for observation (Graham, Holt/Hale, & Parker, 2007) is helpful for characterizing the types of observation questions that are continually on a teacher's mind (figure 8.1). The questions are listed in order of priority.

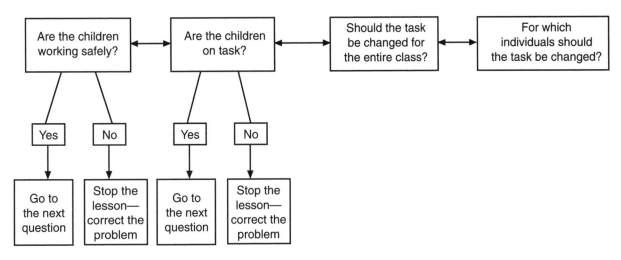

**Figure 8.1** Key observation questions.
Adapted, by permission, from G. Graham, S. Holt-Hale, and M. Parker, 2007, *Children moving: A reflective approach to teaching physical education*, 7th ed. (Mountain View, CA: Mayfield), 121. © The McGraw-Hill Companies.

## Are Children Working Safely?

This is a question teachers must constantly ask. Obviously the content of some lessons (e.g., gymnastics) will require them to ask this question more frequently. With so many children in a class, however, there is a constant need to observe for safety. It is a question that never leaves a teacher's mind (figure 8.1).

## Are Children On Task?

Teachers who spend time at the beginning of the year developing the management protocols (chapter 3) probably need to ask this question less than others. Some classes also stay on task better than others. Nevertheless, this is a question that teachers no doubt ask a number of times during every lesson. My impression is that experienced teachers ask this question subconsciously as they develop a teaching sense that lets them know something is awry almost as soon as it occurs, even when they are not directly observing the children in that area of the gym.

## Is the Task Appropriate?

Another question, typically asked after the first two, relates directly to content development (chapter 9). Is the task or activity appropriate? (figure 8.1). Are children able to work at success rates approximating 80 percent so that they will continue to be motivated to practice (chapter 7)? Does the entire class need a cue, or can I work with children individually to provide feedback?

This is a question constantly asked by teachers in child-centered programs of physical education. Because each lesson is varied for that class of children, teachers continually observe to see whether the task is appropriate and helpful for that class (chapter 9).

## How Are Individuals Using the Critical Component?

In this hypothetical observation schema (figure 8.1), once a teacher has determined that the children are safe and on task and that the activity is appropriate, the next question concerns the use of the critical component featured in that phase of the lesson. Initially the teacher might observe the entire class and then focus on individuals. For example, if the entire class is dribbling a ball, the teacher might look to see if they are using their finger pads rather than their palms. If they are correctly using their finger pads rather than slapping the ball with their palms, then the teacher would decide not to focus on pads. The teacher would choose another critical component such as looking away from the ball as they dribble.

## SUMMARY

The abilities to see with understanding, to observe, and to analyze are critical teaching skills for those who base their decisions on the ability of the children they are teaching (child-centered education). In contrast, for a subject-centered teacher, the ability to observe is far less important. As with so many of the teaching skills described in this book, in actuality there is no chronological order. Teachers are constantly analyzing children, and there are a number of techniques that help them observe more effectively. In addition, there are certain questions that are constantly on a teacher's mind.

## QUESTIONS FOR REFLECTION

1. In some ways observing a class of children can be compared to watching a team sport—it's difficult to see everything that is happening. Describe the strategies one might use to effectively observe a team sport and then compare them to teaching physical education.

2. At times it appears as if a teacher may be teaching games without realizing the game is far too hard or easy for a number of children in the class. What do you think is going through that teacher's mind as the children play the game? What would the teacher tell you if you were able to stop the lesson and ask?

3. Observing is a teaching skill that has to be learned. Why isn't it simply automatic? What's so hard about observing?
4. Think of the sports or activities you know best and those you know least about. Do you think your observation skills might be different for these activities? How do you plan to observe in the areas with which you are unfamiliar?
5. Observing one critical component at a time seems obvious. Why do teachers tend to try to observe many components simultaneously?

# REFERENCES

Arbogast, G., & Chandler, J.P. (2005). Class management behaviors of effective physical educators. *Strategies, 19*(1), 7-11.

Coker, C.A. (1998). Observation strategies for skill analysis. *Strategies, 11*(4), 17–19.

Graham, G., Holt/Hale, S., & Parker, M. (2007). *Children moving: A reflective approach to teaching physical education.* 7th ed. Mountain View, CA: Mayfield.

Hautala, R.M. (1989). The tape recorder teacher. *Journal of Physical Education, Recreation and Dance, 60*(2), 25–28.

National Association for Sport and Physical Education (NASPE). (2004). *Moving into the future: National standards for physical education.* 2nd ed. Reston, VA: NASPE.

Wade, D. (1989). An interview with Harvey Penick—golf teacher for Tom Kite and Ben Crenshaw. *Golf Digest,* (July), 144–147.

## Chapter 9

# Developing the Content

*I once was describing how to dribble a soccer ball with a kindergarten class. I told the kids that the right leg passes to the left leg, and the left leg passes to the right leg. A student raised her hand with her legs twisted and said, "My feet are confused!"*

**Nick Shepard, Redondo Beach, California**
Reprinted with permission from PE Central (www.pecentral.org).

The bottom line in teaching physical education is that children should be *learning!* As a result of the time they spend in physical education, it is reasonable to expect a permanent change of behavior—that is, they will become better runners, throwers, catchers, jumpers, balancers, batters, and so on. Historically in physical education the content, and the way it was delivered (pedagogy), has not led to children becoming skilled movers. The traditional model of doing calisthenics, running a lap, doing a drill or two, and playing a game has been a failure for too many. If you need proof, just observe a high school or college physical education class when they need to throw and catch a ball. You will see far too many of the students, most of whom had elementary school physical education, unable to throw or catch a ball effectively in game situations. In this chapter you will learn an alternative way of developing content, based on the research literature (Rink, 1994, 2006).

Content development is tied directly to planning (chapter 2), but it is far more than simply teaching a few activities that were planned while sitting at a desk or driving to work. Content development refers to the dynamic process of deciding on and implementing a developmental progression of activities so that children will achieve the objectives decided on by the teacher. This is called instructional alignment—matching intended outcomes (lesson objectives) with the teaching process and assessment (Siedentop & Tannehill, 2000; Peterson & Cruz, 2004). Decisions are made as the teacher observes students, reflects on her plan, and asks herself, "What will most benefit this third-grade class that I am teaching at 10:15 on Tuesday morning?"

In developing the content, the teacher is faced with a barrage of instructional alignment questions (chapter 8) he must answer about the tasks or activities he has outlined in his plan:

▶ Is this task (activity) truly helping students to improve?

▶ Should I change the activity now or wait a few minutes?

▶ Is there a cue that will help them improve?

▶ Is the task challenging enough?

▶ Are the tasks, cues, and challenges instructionally aligned so that they will lead to accomplishing my goals for the day? For the unit? For the year?

When a teacher truly develops course content, he is constantly observing his students (chapter 8). This chapter analyzes many of the decisions physical education teachers make as part of the process of developing the content.

## After reading and understanding this chapter, the teacher will be able to

▶ **explain the concept of task progression,**

▶ **analyze ways tasks are made harder or easier for children,**

▶ **explain cues (critical components) and the reason they are a necessary feature of effective teaching,**

▶ **explain challenges and the ways they are used to heighten the student interest in a task,**

▶ **code a teacher's task progression and explain its ramifications,**

▶ **describe a task progression format for planning, and**

▶ **describe the relation between planning (chapter 2) and developing the content.**

# TEACHER CHOICES IN DEVELOPING THE CONTENT

As physical educators, our purpose is to provide children with instruction and practice opportunities designed to lead to the following:

▶ Learning that is faster than trial and error

▶ A developmental progression of content that sequentially leads to improvement

▶ A functional understanding of the correct ways to perform skills so that children don't spend time in later years unlearning bad habits formed through trial and error without instruction or feedback

▶ Instruction in a variety of skills rather than just a few that children might select, only to wish in later years that they had been introduced much earlier to racket sports, for example (NASPE, 2004)

The challenge faced in virtually all programs of children's physical education is a lack of time. There are just not enough days and minutes in a school year to accomplish all that youngsters need. Teachers are thus faced with making some very important instructional alignment decisions about the content of the program and about the progression so that skills and concepts are learned quickly and efficiently. In chapter 2 we discussed the planning process. In this chapter we focus on developing the content by selecting tasks (activities) that are instructionally aligned and truly lead to learning; making tasks harder or easier, based on the observed abilities of students; providing tips for faster and more successful learning; and challenging students to remain interested in practicing activities that are important for improving.

During a lesson, a teacher has essentially three choices after the introductory activity (chapter 5) and the initial explanation (informing) on how students should do an activity. She can choose to

- ▶ change a task (activity) to make it easier or harder,
- ▶ focus on *how* to do the task by providing cues that will make the children more efficient movers, or
- ▶ provide a challenge to the children to give them an opportunity to test their ability and motivate them to continue working on the task.

These three choices are difficult when a teacher is attempting to provide developmentally appropriate practice opportunities for an entire class of children, because classes vary from one to the next, as does the variety of children's ability levels within a class (Graham et al., 1992). It would be much easier, for example, if the teacher simply decided how long to do a task and changed by the clock rather than by the progress the children made (a subject-centered approach; see chapter 8). As one quickly realizes, however, clocks are poor judges of how long children need to practice a given skill and which skill needs to be practiced next. Providing children with experiences that are developmentally appropriate requires a teacher to constantly make decisions about how to develop the content so that the progression of tasks is appropriate.

# Informing

Informing (Rink, 2006) is essentially providing students in a class with information. Most often it resembles a minilecture and might focus on rules, the agenda for that day's class, how to begin a lesson, what to do in case of a fire drill, or other topics. Informing is the function that the layperson would consider to be "the teaching act" and is described in chapter 6. In fact, however, it is only one part of developing the content. The other three functions of developing the content have not yet been discussed in detail.

# Task Progression and Delivery

Task progression implies following a logical, developmentally appropriate sequence of tasks that leads to skill development, physical fitness improvement, or concept understanding. Teachers make a task harder or easier to match the developmental level of their students. It is rather easy to understand this concept. The process of changing tasks, however, so that they match the ability of the children and, just as important, provide them with useful practice opportunities in a logical progression is more difficult. It's easy to find or invent stuff that the children will have fun with. Unfortunately, all too often these experiences are a dead end because they don't lead to improved motor performance. If a teacher just wants to keep children happy, fun activities are appropriate. Schools don't hire professionals, however, solely to keep children entertained.

**See Extending (tasks)**
The DVD that accompanies this text provides one example of a teacher introducing several tasks in a lesson on the skill theme of striking with paddles.

Thus the tasks a teacher presents to students have a definite purpose and progression—they are designed to gradually and sequentially lead children to improved performance and versatility. They have a definite purpose. Box 9.1 shows a progression of tasks from the skill theme of dribbling a ball with the hands (Graham, Holt/Hale, & Parker, 2007).

In addition to being logically sequenced, tasks are designed to provide students with high rates of success (in the 80 percent range; chapter 7). This is why a teacher needs to plan an entire series of task progressions (chapter 2), which then allows him to make a task easier or harder based on student observations (chapter 8).

Development of subject matter expertise and pedagogical content knowledge (chapter 2) takes time and practice to develop. In one study (McCaughtry & Rovegno, 2003), novice physical educators were blaming the children for being off task until they gained the insight that effective task progression and analysis requires a thorough and detailed understanding of children's motor skill development. One student said this about the children: "I thought they (the children) weren't trying. Now I realize that I was the one not paying enough attention. We (other novice teachers) were too stuck on seeing them as a problem to be able to break (the tasks) down and pay attention to what they were doing wrong" (McCaughtry & Rovegno, 2003, p. 364).

## Making Tasks Easier or Harder

It's clear that a teacher needs to have a thorough and practical understanding of the content being taught. This allows her to sequence tasks in a logical progression. When she doesn't understand the content, a progression might be uneven (the difficulty from one task to the next is too large) or unproductive (the tasks don't truly lead to skill improvement) (Hastie & Vlaisavljevic, 1999; Quinn & Carr, 2006; Tjeerdsma, 1997). In general, five factors are typically modified to change the difficulty of a task. Although these factors cannot be applied to every skill we teach, they do provide an overview of how tasks are made easier or harder for children.

### Static to Dynamic

One way tasks are made harder is by changing a movement from static (one movement done in self-space) to dynamic (combining two or more movements and often changing space). It's harder to run and throw a ball than simply to throw from a standing position; it's more difficult to roll after a jump than from a standing position; it's harder to dribble a ball while traveling than while remaining in one place.

### Number of Movements

The number of movements in a task also contributes to its relative difficulty. Jumping and then making a shape in the air is harder than simply making a shape on the floor.

Box 9.1

# Developmental Progression of Tasks for the Skills Theme of Dribbling

## Precontrol Level

Striking a ball down and catching it

Striking down (dribbling) continuously with both hands

Dribbling with one hand

## Control Level

Dribbling at different heights

Dribbling continuously while switching hands

Dribbling with the body in different positions

Dribbling in different places around the body while stationary

Dribbling and traveling

## Utilization Level

Dribbling and changing speed of travel

Dribbling while changing directions (i.e., forward, backward, sideways)

Dribbling in different pathways

Dribbling around stationary obstacles

Dribbling against an opponent: one on one

## Proficiency Level

Starting and stopping; changing directions quickly while dribbling

Dribbling against opponents (e.g., 3 versus 1)

Playing Dribble Tag

Passing with a partner while traveling

Dribbling and passing in game situations

Dribble Keep-Away

Dribbling and throwing at a target

Playing 2 versus 2 basketball

Using Harlem Globetrotters' dribbling and passing routines

Adapted, by permission, from G. Graham, S. Holt-Hale, and M. Parker, 2007, *Children moving: A reflective approach to teaching physical education*, 7th ed. (Mountain View, CA: Mayfield), 524. © The McGraw-Hill Companies.

It's more difficult to jump and then catch or throw a ball. Rolling at different speeds and in varying directions increases the challenge of rolling.

## Number of Children

A third factor influencing task difficulty is the number of children. When we ask children to move in relation to a partner or in a group, the task is typically harder than when moving alone. This is especially true in synchronized movements, in which we challenge children to match the movement of their partners. In the upper grades the task of moving in relation to four or five others in a game or dance is complex. It takes a lot of time and practice to reach a recognizable relationship with one another that can be maintained as the speed and the spaces change. In the same vein, games with two are typically easier to organize and implement than games with six or eight. In addition to the challenge of moving in relation to others, children also learn about cooperating with others to achieve a common goal (chapter 12).

## Modification of Equipment

Equipment is another way to change the difficulty of a task. In the past few years tremendous progress has been made by sporting goods companies in the design of equipment for children. Foam balls, paddles, and hockey sticks are a few examples. Smaller, lighter, more colorful balls that don't hurt when they hit you are another. Basketball goals and nets that can be easily adjusted for height are great aids to the teacher, as are plastic bats and Wiffle balls. In fact, it is becoming increasingly rare to see "adult" equipment used in elementary schools. If this trend continues, wooden bats, softballs (which aren't soft), and official size and weight basketballs, volleyballs, footballs, and soccer balls in elementary schools might some day be as rare as inkwells are now.

## Use of Defenders

A fifth factor influencing many game task progressions is the challenge of eluding opponents. Attempting to dribble, catch, or kick a ball when guarded is far more difficult than attempting to do so unhindered. My sense is that this principle of progression has been violated more than any of the others by physical education teachers in the past. Youngsters were placed in game settings long before they were ready to play against an opponent. I am afraid that, as a result, the poorly skilled child quickly concluded, "I am no good," because he was unable to play a game successfully when it was necessary to elude a defender. My observation suggests that those children quickly resorted to the role of competent bystander (Tousignant & Siedentop, 1983). They could be found in right field, allowing others to take their turns in line, and as far away from the ball as possible in games like soccer and basketball.

One of the ways teachers help the poorly skilled child to succeed is by introducing defenders into games gradually. For example, after children become reasonably competent at dribbling a ball while traveling, the teacher begins by having only one or two children attempt to steal the ball from the entire class. As children become more adept at dribbling against opposition, the number of stealers can be increased to four or five.

Another example of an uneven-sided game is four children trying to maneuver a ball into a goal against one defender (four versus one). As the skill of working in this dynamic setting increases, the game might be changed to three vs. two. The advantage of uneven sides is that the child who is unaccustomed to playing in games with defenders has the chance to ease gradually into this setting without being overwhelmed by the number of defenders. This is also why small-sided games, with two or three on a side, are generally recommended for children in elementary schools (Graham et al., 1992; NASPE, 2008).

As stated at the beginning of this discussion, the progression of tasks the teacher uses to develop the content is crucial if children are going to improve their skills in the limited time allotted for physical education. Children don't learn to throw or jump or balance or move rhythmically in an hour or two—it takes a lot of practice—and they need to have some success if they will continue to practice. Here's another insight gained by a novice teacher in the study by McCaughtry and Rovegno (2004): "You have to find things that can be successful because no one wants to do things they aren't good at. You don't want to swing at a ball all day if you're not going to hit it. They (children) want some success, and that is what we (teachers) should gear ourselves toward" ( p. 362).

## How Many Tries?

A question I often ask is how many tries it takes a student who is a true beginner at a skill to become proficient? Think of a major league pitcher or a professional dancer, for example. How many times did they throw a ball or leap before they became truly proficient? The number is staggering, certainly well into five figures, probably six for most athletes.

## Cues (Critical Elements)

In addition to the developmental progression of tasks the teacher provides, another important aspect of learning involves the most efficient ways to perform various motor skills: the form, proper technique, or strategy. These are often called cues or critical elements (NASPE, 2004). The teacher refines (Rink, 2006) the movement by observing and analyzing the critical components of the movement and then providing cues to students to help enhance the quality of their movement (Buchanan & Briggs, 1998; Gallagher, 1995; Pellet & Harrison, 1995). Obviously a task can be appropriate, but that doesn't necessarily mean students are performing the skill correctly. Cues help children learn a skill quickly and correctly, avoiding bad habits (Masser, 1993; Pellet & Harrison, 1995).

When a teacher is deciding on an appropriate cue, she needs to consider the difficulty of changing, or modifying, the movement given the amount of time available. Some cues, for example, can be changed quickly, whereas others require a total rebuilding of the movement pattern (Coker, 2005). As teachers, our goal is to assist all students in

becoming efficient and effective movers. We need to be realistic, however, when asking a child to make drastic changes to their performance—especially when time (days) is limited. Clearly this is another challenging decision teachers need to make when deciding which cue to provide, and when.

Clearly, one of the teaching skills demonstrated by effective instructors of any sport or physical activity is the ability to provide the right cue at the right time. They are able to provide the proper "mind picture" that lets the learner pay attention to the cue that increases the efficiency of the movement and then provide practice opportunities that encourage children to focus on that cue.

A parent with a minimal background in physical education often uses the cue "keep your eye on the ball" for many skills—catching, batting, kicking, punting, hitting a tennis ball, and so on. Occasionally this is the right cue. More often, however, it is inappropriate—the child is missing the ball but not because of where his eyes are focused. The skillful physical education teacher, in contrast to the uninformed parent, can provide the child with an appropriate cue that enables him to concentrate on an aspect of the movement that leads to an efficient motor pattern for that skill.

**See Refining (cues)**
The companion DVD includes two examples illustrating cues or critical components being emphasized in the lessons.

# The Magic Cue

A popular misconception about teaching physical activity is that there is a magic cue. If a teacher can just find that cue, the learner will instantly improve and become proficient. Golfers are notorious for trying to discover the magic cue. In reality, we know that the cue might be appropriate but that one single trial is not enough to make a cue a habit. It won't automatically help the first time it is explained and demonstrated. When I was learning to downhill ski, for example, the cue that initially helped me the most was to "keep my weight forward." But the first time I heard that cue and concentrated on it, I didn't magically ski the hill without falling. Fortunately, my instructor kept repeating it, and eventually I incorporated the cue into my motor pattern and began to fall less and less (Schmidt & Wrisberg, 2008).

As with the process of extending tasks, teachers need to understand the critical components of a movement and their sequence of development in children to know which cues to focus on and when. The cues teachers use for beginners will not be very helpful for advanced students, and vice versa. Box 9.2 provides a general idea of the types of cues that might be helpful for beginners and those for more advanced students. The children's physical education teacher faces the challenge of understanding many skills for many activities as she attempts to introduce the cues taught in elementary school. In contrast, the high school track coach can use the cues appropriate for advanced performers of a single sport.

---

**Box 9.2**

# Examples of Cues for Beginners and More Advanced Students

## Beginner Cues

- How to hold or grip an implement (e.g., a racket, a ball)
- Appropriate stance (e.g., knees bent, side to target)
- Movement concept (e.g., like a wheel, level, slow to fast)
- Use of body parts (e.g., arms spread, elbow leads, step with front foot)

## Advanced Cues

- Body parts move sequentially (e.g., hips then shoulders)
- Concentrate on how others are moving
- To change the speed, direction, angle of the object . . .
- As you move in relation to others think about . . .

---

## One Cue at a Time

Because we do know skills so well and because time is so short, one tendency of physical educators is to overload children with more information than they can possibly remember or use (chapter 6). In the past, physical educators explained and demonstrated five or six cues at the beginning of the lesson—and expected children to remember all of them! Today we know that it is more effective to focus on a single cue at a time (e.g., tucking the chin to the chest during a forward roll; Schmidt & Wrisberg, 2008). Instruction includes a brief explanation and demonstration, and then feedback (chapter 10) focuses on this single cue. Using this format, the children and the teacher are thinking about the same cue ("tuck the chin to the chest"). When a variety of cues are explained at the same time, children might think about one cue and the teacher another cue, thereby making the feedback incongruent (chapter 10).

A question I am often asked is "How do you know which cue to focus on?" Beginners need to concentrate on so many cues. But what typically happens is that so many cues are provided that children don't really remember any of them. The challenge of teaching is to select one cue to help children most, then focus on that cue until the children know it, and then move to another one.

Thousands of adults throw and step with the same hand and foot (no opposition). Many of them were in physical education classes. They were reminded to step with the opposite foot, but they weren't reminded often enough to have learned it. One or two lessons focused only on this cue is sufficient for most children to learn the concept, assuming, of course, that the skill will be quickly revisited throughout the years.

Typically, children can describe a cue before they can actually do it. First they understand it. Then they begin to incorporate it into the schema of that movement. Eventually, after a lot of practice, the skill becomes automatic.

One way to understand the importance of cues and of teaching them one at a time is to think of learning to drive a car that has a stick, rather than an automatic, shift. When we start, we understand that to shift without grinding gears we have to step on the clutch. We understand it. We can't do it, however. After many attempts at shifting, the process becomes internalized, and we no longer have to think about stepping on the clutch as we shift. At that point in learning to drive, however, the proper way to step on the clutch is the cue we need. Until we learn this, it doesn't make much sense for our instructor to tell us how to drive in snow or enter a freeway at high speeds. We belong in the parking lot, not on the freeway.

The same principle applies to learning other motor skills. The right cue at the right time is crucial for enhanced and enjoyable learning. When one or two cues are presented many times throughout a class while a teacher focuses on proper technique, it is obvious to the observer which of the cues is being emphasized—and, most important, it is clear to the children. During closure (chapter 13), they are able to recall the cues because they have heard and observed them throughout the lesson.

Finally, it is important to make the point that in a single lesson several cues might be emphasized, depending on the children and how quickly they grasp the concept and are able to incorporate it into their motor patterns. Ideally, however, cues are emphasized one at a time rather than together for the reasons I have explained.

## Which Cue?

One of the difficulties faced by teachers who see their children only one or two days a week is deciding what to include in the curriculum. There just isn't time for children to learn everything (chapter 2). Generally, however, it is agreed that children can at least learn basic cues for the more common skills, such as throwing, jumping, balancing (NASPE, 2004). They might not always use them in their movements, especially when playing games or performing a sequence in front of classmates, but they can verbally describe the cues so that they can recall them when they are "on their own" and no teacher is present. Chapter 13 provides practical suggestions for ways a teacher can realistically assess which cues students know as a result of the program.

## Challenges

Cues aren't learned just because they are explained and demonstrated. They require practice. Children, however, don't necessarily see the value in continuing to practice a skill. The connection between practicing and learning is neither understood nor valued by most children. The dilemma faced by the teacher is how to maintain students' interest in a task so that they can continue to focus on the cue until it is internalized. Challenges, also called applications (Rink, 2006), are one way to maintain the interest of children in continuing to practice a task without making the task more difficult for those who are not yet ready.

**See Applying (challenges)**
The DVD that accompanies this text demonstrates the use of challenges to motivate youngsters to practice the skills of volleying and using quick feet in a dodging game.

An example from math might help illustrate how challenges are used by teachers. When a math instructor is teaching a simple strategy, such as how to carry a number in long division, the successful math instructor uses her pedagogical content knowledge to devise a variety of ways to keep children involved with that concept until they have learned it and can apply it to other problems. The ineffective teacher covers the process, but the children don't really learn it and, consequently, they have difficulties later when they are expected to be able to carry numbers correctly in long division problems.

The process works the same in physical education. When children can't volley a ball thrown gently to them or strike a ball accurately with the hand, it makes little sense for them to be required to play an official game of volleyball. Children who have yet to learn the prerequisite skills need to continue to practice those skills; those who have the necessary skills are ready to begin games using these skills (chapter 7).

## Teacher, You Just Left Me Behind . . . Again

One of the criticisms of education (not only physical education) is that we leave children behind who don't learn as quickly as others. Tumbling comes immediately to mind. Teachers often start, for example, with a log roll, then progress to a forward roll, a backward roll, a cartwheel, headstand, handstand, and so forth. Many of us needed to stay at the backward roll. We hadn't learned it, but the teacher kept introducing new skills. The process of challenging children, as described in this chapter, provides a way for the teacher to maintain the interest of the children who have learned the backward roll while still working with those who are slower to grasp the cues. Here are some examples:

- **"Some of you might want to try two backward rolls in a row."**
- **"Can you and your partner start and stop your backward rolling at the same time?"**
- **"If this is easy for you, you might want to combine a forward roll and a backward roll."**

Providing challenges is a technique for maintaining the interest of the children without changing the task. As with task development, there are a number of ways that teachers have devised to challenge children.

## Repetitions

One of the simplest ways teachers challenge children, without making the task harder, is to provide self-tests that encourage the children to meet a goal suggested by the teacher. In these examples children are already doing the task (e.g., jumping over a hoop, attempting to catch a ball, or dribbling a ball). They continue the task, but the teacher challenges them to see if they can meet a standard or goal:

▶ "Can you jump over the hoop and land without falling three times in a row?"

▶ "How many times can you catch the ball on a fly?"

▶ "See if you can beat your old record."

▶ "Bounce the ball for each letter of your first name (the name of the school, the capital of California, the president of the United States)."

## Cognitive Challenges

Another way teachers find to interest children in continuing to practice a task is by using cognitive challenges. These challenges reinforce what children are learning in the classroom while making the task more enjoyable and fun.

▶ "This time strike the ball with your paddle as many times as the answer to this problem—10 divided by 2.

▶ Children dribble to pieces of papers taped to the wall (floor) and answer the question on the paper, such as: What is the capital of Virginia?

▶ Children jump over vocabulary words (taped to the floor) they are studying in class and say the word out loud while in the air.

▶ An obstacle course is set up in the gym. Each time children successfully complete part of the obstacle course (e.g., skip along a bench, crawl through a hoop backward without knocking it down), they take a word from one of the buckets placed on the obstacle course. Challenge them to make a complete sentence with the words they find.

Needless to say, classroom teachers and principals are delighted when physical educators can reinforce concepts being taught in the classroom.

## Timing

Another self-testing technique is competing against the clock. Here are examples:

▶ Children are attempting to jump and land in a balanced position. The teacher challenges them by asking, "Can you hold the balance for at least five seconds?"

▶ Children are throwing and catching, or kicking or striking a ball with a paddle to a partner. The teacher challenges them to keep the ball going for 30 seconds.

▶ Children are jumping rope, and the teacher challenges them to jump continuously for 10 seconds, 15 seconds, and so on.

## Keeping Score

Some skills (movements) lend themselves to keeping score. When fourth graders or fifth graders are playing a game with defenders (e.g., 2 versus 2) , they might be challenged to figure out a way to keep score. This will motivate some to continue practicing a skill longer than if score isn't kept. Sometimes scores can be cooperative (how long can one pair keep a ball going?). Although it is not always feasible, scoring seems to work best when children are provided with a choice—keep score only if you want to (chapter 7).

Typically, more skillful children are interested in competing with others; they find this challenging because they have mastered the skill in static environments. These children truly enjoy and benefit from opportunities to use their skills in competition with others.

## Replays

Replays, as a way to challenge children, are used more in gymnastics or dance settings. "Can you repeat the movement exactly so that both tries appear identical?" This is a true challenge for children, especially if they are trying to repeat a sequence of several movements. It's even harder when the sequence is performed with a partner. Thus teachers often use replays to heighten the challenge for children: "Imagine that I videoed your sequence. Let's see if you can do it again exactly as I recorded it."

## Video

In the example just cited, the video was imaginary. When video recording is available, however, encouraging children to work on their sequence or dance to improve it to performance quality for videoing can be highly motivating. Children enjoy seeing themselves on TV. The possibility of being videoed often provides incentive to continue working on a project that might otherwise be abandoned early because of lack of interest. Obviously the teacher is attempting to motivate children to continue improving the quality of their movements.

Another technique that is used is similar to pinpointing (chapter 6). Children are asked to show others in the class how they are doing a task. Rather than attempting to teach the children, however, this challenge is used to motivate them to continue practicing so that they can show others. This technique can be used in several ways:

▶ "All those on this side of the gym will do their sequences three times. After that we will switch, and that half of the class can sit down and become spectators."

▶ "Who would like to demonstrate their game for the rest of the class?"

▶ "I am looking for routines that clearly show the different speeds and levels that can be shown to the class at the end of the lesson."

▶ "Steve and Jenny have found a different way to make their balance. Let's see how they have solved the problem."

## Challenges for the Young Child

Young children have a limited movement vocabulary. Thus it is difficult to challenge them by combining two skills because they are unable to do the skills by themselves, let alone when skills are combined. Because of the limited vocabulary and the short attention span of these youngsters, teachers find that a minor change in a task (it is embellished more than changed) is often satisfying to the four- or five-year-old child. The following examples are truly minor changes, yet they interest young children because they are developmentally appropriate for them. Young children perceive minor changes as new challenges.

▶ "Now find a different carpet square to balance on." (The balance might be the same, but now it is on a blue rather than a brown carpet square.)

▶ "After you throw five times, find a different-colored beanbag to throw." (The throw is the same except it is now done with a yellow instead of a red beanbag.)

▶ "Now see if you can walk on a blue line without falling off." (They are challenged to find the color blue although they are still focusing on balancing on a line.)

▶ "Make a different shape with your rope. Then continue trying to jump over the rope and land without falling." (The focus is still on jumping and landing; the shape of the rope is different.)

▶ "Now turn and skip the other way around the hoop." (The task has been changed from a clockwise to a counterclockwise skip.)

In each of these examples the challenge remains the same. The children, however, are motivated by the opportunity to try the task in what is (for them) a new setting.

# CONTENT DEVELOPMENT PATTERNS

One of the fascinating aspects of teaching is the difficult process of deciding when to change a task, provide a cue, or offer a challenge to the class. Ideally, these decisions are based on the progress made by the children rather than arbitrary factors such as time or number of tasks to be covered in a day. Few would argue with this concept; in reality, however, it's hard to know when to change from one to another. But successful teachers can do it in a way that is interesting to the children and also leads to motor skill, fitness, and concept development.

A number of content development patterns evolve as teachers work with different classes. A brief description of these patterns might help explain how teachers vary tasks, cues, and challenges in their teaching. These patterns can be graphed to aid understanding (figure 9.1). The vertical axis contains tasks, cues, and challenges. The horizontal axis simply numbers each task, cue, or challenge so that the pattern of use can be understood. Each time the teacher stops the entire class, the observer writes down what he says (summarizes the key points) and codes it later as a task, cue, or challenge. This is easily done from a video as well. The way the content was developed can then be interpreted by the teacher to determine the pattern he used.

## All-Task Pattern

When a teacher initially works with a class of children, it is not uncommon to observe changes from one task to another very quickly. This occurs as the teacher attempts to discover the skill level of the children in that class (figure 9.2). This pattern is also observed frequently with beginning teachers who have yet to use challenges to keep

Teacher's name_____ Observer_____

Class taught_____ Date_____

Lesson focus_____

*Directions:* Write down the statements the teacher makes to the entire class—not to groups or individuals—about motor skills—not about behavior or management.  At times you may need to abbreviate, but try to capture the intent of the meaning.  When the lesson is over, classify each statement as extending (tasks), refining (cues), or applying (challenges). Then graph the statements in the order in which they occur.  You may need to use the back of the sheet to record all of the statements.

1.

2.

3.

4.

5.

6.

7.

8.

9.

10.

(continue on back)

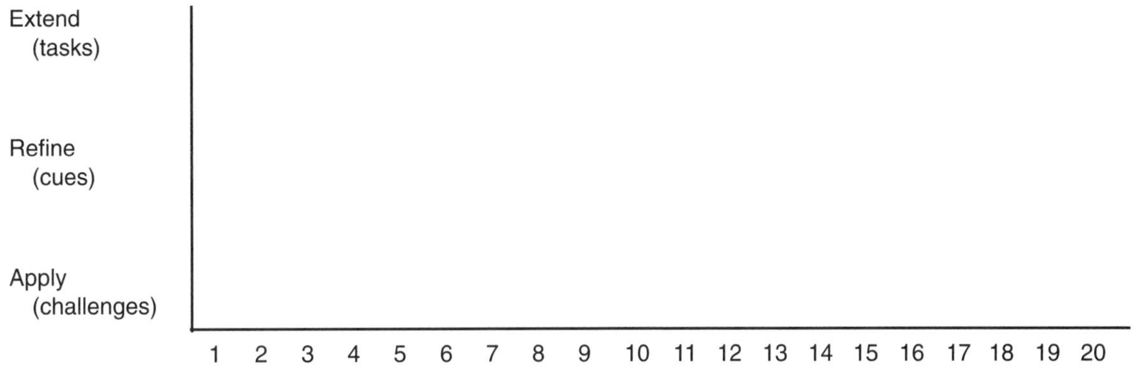

Extend
  (tasks)

Refine
  (cues)

Apply
  (challenges)

    1   2   3   4   5   6   7   8   9   10  11  12  13  14  15  16  17  18  19  20

**Figure 9.1**  Assessing your pattern of content development.

From G. Graham, 2008, *Teaching Children Physical Education,* 3rd ed. (Champaign, IL: Human Kinetics).

Teacher's name _____ Ron _____ Observer _____ Julie _____

Class taught _____ Mrs. Speck's, 2nd Grade _____ Date _____ Dec. 5 _____

Lesson focus _____ Dribbling with hands _____

*Directions:* Write down the statements the teacher makes to the entire class—not to groups or individuals—about motor skills—not about behavior or management. At times you may need to abbreviate, but try to capture the intent of the meaning. When the lesson is over, classify each statement as extending (tasks), refining (cues), or applying (challenges). Then graph the statements in the order in which they occur. You may need to use the back of the sheet to record all of the statements.

1.  Bounce the ball with 2 hands; stay on your carpet square.

2.  Bounce the ball with 1 hand; stay on your carpet square.

3.  Bounce the ball at low level only; stay on your carpet square.

4.  Bounce the ball with your other hand; stay on your carpet square.

5.  Walk around your carpet square and dribble the ball.

6.  Walk in general space and dribble the ball.

7.  Walk in general space and dribble the ball at low level.

8.  Jog and dribble in general space.

9.  Skip and dribble in general space.

10.  When the drum beats, stop traveling, but continue dribbling.

(continue on back)

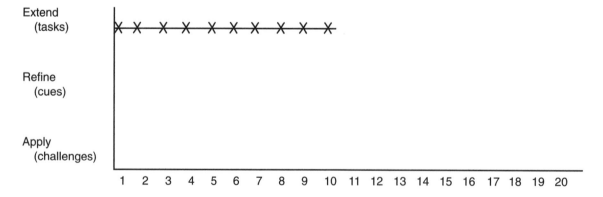

**Figure 9.2**  All-task pattern of content development.

From G. Graham, 2008, *Teaching Children Physical Education,* 3rd ed. (Champaign, IL: Human Kinetics).

children working at the same task. Instead, they make the task harder when they think children are becoming bored, rather than providing them with a challenge while keeping the task the same.

Another common content development pattern is a repetition of task, cue, task, cue, and so on (figure 9.3). In this instance the teacher might be reviewing previously taught tasks. If a lesson is not a review, however, and if the cue is different each time, this suggests that children might not be learning the cues because of the limited practice time and opportunities to understand the critical component the teacher is emphasizing. This is probably what happened for many adults today who have failed to grasp the concept of opposition when throwing.

## Task-Cue-Cue Challenge Pattern

The pattern of starting a task, followed by instruction and demonstration of the same cue several times, followed by a challenge (figure 9.4) suggests that a teacher is truly developing the content so that children can learn it (i.e., she is emphasizing the quality of the movement and keeping children on the same task because it is appropriate for their ability level). This pattern is often observed in experienced teachers who are familiar with the process of content development and who strive to help their students learn the critical components of the various skills (Masser, 1987).

## Interpreting Content Development Patterns

A pattern of content development can be observed and analyzed rather easily by a teacher who wants to determine the way he is developing the content in a class. The patterns, however, provide a teacher with information only about the number of tasks, cues, and challenges and their sequence. That's helpful to know.

It's at least as important, however, to make a judgment about the quality of the tasks, cues, and challenges. Just because a teacher uses a particular content development pattern doesn't necessarily mean that it was a good or poor lesson. The pattern always needs to be interpreted within the context of the lesson, considering such factors as the skill level and experience of the children in the class, the number of times the skill has been taught previously, and the progression in which tasks were presented.

In addition, the quality of tasks, cues, and challenges can also be judged in terms of their appropriateness and effectiveness. Did the pattern work with that class? Why? Why not? How might it be improved? These decisions are based on the way the children are moving, as determined through observation. Let's assume the teacher videos a lesson and then reviews it that evening at home. She might ask herself these questions:

▶ Did the children understand and use the cues being emphasized during the lesson? Were they actually moving quickly to the ball (a cue for that lesson)? If I ask them in two weeks (six months), will they remember the cue?

▶ Was the cue appropriate? Was it the one they really needed at that point in their skill development?

▶ Was the progression of tasks too hard? Too easy? (She would look at the success rate of the children and also make a judgment about the children's interest in the tasks.)

Teacher's name_____Kakki_____Observer_____Marilyn_____

Class taught_____Ms. Bray's, 2nd Grade_____Date___Dec. 5_____

Lesson focus_____Dribbling with hands_____

*Directions:* Write down the statements the teacher makes to the entire class—not to groups or individuals—about motor skills—not about behavior or management.  At times you may need to abbreviate, but try to capture the intent of the meaning.  When the lesson is over, classify each statement as extending (tasks), refining (cues), or applying (challenges). Then graph the statements in the order in which they occur.  You may need to use the back of the sheet to record all of the statements.

1. Walk around your carpet square and dribble your ball.

2. Use your finger pads, not your palms.

3. Walk in general space and dribble the ball.

4. Look up from the ball.

5. Walk in general space and dribble the ball at low level.

6. Look up from the ball.

7. Jog and dribble in general space.

8. Try to push the ball ahead of you.

9. Skip and dribble in general space.

10. Try to push the ball ahead of you.

(continue on back)

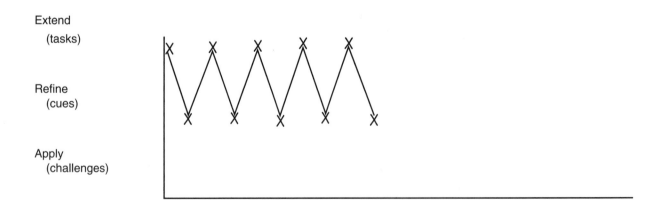

**Figure 9.3**  Task-cue-task-cue pattern of content development.
From G. Graham, 2008, *Teaching Children Physical Education,* 3rd ed. (Champaign, IL: Human Kinetics).

Teacher's name _____ Steve _____ Observer _____ Vickie _____

Class taught ___ Ms. Sander's, 2nd Grade _____ Date ___ Dec. 5 ___

Lesson focus _____ Dribbling with hands _____

*Directions:* Write down the statements the teacher makes to the entire class—not to groups or individuals—about motor skills—not about behavior or management. At times you may need to abbreviate, but try to capture the intent of the meaning. When the lesson is over, classify each statement as extending (tasks), refining (cues), or applying (challenges). Then graph the statements in the order in which they occur. You may need to use the back of the sheet to record all of the statements.

1.  Walk in general space and dribble the ball.

2.  Use your finger pads, not your palms.

3.  Look over the ball.

4.  When I hold up my fingers, tell me how many.

5.  Jog and dribble in general space.

6.  Look over the ball.

7.  Try to push the ball ahead of you.

8.  When you pass someone, call out their name.

9.  Skip and dribble in general space.

10. Look over the ball.

(continue on back)

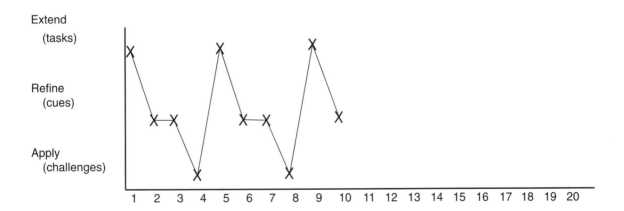

**Figure 9.4** Task-cue-cue challenge pattern of content development.
From G. Graham, 2008, *Teaching Children Physical Education,* 3rd ed. (Champaign, IL: Human Kinetics).

▶ Were tasks changed unnecessarily or too quickly? (This often happens when a teacher has taught the same skill to five or six classes in a row and is tired of it, but the children might not be.)

▶ Did the challenges truly motivate the children to practice longer?

▶ Were tasks appropriate to accomplish the objective for the lesson? Did they truly provide the children with plenty of appropriate practice?

As a teacher views a video in the relative solitude of an office or a home, she can see many more things than she can during the turmoil of teaching. This is the time to truly evaluate the quality of her content development.

# SUMMARY

Many children can learn to leap, roll, play basketball, bat a ball, and jump rope with no help from adults—if they want to. They don't learn as quickly or as efficiently as they might with instruction, however. And, as with eating vegetables, they tend to choose only the skills and activities they like.

Developing the content refers to the process of helping children learn the various motor skills that are typically taught in physical education. As part of this process, teachers decide how long children should practice a task, which tasks and cues are most appropriate, and how to challenge children so they will continue meaningful practice.

# QUESTIONS FOR REFLECTION

1. In contrast to developing the content to help children truly learn, some teachers simply "teach" fun activities to children with little thought about progression or cues. Their goal appears to be to keep them busy, happy, and good but not necessarily learning. Why do you think that is so?

2. Think about your own background. Which skills do you know the most about? What are five cues that would help children learn this skill? What about a skill you know very little about? Describe five cues for this skill if you can.

3. Again think about your background. Select a skill you know best. Can you outline a progression of tasks from simple to complex (similar to that in box 9.1)?

4. Throughout this chapter I have mentioned that the teacher relies on a plan to develop the content. It has been implied, however, that the teacher doesn't follow this plan without reflecting on it and making changes as necessary. Why is it important to base content development on a plan but also to make changes if appropriate?

5. Challenges are an important part of the teaching process. Briefly describe what might happen if teachers did not use challenges.

# REFERENCES

Buchanan, A., & Briggs, J. (1998). Making cues meaningful: A guide for creating your own. *Teaching Elementary Physical Education, 9*(3), 16–18.

Coker, C. (2005). Faulty mechanics: To fix or not to fix? *Strategies, 19*(1), 29–31.

Gallagher, J.D. (1995). Critical cues: Can they really help me teach children? *Teaching Elementary Physical Education, 6*(1), 15–16.

Graham, G., Castenada, R., Hopple, C., Manross, M., & Sanders, S. (1992). *Developmentally appropriate physical education for children: A position statement of the Council on Physical Education for Children (COPEC).* Reston, VA: National Association for Sport and Physical Education.

Graham, G., Holt/Hale, S., & Parker, M. (2007). *Children moving.* 4th ed. Mountain View, CA: Mayfield.

Hastie, P.A., & Vlaisavljevic, N.C. (1999). The relationship between subject-matter expertise and accountability in instructional tasks. *Journal of Teaching in Physical Education, 19,* 22–33.

Masser, L. (1987). The effect of a refinement on student achievement in a fundamental motor skill in grades K through 6. *Journal of Teaching in Physical Education, 6,* 174–182.

Masser, L. (1993). Critical cues help first-grade students' achievement in handstands and forward rolls. *Journal of Teaching in Physical Education, 12*(3), 301–312.

McCaughtry, N., & Rovegno, I. (2003). Development of pedagogical content knowledge: Moving from blaming students to predicting skillfulness, recognizing motor development, and understanding emotion. *Journal of Teaching in Physical Education, 22,* 355–368.

National Association for Sport and Physical Education (NASPE). (2004). *Moving into the future: National standards for physical education.* 2nd ed. Reston, VA: NASPE.

National Association for Sport and Phyiscal Education (NASPE). (2008). *Appropriate practices in elementary physical education.* Reston, VA: NASPE.

Pellet, T.L., & Harrison, J.M. (1995). The influence of refinement on female junior high school students' volleyball practice success and achievement. *Journal of Teaching in Physical Education, 15*(1), 41–52.

Peterson, S., & Cruz, L. (2004). What did we learn today? The importance of instructional alignment. *Strategies,* May/June, 33–36.

Quinn, R., & Carr, D. (2006). Developmentally appropriate soccer activities for elementary school children. *Journal of Physical Education, Recreation and Dance, 77*(5), 13–17.

Rink, J.E. (1994). Task presentation in pedagogy. *Quest, 46,* 270–280.

Rink, J. (2006). *Teaching physical education for learning.* 5th ed. New York: McGraw-Hill.

Schmidt, R.A., & Wrisberg, C.A. (2008). *Motor learning and performance.* 4th ed. Champaign, IL: Human Kinetics.

Siedentop, D., & Tannehill, D. (2000). *Developing teaching skills in physical education.* 3rd ed. New York: McGraw Hill.

Tjeerdsma, B. L. (1997). A comparison of teacher and student perspectives of tasks and feedback. *Journal of Teaching in Physical Education, 16*(4), 388–400.

Tousignant, M., & Siedentop, D. (1983). A qualitative analysis of task structure in required secondary physical education classes. *Journal of Teaching in Physical Education, 3*(1), 47–57.

# Providing Feedback

*We were beginning striking with paddles in the kindergarten classes. The classes were receiving instruction on how to keep the wrist stiff when contacting the piece of equipment being struck. The classroom teacher came to pick them up and one student proceeded to exclaim, with much excitement, "I had fun playing with those 'skillets!'" I guess the association came from the use of "flipping pancakes" while we were tossing and catching beanbags with a stiff wrist.*

**Paula Green, Price's Fork Elementary School, Blacksburg, Virginia**
Reprinted with permission from PE Central (www.pecentral.org).

When a teacher observes a class and makes a decision that

  ▶ the task is appropriate for the children,
  ▶ they don't need a challenge because they are practicing the task intended, and
  ▶ the cue or critical component has been understood,

that is a good time to provide feedback. The teacher observes children individually and apprises them of how they are moving and what they can do to improve. The purpose of this chapter is to describe and analyze the various types and uses of feedback.

## After reading and understanding this chapter, the teacher will be able to

▶ describe the advantages and uses of feedback,

▶ assess who is getting feedback from the teacher,

▶ analyze various types of feedback, and

▶ explain the value of feedback for teachers of children's physical education.

# TYPES OF FEEDBACK

The use of feedback by a teacher has several advantages:

▶ Feedback encourages children to continue practicing because it lets them know you are watching them move (Silverman, Tyson, & Krampitz, 1992).

▶ When teachers provide feedback, they also tend to travel around the teaching area, as opposed to standing in one spot, an effective teaching behavior (chapter 4).

▶ Feedback helps children assess their performances, which they can't really see or feel on their own.

▶ Feedback lets teachers assess individuals to determine how quickly (and correctly) they are learning the skill being taught (Stroot & Oslin, 1993).

## KP or KR?

Feedback can be classified in many ways (Lee, Keh, & Magill, 1993; Schmidt & Wrisberg, 2008; Silverman, Tyson, & Krampitz, 1992). One of the more common distinctions is between knowledge of performance (KP) and knowledge of results (KR). Knowledge of results refers to the outcome or product of the movement (e.g., the ball hit the target). Knowledge of performance refers to the characteristics of the movement (the cues or critical components), also referred to as the process of the movement (Boyce, Markos, Jenkins, & Loftus, 1996; Schmidt & Wrisberg, 2008). The discussion of feedback in this chapter focuses on knowledge of performance or the movement process.

Successful teachers provide various amounts and types of feedback to accomplish these purposes (Nicaise, Cogerino, Bois, & Amorose, 2006). Typically, feedback provided by successful teachers can be categorized as specific, congruent, simple, and generally positive or neutral (Sharpe, 1993).

## Specific to General Feedback

Feedback is specific when it contains information that allows children to know exactly what they need to practice or how they are moving (Claxton & Fredenburg, 1989; Mustain, 1990; Pellett & Harrison, 1995; Rink & Werner, 1987; Silverman, Tyson, & Krampitz, 1992). Feedback is general when it might refer to any of several factors, such as children's movement, behavior, or dress.

Probably the most commonly used expression of general feedback in education today is "Good!" Unfortunately, this really doesn't provide the child with the necessary information to improve—was it the outcome, result, or process (performance) that was good? Or was it simply a good try?

Expressions such as "good," "great," "terrific," "wow," and "all right" are helpful for promoting a positive and warm learning environment, especially with young children who desire teacher approval and have yet to achieve the skill level that allows them to obtain intrinsic satisfaction from being able to move in accomplished ways (Sharpe, 1993). Teachers often use general feedback to encourage children to continue to move and continue to try.

As children mature, they benefit from the information the teacher provides that they can't know themselves. They know, for example, that the ball isn't going where they want it to—they just don't know what they need to do differently. This is when specific feedback is valuable because it tells them exactly what they need to focus on, for instance, to get the ball into the air or to make it go straight.

Here are some examples of specific feedback (knowledge of performance):

▶ "This time see if you can bend both your knees and your ankles."
▶ "Be sure to turn your side toward the target."
▶ "Great. That time you both started at the same time."
▶ "Can you make your shape even wider?"
▶ "This time see if you can make the slow part even slower."
▶ "Try to follow through so that your hand and arm go right to the target."

At times, when children are familiar with the terminology the teacher uses, one or two reminder words (chapter 6) can provide individuals with specific feedback about how they are moving. Typically this occurs when the feedback relates to a cue or refinement recently explained by the teacher. "Side" or "wait" or "bend" might be the single word that the teacher says in these instances (table 6.1).

## Congruent and Incongruent Feedback

When feedback focuses on the cue or refinement just explained (chapter 9) and often demonstrated to the entire class (chapter 6), this is termed congruent feedback (i.e., it corresponds to the idea just presented to the children that, ideally, they are thinking about as they move) (Masser, 1993; Pellett & Harrison, 1995; Rink & Werner, 1987). An example will help make the point.

The lesson is focused on learning to strike with a paddle. The task the fourth graders have been working on is striking the ball back and forth with a partner. The teacher stops the class and demonstrates the concept of "quick feet" (moving quickly to be in a position to hit the ball). He then asks them to continue striking with their partners and thinking about "quick feet"; he begins to circulate and provide feedback. If he provides congruent feedback, we will hear him tell the children how they are (or are not) using "quick feet" to move to the ball.

If he provides incongruent feedback, we might hear him tell the children about how to hold the paddle, to watch the ball, to follow through, to extend the elbow, and other important components related to striking with paddles. These examples of incongruent feedback are often used by teachers. They are not wrong—just incongruent because they are inconsistent with what the children have been asked to think about and pay attention to as they practice.

When teachers provide congruent feedback, they attempt to limit their feedback to the information most recently provided as they explained the cue to the entire class. This doesn't mean that some children don't need feedback about other cues—often they do. Congruent feedback, however, lets children know how their practice of the cue is going; they receive feedback about what they are thinking and practicing. This is often reinforced through pinpointing (chapter 6), in which certain children are asked to demonstrate the cue to the entire class.

**See Teacher Feedback**

The DVD that accompanies this text provides an example of a teacher emphasizing the cue "elbow to ear" as children play a game involving throwing and catching.

## Simple Feedback

One of the advantages of providing congruent feedback for the teacher is that the teacher focuses on only one component at a time (chapter 8). This is referred to as simple feedback. This is far easier and no doubt more accurate than attempting to do a complete biomechanical analysis of all children in the class as the teacher moves around, attempting to quickly observe and review the correct use of four, six, or even eight critical components (chapter 8).

In addition to being easier for the teacher, the children benefit because they continually hear (see) the cue being repeated as the teacher moves about providing feedback. Obviously, this repetition promotes learning (Sharpe, 1993). It also gives the teacher a better idea of when to change the cue because she knows when children are incorporating it into their movement.

Let's look at another example of simple feedback. When the most recently taught cue relates to the use of the finger pads in dribbling, this might be the feedback pattern we hear:

▶ "Pads, Mark."

▶ "Nice pads, Rosa."

▶ "Ferman, are those your finger pads?"

▶ "Liz, good pads."

▶ "Pads, Verenda."

▶ "Use your pads, Shawn."

Simple feedback can often consist of a word or two; reminder words used to describe the cue during instruction (chapter 6) are repeated as feedback. When a teacher provides specific, congruent, simple feedback, it's easy to tell what is being emphasized. In fact, those teachers who say "pads" hundreds of times during their eight or more classes are sick of the word by the time the day is over. But they have the satisfaction of knowing that when the 200 to 300 children they teach in a day go home, they can answer the question, "What did you learn in PE today?" Well, realistically, many of the children will be able to answer the question.

## Positive, Neutral, and Negative Feedback

Overall, the best feedback is positive feedback (Schmidt & Wrisberg, 2008; Sharpe, 1993; Silverman, Tyson, & Krampitz, 1992). It is encouraging to youngsters and creates a warm, pleasant atmosphere as compared to a nagging, harsh environment where youngsters are made to feel that they are continually doing something wrong. Review the previous examples and you will notice that the examples of feedback are either positive ("nice, good") or neutral ("pads"). Negative feedback is not used by many teachers (Silverman, Tyson, & Krampitz, 1992). Overall, it is effective for teachers to vary the affective message of the feedback: sometimes positive, sometimes neutral, occasionally negative (Kniffen, 1988). It is also helpful when the teacher provides feedback both verbally and visually by demonstrating a skill and, when appropriate, physically guiding the student through a movement (Sharpe, 1993). This way teachers ensure that youngsters truly grasp concepts being emphasized.

Feedback can influence performance of a skill and might also affect perceived competence (Nicaise, Cogerino, Bois, & Amorose, 2006). Feedback from teachers, parents, and coaches can influence how children feel about their ability to perform a task or assume a role in a game or group work. This is another reason for teachers (and coaches) to be sensitive to the type, and tone, of the feedback they give to children.

## Coaches' Feedback

My recollection of the type of feedback I received from coaches in team sports is that it was predominantly negative. If I did something right, I didn't hear much about it. But if I messed up, I sure received feedback in a hurry, and it was often negative—and loud! Why was that so? Are athletes on a team different from children in a physical education class? Does one's skill level influence the type of feedback that might be useful? Are coaches today different from the coaches of 20 years ago?

Although negative feedback is rarely recommended, I find that teachers who provide feedback that is specific, congruent, and simple can use negative feedback occasionally to let children know that they still aren't using a cue correctly. Although this feedback is negative, my experience suggests that it can be done in such a way that it is helpful, not damaging, to a child. A private statement, such as "Jenelle, those are your fingertips, not your pads," is technically negative but realistically helpful to the child. An occasional use of negative feedback, interspersed with predominantly positive and neutral feedback, can be effective.

Negative feedback is especially useful for the child who just doesn't understand the cue and fails to realize, after repeated feedback, that the cue still isn't being used. It's also particularly useful for the occasional youngster who is an athlete, or highly skilled, and doesn't bother to listen carefully to a teacher. The child has played on the basketball team since second grade and thinks he knows everything there is to know about the game and certainly everything about a simple skill such as dribbling. This might sound harsh to inexperienced teachers, but veterans will quickly recognize my characterization of the athlete who "knows it all."

## Pro or Con?

What do you think about the use of negative feedback? Should it never be used? Used sparingly? Is it damaging to a child's self-concept? How much depends on the way the teacher provides negative feedback? What is an example in which negative feedback would be harmful?

Brophy and Good (1986), as part of an analysis of effective teaching, provided guidelines for praising children effectively (table 10.1). When you review that table you will see that many of the principles described in this chapter for effective feedback—specific, simple, congruent, and generally positive—are summarized.

In the previous sections the assumption has been made that all feedback is directed to individual students when the teacher is nearby. That is often the case, but there are times when feedback may be directed to a single student, or a group of students, from across the class so that the other children can hear it (Ryan & Ratliffe, 2000). This has been termed "crossgroup feedback." It has the advantage of focusing children on the cue and also reminds them that their practice attempts are being watched. Crossgroup feedback is another effective tool to have in your teacher tool box.

Table 10.1   Guidelines for Effective Praise

| EFFECTIVE PRAISE | INEFFECTIVE PRAISE |
|---|---|
| 1. Is delivered contingently | 1. Is delivered randomly or unsystematically |
| 2. Specifies the particulars of the accomplishment | 2. Is restricted to global reactions |
| 3. Shows spontaneity, variety, and other signs of credibility; suggests clear attention to the students' accomplishments | 3. Shows a bland uniformity that suggests a conditioned response made with minimal attention |
| 4. Rewards attainment of specified performance criteria(which can include effort criteria, however) | 4. Rewards mere participation, without consideration of performance processes or outcomes |
| 5. Provides information to students about their competence or the value of their accomplishments | 5. Provides no information at all nor gives students information about their status |
| 6. Orients students toward better appreciation of their own task-related behavior and thinking about problem solving | 6. Orients students toward comparing themselves with others and thinking about competing |
| 7. Uses students' own prior accomplishments as the context for describing present accomplishments | 7. Uses the accomplishments of peers as the context for describing students' present accomplishments |
| 8. Is given in recognition of noteworthy effort or success at difficult (for *this* student) tasks | 8. Is given without regard to the effort expended or the meaning of the accomplishment |
| 9. Attributes success to effort and ability, implying that similar successes can be expected in the future | 9. Attributes success to ability alone or to external factors such as luck or low task difficulty |
| 10. Fosters endogenous attributions (students believe that they expend effort on the task because they enjoy the task and/or want to develop task-relevant skills) | 10. Fosters exogenous attributions (students believe that they expend effort on the task for external reasons—to please the teacher, to win a competition or reward, etc.) |
| 11. Focuses students' attention on their own task-relevant behavior | 11. Focuses students' attention on the teacher as an external authority figure who is manipulating them |
| 12. Fosters appreciation of, and desirable attributions about, task-relevant behavior after the process is completed | 12. Intrudes into the ongoing process, distracting attention from task-relevant behavior |

Reproduced, by permission, from J. Brophy, 1981, *Teacher praise, A functional analysis* (American Educational Research Association).

# WHO GETS YOUR FEEDBACK?

If we're honest with ourselves, we probably tend to favor one type of child over another. Some of us prefer to teach the highly skilled, others, the less skilled. Ideally, we provide equal amounts of feedback to youngsters of all skill levels (Sharpe, 1993; Tjeerdsma, 1997).

Physical attractiveness of youngsters may also influence our feedback tendencies. Martinek (1983), for example, found that attractive children tend to get more teacher

attention than unattractive children. Some teachers provide more feedback to boys; others give more to girls.

Figure 10.1 is a form to help you determine which children in a class receive your feedback. It is also designed to let you know the type of feedback they receive. To use this form, list the names of all the children in a class in the left-hand column. Video yourself teaching the class (if possible using a wireless microphone so you can hear your individual interactions with the children). You can also use an audiotape to assess your feedback by wearing a small tape recorder on your belt. (The problem with an audiotape recorder is that you don't know who you are talking to unless you remember to call each child by name.) When the lesson is finished, you can use the form to tally and analyze the feedback statements made to the students. Some of the questions you can answer will be

▶ Which (if any) children did not receive feedback from you?

▶ Did you tend to favor any particular group—the highly skilled, the more personable children? Boys? Girls? (Nicaise, Cogerino, Bois, & Amorose, 2006).

▶ Do you tend to use specific or general feedback?

▶ Was your feedback congruent with your cues?

▶ Are you satisfied with the ratio of positive to neutral to negative?

▶ Did you vary your use of positive terms? Or did "good" or "all right" predominate?

Obviously, you could also ask a number of other questions about your feedback. This type of analysis, done periodically, helps you better understand and analyze your teaching.

# RESEARCH ON PHYSICAL EDUCATION TEACHER FEEDBACK

Historically, physical education teachers have been taught that teacher feedback is an important technique to help students learn motor skills. No doubt this is true. But some suggest that feedback might be overrated in terms of its value as a teaching skill (Lee,

# Feedback analysis form

Date ___11/20___ Class ___Ms. Browne___ Grade ___4th___

Topic of lesson ___Gymnastic sequences-smooth rolls into balances___

| Names | General feedback | Behavior | | | Skill | | | Cong | |
|---|---|---|---|---|---|---|---|---|---|
| (May not want to list entire class) | (No specific referent) | + | 0 | — | + | 0 | — | Yes | No |
| 1. Jacob | I | | | | I | I | | I | I |
| 2. Kathy | I | | | II | | | | | II |
| 3. Nathan | | | | | II | I | | I | II |
| 4. John | | | I | | | I | I | II | I |
| 5. Lois | | | | | I | II | | III | |
| 6. Jim | I | | I | | | | I | I | I |
| 7. Peggy | | | | | III | | | III | |
| 8. | | | | | | | | | |
| 9. | | | | | | | | | |
| 10. | | | | | | | | | |
| 11. | | | | | | | | | |
| 12. | | | | | | | | | |
| 13. | | | | | | | | | |
| 14. | | | | | | | | | |
| 15. | | | | | | | | | |
| 16. | | | | | | | | | |
| 17. | | | | | | | | | |
| 18. | | | | | | | | | |
| 19. | | | | | | | | | |
| 20. | | | | | | | | | |
| 21. | | | | | | | | | |
| 22. | | | | | | | | | |
| 23. | | | | | | | | | |
| 24. | | | | | | | | | |
| 25. | | | | | | | | | |
| 26. | | | | | | | | | |
| 27. | | | | | | | | | |
| 28. | | | | | | | | | |
| 29. | | | | | | | | | |
| 30. | | | | | | | | | |

**Figure 10.1** Feedback analysis form.

From G. Graham, 2008, *Teaching Children Physical Education,* 3rd ed. (Champaign, IL: Human Kinetics).

Keh, & Magill, 1993; Nicaise, Cogerino, Bois, & Amorose, 2006; Silverman, Tyson, & Krampitz, 1992).

Essentially, the value of feedback has been documented in laboratories by motor learning researchers (Lee, Keh, & Magill, 1993; Schmidt & Wrisberg, 2008; Silverman, Tyson, & Krampitz, 1992). In these labs they are able to create settings where a subject receives absolutely no feedback whatsoever. The subject presses a button, for example, and has no idea if she pressed it too soon or too late. The researcher can then provide the subject with any type of feedback that is being tested. In studies of this type, feedback is superior to no feedback.

In contrast, when students are learning a motor skill on the playground, they always receive some type of internal feedback—they know, for example, where the ball went, how far it went, or how high. If they were rolling or jumping, they have some sense of how it felt and where they ended up. Although different from feedback provided by a teacher or researcher, the students' knowledge of results lets them know how they are moving.

Some of the feedback studies done in gyms and on playgrounds have also suggested that feedback is valuable (Pellett & Harrison, 1995; Sharpe, 1993; Silverman, Tyson, & Krampitz, 1992; Stroot & Oslin, 1993). Unfortunately, it is often difficult to control for the amount of practice the students receive. Typically, when teachers are providing feedback, students are practicing. Thus students who received higher amounts of feedback sometimes learned more—or better. They also practiced more, however, making it difficult for the researcher to know whether their improvement was a result of teacher feedback or simply more practice opportunities. As more researchers begin to control the amount of practice so it is equal for students under varying practice conditions (Goldberger, Gerney, & Chamberlin, 1982) and to set their studies in the real world of physical education, we will gain an increased understanding of teacher feedback and its contribution to student learning.

Today we think that teacher feedback is important, especially when it is specific, congruent, simple, and mostly positive and neutral. We know, however, that lots of practice at high rates of success contributes to student learning and obvious feelings of satisfaction and enjoyment. Keeping this in mind, the effective teacher first makes sure that all students are practicing appropriately. Only then does he begin to provide individual feedback. When a teacher spends time with individuals, and many of the class drift off task, the provision of individual feedback is probably counterproductive.

# SUMMARY

Feedback is important to children. They want and need to know how they are doing. Ideally, children receive reasonable amounts of feedback from a teacher and they are not neglected. Feedback that is specific (rather than general), congruent (rather than incongruent), simple (rather than complex), and positive or neutral (rather than negative) is most effective with children.

# QUESTIONS FOR REFLECTION

1.  Why is providing feedback an important teaching skill? What is the impact when a teacher provides no feedback at all to children?

2. Can you think of some instances in which general feedback might be useful to some classes of children? Try to provide several examples.
3. Think of your physical education experiences as a student. Was feedback important to you? Can you remember the types of feedback you received? If you were an athlete, it might be interesting to compare the feedback you received from a coach to that from a teacher.
4. Why is congruent, simple feedback so rare in physical activity lessons? Why do instructors tend to overload students?
5. Can you think of several instances in which a lot of feedback might not necessarily be beneficial to a lesson? To children?

# REFERENCES

Boyce, B.A., Markos, N.J., Jenkins, D.W., & Loftus, J.R. (1996). How should feedback be delivered? *Journal of Physical Education, Recreation and Dance, 67*(1), 18–22.

Brophy, J., & Good, T.L. (1986). Teacher behavior and student achievement. In C.M. Wittrock (Ed.), *Handbook of research on teaching.* 3rd ed., 328–375. New York: Macmillan.

Claxton, D., & Fredenburg, K. (1989). Coaching young athletes: Strategies for success. *Strategies, 2*(2), 5–8, 19.

Goldberger, M., Gerney, P., & Chamberlin, J. (1982). The effects of three styles of teaching on the psychomotor performance and social skill development of fifth grade children. *Research Quarterly for Exercise and Sport, 53,* 116–124.

Kniffen, M. (1988). Instructional skills for student teachers. *Strategies, 1,* 5–10.

Lee, A.M., Keh, N.C., & Magill, R.A. (1993). Instructional effects of teacher feedback in physical education. *Journal of Teaching in Physical Education, 12*(3), 228–243.

Martinek, T. (1983). Creating Golem and Goleta effects during physical education instruction: A social psychological perspective. In T. Templin & J. Olson (Eds.), *Teaching in physical education,* 59–70. Champaign, IL: Human Kinetics.

Masser, L. (1993). Critical cues help first-grade students' achievement in handstands and forward rolls. *Journal of Teaching in Physical Education, 12*(3), 301–312.

Mustain, W. (1990). Are you the best teacher you can be? *Journal of Physical Education, Recreation and Dance, 61*(2), 69–73.

Nicaise, V., Cogerino, G., Bois, J., & Amorose, A.J. (2006). Students' perception of teacher feedback and physical competence in physical education classes: Gender effects. *Journal of Teaching in Physical Education, 25*(1), 36–57.

Pellett, T.L., & Harrison, J.M. (1995). The influence of a teacher's specific, congruent, and corrective feedback on female junior high school students' immediate volleyball practice success. *Journal of Teaching in Physical Education, 15*(1), 53–63.

Rink, J., & Werner, P. (1987). Student responses as a measure of teacher effectiveness. In G.T. Barrette, R.S. Feingold, C.R. Rees, & M. Pieron (Eds.), *Myths, models, and methods in sport pedagogy,* 199–206. Champaign, IL: Human Kinetics.

Ryan, S., & Ratliffe, T. (2000). Keeping kids on-task with crossgroup feedback. *Strategies,* July/August, 34–35.

Schmidt, R.A., & Wrisberg, C.A. (2008). *Motor Learning and Performance.* 4th ed. Champaign, IL: Human Kinetics.

Sharpe, T. (1993). What are some guidelines on giving feedback to students in physical education? *Journal of Physical Education, Recreation and Dance, 64*(9), 13.

Silverman, S., Tyson, L., & Krampitz, J. (1992). Teacher feedback and achievement in physical education. *Teaching and Teacher Education, 8*(4), 333–334.

Stroot, S.A., & Oslin, J.L. (1993). Use of instructional statements by preservice teachers for overhand throwing performance of children. *Journal of Teaching in Physical Education, 13*(1), 24–25.

Tjeerdsma, B.L. (1997). A comparison of teacher and student perspectives of tasks and feedback. *Journal of Teaching in Physical Education, 16*(4), 388–400.

## Chapter 11

# Building Critical-Thinking Skills

*During a lesson with students in kindergarten, they were practicing pencil rolls. I saw a student who was doing the pencil roll with his legs and arms bent. When I went over to provide feedback on how to do a pencil roll correctly the student replied, "Oh, I am not trying to do a pencil roll. This is the broken pencil roll!"*

**Rich Wood, Paddy Hill Elementary School, Rochester, New York**
Reprinted with permission from PE Central (www.pecentral.org).

It's time to switch gears. The first 10 chapters have assumed that the teacher is using a direct style of teaching (Mosston & Ashworth, 2002) in which the teacher tells the students what to do and when to do it, and the students comply (Lee, Landin, & Carter, 1992). My sense is that the majority of teachers use this style for the majority of their lessons. Some lessons, however, may be taught using a more indirect style of teaching, involving children in problem solving as they respond to questions posed by the teacher (Mosston & Ashworth, 2002). In these lessons we want children to explore, discover, create, and generally experiment with a variety of ways of moving—both for enjoyment and as a way to stimulate their cognitive involvement in physical education (NASPE, 2004). In fact, physical activity is an excellent medium for providing children with critical-thinking opportunities (Blitzer, 1995; Cleland & Pearse, 1995; Cone, Werner, Cone, & Woods, 1998; Hautala, 1996; Johnson, 1997; McBride, 1992; Mosston & Ashworth, 2002; Schwager & Labate, 1993).

This chapter describes and analyzes the teaching skills of questioning and setting problems as alternatives to more direct styles of teaching.

## After reading and understanding this chapter, the teacher will be able to

▶ explain the value of critical-thinking activities in physical education for children,

▶ describe the differences between convergent and divergent problem solving, and

▶ analyze the teaching skills and characteristics of teachers who are effective at providing critical-thinking learning experiences.

# VALUE FOR THE CHILDREN

Critical-thinking experiences use movement as a catalyst to stimulate the higher-order thinking skills of children as they are challenged to explore and create solutions to the movement problems posed by the teacher (Blitzer, 1995; Cleland & Pearse, 1995; Hautala, 1996; Johnson, 1997; McBride, 1992; Metzler, 2000; Mosston & Ashworth, 2002; Schwager & Labate, 1993). As children grow accustomed to this type of lesson, it is fascinating to observe their concentration and interaction as they work through their responses. It is especially interesting and rewarding when children are able to work cooperatively in these types of lessons.

As any teacher who uses a questioning or problem-solving approach will attest, it takes time and practice to learn to use this style of teaching successfully. Used adeptly, this method provides children with an intellectually challenging learning environment. Used ineptly, it often results in puzzlement, which leads to bewilderment and eventually off-task behavior by the children. Successful teachers ask questions and pose problems that are productive, thought-provoking, and conducive to worthwhile experiences that are understood and enjoyed by the children.

As with any method or teaching strategy, this approach works better with some than others. Alyssa, a middle school student in one study (Cothran & Kulinna, 2006), offered the following insight about alternatives to direct instruction: "I think this would be good. They (teachers) usually make us sit there and lecture you, like 'So try this and this and this', and then they are talking too much and they don't let you get a chance to try it. But if they just simply ask you and then you go on to then do it that would be good because you are thinking about it, and you are more focused, and it gives you a chance to try it" (Cothran & Kulinna, 2006, p. 176).

## *Children With No Bodies*

From time to time I become involved in a discussion about the value of physical education in schools—especially when budgets are being cut. One argument I use to support the importance of physical education is that schools are responsible for educating the whole child, not just the child's head. If this weren't the case—I argue facetiously when I am losing the discussion—just think of the money that could be saved in busing and classroom space if parents just sent their children's heads to school and kept their bodies at home. This same argument can be turned around to make the point that when children come to physical education, both their bodies and their heads are present. Clearly our unique responsibility as physical educators is to focus primarily on the physical, but we certainly do not want to neglect the cognitive and affective development of the child (NASPE, 2004). A questioning and problem-solving approach might take more time but seems a valuable approach in the tool box of master teachers for use at appropriate times throughout the year.

In this chapter we will discuss both convergent and divergent problem solving, including specific teaching behaviors used in each approach. In addition, the teaching skills of asking questions and setting problems are discussed, along with some recent thinking about verbal, rather than movement, problem solving.

# CONVERGENT PROBLEM SOLVING

In a convergent problem-solving lesson, the teacher guides children to discover one or more solutions to a problem. There is a right answer, sometimes several. But rather than simply telling the children the answer, the teacher leads the children to discover the solution gradually (Blitzer, 1995; Johnson, 1997). For this reason, convergent problem solving is also referred to as guided discovery (Mosston, 1981; Moston & Ashworth, 2002).

My favorite example of convergent problem solving is Mosston's (1981) now classic "slanty rope" lesson. (This concept was also discussed in chapter 7 as a way to design tasks to accommodate different skill levels.) Imagine a class of children organized into small groups. Each group has two ropes placed parallel on the ground about 12 inches apart. The children are challenged to jump the imaginary river formed by the two ropes without getting wet or being swallowed by the alligators. They all succeed. Now they are asked to widen the river so that it is 24 inches apart and see if they can still jump it. Gradually they continue to widen the river, and some children are unable to jump it successfully. Now groups are ready to hear the problem: "Is there a way you can set up the ropes so that everybody in your group will be able to jump the river successfully?"

There are at least two solutions to this problem. One solution is to arrange the ropes so that at one end they are close together and at the other end farther apart (see the cartoon in chapter 7). The other solution is to keep one rope straight and curve the other so that the river is narrower in the middle and wider at the ends.

This is one example of a convergent problem-solving lesson. Other approaches suitable for this type of lesson include the following:

▸ "What are the five basic ways we can take off and land when we jump?"

▸ "What are the most balanced and least balanced positions you can make?" (Later there will be an example of how this might be developed in a lesson.)

▶ "How do you land from a jump so that the landing is soft and quiet?"

▶ "What is the quickest way to mount the bench (box, table, beam, bars)?"

▶ "How can you stand so that you are ready to move quickly?"

▶ "In your game you may pass the ball to your partner using only two hands at middle level." (After playing for some time, children are guided to understand the need for developing the ability to pass the ball at a variety of levels, using both one and two hands.)

## Never Tell the Answer

The most obvious guideline in this approach to teaching is that the teacher never tells the answer. If the teacher does tell the answer, children become less willing to truly explore the solutions, knowing the teacher will eventually provide the answer. In fact, it's not at all unproductive to finish a lesson that the children still haven't discovered an answer to. Wonder and curiosity are valuable mental processes that can be readily stimulated through physical activity. And, after all, what's so bad about children leaving a class and still not knowing the answer the teacher had in mind?

## Responding to Incorrect Solutions

In convergent problem solving there is at least one correct answer, and sometimes more. When children reach a conclusion that is incorrect, rather than telling them they are wrong, many teachers will ask, "Do you need more time?" or "Have you checked your answer?" or "Can you explain your answer to me?" This preserves the atmosphere of discovery and problem solving, in contrast to lessons in which the teacher provides the answers.

## *Look at It This Way*

My experience is that children have a much more creative and mirthful way of interpreting our questions. Two examples come to mind. I remember asking one class to make a narrow shape with their bodies. As I looked at one child, she definitely had a wide shape: arms and feet spread wide apart. When I queried her about her "narrow" shape, she said, "You're looking at it the wrong way. Look at it from the side." She was right! Viewed from the side, her shape was narrow. Asking children to balance with $x$ number of body parts touching the floor is also fascinating. Some children, for example, view a foot as one part; others count each toe, so a one-foot balance, for them, is interpreted as five parts. Some count their rear end as one part, others as two.

Convergent problem solving is probably easier with young children who have little or no prior knowledge or habits related to the problem posed by the teacher. They are eager to explore movement. Older children, unfortunately, have had some of their curiosity dampened and often are more interested in "right" answers. Typically they will respond quickly by recalling previous experiences if the problem posed by the teacher is not unique to their background. This is not to say that convergent problem solving cannot be used with older children—just that it is more challenging for the teacher to develop truly interesting lessons using this approach.

## Discussing Solutions

During closure (chapter 13), many teachers discuss responses with students. Some do not. It depends on the teachers and the importance they place on children discussing the concepts taught during the lesson. Some teachers, for example, want children to be able to verbalize their movement responses (e.g., to verbally describe a stable or unstable balance); others are satisfied if children can provide movement answers (e.g., to physically demonstrate stable and unstable balances).

**See Checking for Understanding**

The section Checking for Understanding in your companion DVD illustrates an example of a teacher asking children to describe concepts of bound and free flow as they exit the gym.

# DIVERGENT PROBLEM SOLVING

In contrast to convergent problem solving, divergent problem solving asks children to explore alternatives and discover many different ways to solve a problem (Cleland & Gallahue, 1993; Mosston & Ashworth, 2002). Convergent problem solving has one or more correct answers; divergent has an infinite number of responses. There is no limit to the diversity and range of possible answers. Whereas convergent problem solving leads children to focus on the depth of an answer, divergent problem solving emphasizes a breadth of responses. The exciting part of this approach is the variety of unique solutions children create as they explore answers to questions posed by the teacher.

Examples of topics that might be developed in divergent problem-solving lessons include

- different ways to travel in general space;
- different ways to balance on the floor or on apparatus;
- the number of different, safe ways one might mount or dismount a bench, table, or vaulting box;
- ways to outmaneuver opponents in a game;
- alternative ways to "pass" a ball when guarded by an opponent;
- sequences of gymnastics or dancelike movements;
- ways of passing a ball from player A to player B; and
- ways of creating a game.

**See Problem Solving**

The companion DVD illustrates children in a problem-solving process as they design their own games.

## Asking the Divergent Question

There are many ways of asking questions leading to divergent movement. Some are better than others. Mosston (1981) suggests that two frequently used questions might be counterproductive:

▶ The question "Can you . . . ?" might result in the response "No, I can't."

▶ The question "How many ways . . . ?" might lead some children to respond with only one movement or to become intimidated because they can hardly think of one response, let alone several.

He recommended that divergent questions take the following form:

▶ "What are three possible ways to . . . ?" When (if) children discover three ways, the teacher can then ask for several more ways. This format of questioning allows children to be successful at finding three solutions.

The way the question is asked is more important when a teacher is first beginning to teach using a divergent problem-solving approach. In time, when children become accustomed to problem solving in the gym, the form used to ask the question (not the content) becomes less crucial. Children enjoy the uncertainty of exploring and discovering movement alternatives. They also realize that the teacher can be trusted to present interesting, fun problems to solve.

## Learning Atmosphere

If divergent problem solving is going to be effective, teachers need to create supportive environments in which children feel comfortable exploring and attempting new concepts and ideas. Most of the feedback statements are neutral (chapter 10) as the teacher encourages children to continue exploring alternatives. For example, a teacher might say to a child who has found two ways to move at low level, "That's two different ways. Can you find a third?" When a response simply does not address the question, it is most effective to explain why the response is inappropriate so that children are clear on the problem that they are to solve.

## Pinpointing

Pinpointing (chapter 6) can be helpful for showing children the diversity of responses that you encourage. In the beginning children are often looking for the "right" answer and fail to understand that there is no single answer that the teacher is looking for. In these instances the teacher can pinpoint several children who are making appropriate responses so the others can see the type of diversity that the teacher encourages.

If the teacher has asked for different ways to travel in general space, for example, many children might be traveling on their feet. The teacher might pinpoint children traveling at low level on their hands and knees or those transferring weight (as in a cartwheel) to encourage children to explore the alternatives. In this instance, the teacher should explain that she is looking for ways to move other than those that were just pinpointed. If this is not clear to the children, they will instantly mimic the movements previously pinpointed—the opposite of what you are searching for in divergent problem solving.

# VERBAL PROBLEM SOLVING

Up to this point we have assumed that the responses of the children will involve movement rather than verbal responses. But clearly there are times when teachers ask for verbal responses to questions. There are two guidelines we have devised, based on classroom research, about verbal responses to questions. One involves children calling out answers; the other involves waiting for an answer from the children.

## Callouts

One clear finding is that callouts (situations in which children respond immediately and simultaneously) are not as effective as calling on children who have their hands raised. We have all asked questions to a class of children only to have eight children answer at once. Children in another class at the same school—when asked the same question—might respond by raising their hands but remaining silent. Clearly the way they respond is based on the protocol the classroom teacher established at the beginning of the year (chapter 3).

Generally it is thought that asking children to respond by raising their hands to be recognized by the teacher is more effective than simply allowing children to call out (Johnson, 1997). The exception to this generalization is for those truly unmotivated classes that seem to respond better in a rapid-fire question-and-answer setting—the type often depicted in the movies.

## Wait Time

One of the reasons children are taught to raise their hands is so the teacher can pause for several seconds (three is suggested) before calling on a child to respond (Johnson, 1997). This allows every child to think about the answer without knowing who will be called on. It seems that once a teacher names a child, the others tend to relax and stop thinking. The three seconds or so of wait time also allows children to formulate better responses. We have all observed kindergarten and first-grade classes in which all children raise their hands to respond to every question asked by the teacher. When no time is allowed for thought (and even sometimes when it is), it is common to call on a child only to realize that she didn't really have an answer but just wanted to see if she could be the one recognized by the teacher from the field of waving hands.

The concept of wait time (pausing three seconds or more) before calling on a child is an interesting teacher behavior to begin to use. Initially, three seconds might seem like an eternity. Over a series of lessons, however, both children and the teacher become accustomed to wait time, and the children benefit more from this type of questioning than when they are called on immediately. It's obviously even less productive when a child is named to answer the question before it is asked.

# EFFECTIVE QUESTIONING AND PROBLEM SETTING

As with any aspect of pedagogy, there are a variety of related teacher behaviors and characteristics that blend together to compose an effective method or technique. Asking questions and setting problems is no different. Teachers who challenge and motivate students to think about movement in creative and intellectually challenging ways have patience, a good knowledge of the content and developmental level of their students, and are positive and accepting.

## Patience

Teachers who successfully develop lessons using a problem-solving approach have patience. Problem solving takes time; it's a much slower process than simply telling students the answers. This might be why we see problem solving less often than we see other types of lessons—the process takes longer, and most programs are severely limited in time.

Initially, it takes time just for the children to learn to effectively explore solutions to a problem. Children aren't instantly terrific problem solvers. Naturally this depends on what they are accustomed to in the classroom. If problem solving is used in the classroom, it is reasonable to expect that class to be adept at the process. In contrast, a class that is taught using only a direct approach will take much longer to learn to problem solve effectively.

Once a class of children has learned the process, it still takes much longer for them to discover a solution or explore various alternatives on their own than it would if the teacher simply told or showed them an answer. Obviously, however, certain content we teach lends itself to problem solving, and this is the reason many teachers use this approach. It might take longer, but children benefit from the process.

One indicator I have always used to determine how well children are adapting to the problem-solving approach is the amount of time they remain involved in a problem. Initially children are satisfied with a sequence or game created in just a few minutes. As they have more experience with the process, however, it seems that they always need more time. As children expand their movement repertoires they often need more time to refine their gymnastics sequence or game so that it is truly satisfying to them. The fifth-grade class who initially had their sequence finished in five minutes might need two or three class periods once they understand all that is involved in creating and polishing a routine so that it is interesting and satisfying.

## Content Knowledge

In addition to patience, another skill needed by a teacher to successfully pose questions and set problems is a thorough knowledge of the content that is the topic for that lesson. Ideally this is true for every lesson we teach, but it seems that it is even more so in this approach because the teacher is gradually leading the children to one or more solutions. An example of teaching the concept of balance to a class of young children will help illustrate (Mosston, 1981, p. 176):

"What does the word balance mean?"

"Right. It means that you are not falling down and that you are able to remain steady."

"Show me one way to balance with your body."

"Now let's see how you can make that balance even steadier."

"Is this your most balanced position?" (In time, under the guidance of the teacher, the children will realize that the lower and wider the position, the more stable the balance. A few children may actually lie flat on the floor.)

"Now let's see how you can change your balance to make it less steady."

"Even less steady?"

"Show me your least-balanced position."

During closure (chapter 13), the teacher can discuss ways children changed from most to least balanced (i.e., the characteristics of balance). This basic concept is one example of content that lends itself well to problem solving because the children easily and accurately grasp the essence of balance through this process.

In the next example, the teacher uses problem solving with content (the overhand throw) that leads to a possible misunderstanding by students. This lesson uses problem solving to attempt to help children understand the concept of using the opposite foot when forcefully throwing overhand:

"Using an overhand throw, throw the ball hard against the wall." After a number of tries, the teacher might ask, "Which foot do you step with? The one on the same side as the throwing hand? Or the one on the opposite side?"

"Try some throws now and use the other foot—the one you haven't been stepping with. Does the ball travel faster when you step with one foot or the other?" This process might continue for some time as the teacher continues to ask children to change feet, sometimes using opposition, sometimes an ipsilateral step.

During closure the teacher might then ask, "Which foot do you step with to make the ball go faster—the one on the same side as the throwing arm or the one on the opposite side?"

My experience and my observation of other teachers suggests that this teacher would probably receive a mixed response. Some students would argue for opposition, others would not.

Compared with the concept of balance, opposition might not be a good topic to use in a guided discovery lesson (the teacher attempting to gradually lead the children to discover that it is better to use opposition than a unilateral stepping pattern). The reason it is not a very effective lesson is that the child who does not use opposition when he throws is not quickly comfortable. He is also not convinced that opposition improves his throwing ability. Because it is a new and awkward feeling for the child, his throw doesn't necessarily go farther or harder, and the child concludes that a unilateral stepping pattern results in better throws for him. The teacher is then faced with a dilemma: whether to tell the child he has drawn the wrong conclusion, causing him to distrust his ability to discover, or to allow that solution to stand until a lesson later in the year (Ainsworth & Fox, 1989).

Obviously there might be ways of guiding children to discover the effectiveness of opposition that are not counterproductive. Over the years, however, I have observed this lesson taught by enough different teachers to conclude that some content lends itself well to problem solving, whereas other content is harder to teach using this approach. The important point is that, in addition to patience, a teacher needs to know the content well to design and implement an effective problem-solving lesson.

# Children's Developmental Level

Along with knowing the content being developed, teachers should be familiar with the age and developmental level of their students. Teachers need to know what type of question or problem will be interesting and provocative at various grade levels (box 11.1).

**Box 11.1**

# Critical-Thinking Skills: Levels of Complexity

Teachers can ask questions that promote critical thinking at various cognitive levels from lower-order (level 1) to more complex or higher-order thinking (level 3) (Schwager & Labate, 1993). The three levels of complexity are as follows:

**Level 1:** Count, describe, match, name, recite, recall, select, and tell. *Examples:* "Did you hop, jump, or leap over the rope?"; "Describe how high you need to toss the ball to serve it overhand."

**Level 2:** Analyze, compare, contrast, classify, distinguish, explain, infer, reason, sequence, solve. *Examples:* "Sarah, what was the difference between your way of traveling over the rope and Tom's?"; "How does the height of your toss compare with the toss Joachim and Stian just demonstrated?"

**Level 3:** Apply a principle, estimate, evaluate, forecast, hypothesize, imagine, judge, predict, make an analogy, speculate. *Examples:* "Can you think of a way of traveling over the rope that would get you high into the air?"; "Why do you think you would get higher with a leap than a hop?"; "Why do you think most of your serves are hitting the net? Do you think you need to adjust the swing of your racket, the height of your toss, or both?"

Adapted, by permission, from S. Schwager and C. Labat, 1993, "Teaching for critical thinking in physical education," *Journal of Teaching in Physical Education* 64(5): 24-26.

The two examples related to balance and opposition are appropriate for primary-grade children. With intermediate-grade children, however, they won't be of much interest. If children don't already understand these concepts, they probably aren't interested in spending much time exploring solutions.

They are often interested, however, in working in small groups to design and synchronize a series of movements (as in a gymnastics or dance routine) or to design a game. Identifying strategies used in escaping from a defender is another problem that fascinates many older children. The following examples are often interesting to children in grades four through six:

▶ With a partner, design a sequence that has at least one roll, one balance, one weight transfer, and a beginning and ending shape. Repeat it three times, each time varying the speed of the sequence.

▶ In a group of four to six, make up a game. The game must have kicking (a ball) in it. Use cones to clearly define your boundaries.

▶ In groups of three or four, see if you can find at least three ways to form a counterbalance. Everyone must keep at least one foot on the floor. When it is finished I will take a picture of it for other classes to see. I will also put some pictures on our school Web site for your parents to see.

**See Problem Solving**

The Problem Solving section of the companion DVD illustrates children designing a game that focuses on dribbling with their hands.

## Positive and Accepting

In addition to being patient and having a good knowledge of the content and the developmental level of their students, teachers also need to create an environment in which students feel comfortable trying out new ideas and solutions without fear of failure. Teachers typically create this environment by being positive and accepting with students.

As children offer solutions, either verbally or in movement, they naturally explore some ideas that are recognized by the teacher as counterproductive—silly or uninventive, or lacking in much effort. What is important to remember, however, is that the teacher is a more sophisticated problem solver who typically knows many of the solutions. The children do not. Thus, part of the process is encouraging children to continue to work and try even though they might appear to be a long way from the solution.

When a teacher isn't positive and accepting, students might sense it and become unwilling to genuinely participate in the process. This is especially true when the teacher makes the children feel as if their responses are not worthwhile or appropriate. The challenge for the teacher, of course, is to distinguish between the child who is off task and just goofing around and the child who is creatively working at solving the problem. The off-task child needs to be refocused; the creative child needs to be reinforced for her efforts.

## The Highly Skilled Child as a Problem Solver

My experience has been that the highly skilled child often finds it harder to problem solve in physical education than the lower-skilled child. This might be true because highly skilled children already have a movement repertoire that has been polished and refined through practice. They have a series of responses to questions posed by the teacher and thus see no need to search for alternatives. I am particularly reminded of children who are excellent gymnasts. My experience has been that many of them, when asked to create a sequence, will rely totally on their predesigned stunts so that their sequence appears very similar to an Olympic gymnastics floor exercise routine. Personally I find these routines far less interesting than those of the children who are less skilled and yet able to discover creative solutions to movement problems. As I work with highly skilled children who rely solely on traditional rolls, balances, and weight transfers, I want to tell them that they can't use any of these movements in their sequences. I remind myself, however, that that's *my* need, and I try to remain patient and accepting of their efforts.

# SHOULD I USE A DIRECT OR INDIRECT APPROACH?

Successful teachers are always searching for better ways to help and motivate children to learn. Choosing the teaching approach to use for various lessons is one decision they continually face: Would a direct or an indirect approach be better with this lesson?

Some questions to consider relate to the role of the teacher and the children. Ainsworth and Fox (1989) have developed a helpful analysis comparing what they term a traditional (direct) and a cognitive processes (indirect) approach to learning in physical education (table 11.1). Although the analysis doesn't fit exactly with the approaches discussed in this chapter, it is a helpful summary for teachers as they decide which approach to use in their classes.

**Table 11.1**  Comparison of Traditional Behavioral (Direct) and Cognitive Processes (Indirect) Approach

| TRADITIONAL (BEHAVIORAL) APPROACH | COGNITIVE (PROCESSES) APPROACH |
| --- | --- |
| Subject centered | Learner centered |
| Teacher tells | Learner explores |
| Ignores learners' rich repertoire of movement memories | Utilizes learners' rich repertoire of movement memories |
| Learner plays relatively passive role in the process | Learner assumes a major responsibility for his/her own learning |
| Teacher identifies errors and prescribes corrections | Learner identifies errors and makes adjustments |
| May be less time-consuming in early stages | May be more time-consuming in early stages |

Reprinted, by permission, from J. Ainsworth and C. Fox, 1989. "Learning to learn: A cognitive process approach to movement skill acquisition," *Strategies* 3(1): 20-22.

# SUMMARY

A master teacher is one who is adept at different styles of teaching, both direct and indirect. Questioning and problem solving represent an indirect style of teaching. Convergent problem solving (discovering answers to a problem) and divergent problem solving (searching for a variety of alternatives rather than one or more answers) are two ways teachers can involve children in higher-level thinking skills in physical education. To be effective, teachers must use certain teaching skills and characteristics. Obviously teachers must know and understand children, the content, and their own characteristics as teachers if they are going to effectively lead children in problem-solving activities.

# QUESTIONS FOR REFLECTION

1. List five concepts or skills typically taught in physical education. Which of them might be taught using a divergent problem-solving approach? Which might be taught with a convergent problem-solving approach?
2. Do you think problem solving is widespread, or barely used, in physical education classes today? Explain the reasons for your answer and why this might be the case.

3. Problem solving requires more time than a direct teaching approach. Why is this so?

4. When you think of your characteristics as a teacher, are you more or less apt to use a problem-solving approach? Can you understand the reasons for your answer?

5. It seems that teachers in the classroom are reluctant to use problem-solving lessons that involve children in movement. Outline the argument you would use to convince a classroom teacher that higher-order thinking skills can be developed in the gym as well as they can when children sit at a desk.

# REFERENCES

Ainsworth, J., & Fox, C. (1989). Learning to learn: A cognitive process approach to movement skill acquisition. *Strategies, 3*(1), 20–22.

Blitzer, L. (1995). "It's a gym class . . . what's there to think about?" *Journal of Physical Education, Recreation and Dance, 66*(6), 44–48.

Cleland, F.E., & Gallahue, D.L. (1993). Young children's divergent movement ability. *Perceptual and Motor Skills, 77*(2), 535–544.

Cleland, F., & Pearse, C. (1995). Critical thinking in elementary physical education: Reflections on a yearlong study. *Journal of Physical Education, Recreation and Dance, 66*(6), 31–38.

Cone, T.P., Werner, P.H., Cone, S.L., & Woods, A. (1998). *Interdisciplinary teaching through physical education.* Champaign, IL: Human Kinetics.

Cothran, D.J., & Kulinna, P.H. (2006). Students' perspectives on direct, peer, and inquiry teaching strategies. *Journal of Teaching in Physical Education, 25,* 166–181.

Hautala, R. (1996). Gym class with "Coach Piaget": How cognitive development theories can be used in PE. *Teaching Elementary Physical Education, 7*(1), 20–22.

Johnson, R. (1997). Questioning techniques to use in teaching. *Journal of Physical Education, Recreation and Dance, 68*(8), 45–49.

Lee, A.M., Landin, D.K., & Carter, J.A. (1992). Student thoughts during tennis instruction. *Journal of Teaching in Physical Education, 11*(3), 256–257.

McBride, R. (1992). Critical thinking—an overview with implications for physical education. *Journal of Teaching in Physical Education, 11*(2), 112–125.

Metzler, M. (2000). *Instructional models for physical education.* Boston: Allyn and Bacon.

Mosston, M. (1981). *Teaching physical education.* Columbus, OH: Bell & Howell.

Mosston, M., & Ashworth, S. (2002). *Teaching physical education.* 5th ed. New York: Benjamin Cummings.

National Association for Sport and Physical Education (NASPE). (2004). *Moving into the future: National standards for physical education.* 2nd ed. Reston, VA: NASPE.

Schwager, S., & Labate, C. (1993). Teaching for critical thinking in physical education. *Journal of Teaching in Physical Education, 64*(5), 24–26.

**Chapter 12**

# Building Positive Feelings

*While teaching a parachute lesson to our preschoolers we always have the kids raise their hands and tell us a few rules about the parachute. Important rules are "do not walk on the parachute" and "do not pull on the parachute." One little girl raised her hand and said, "Do not pick your nose and rub it on the parachute."*

**Craig Wilson, Mount Paran Christian School, Kennesaw, Georgia**
Reprinted with permission from PE Central (www.pecentral.org).

As I begin this chapter, Funky Winkerbean, the cartoon character created by Tom Batiuk, is hanging from a climbing rope. He can't get down. He's been stuck on the rope all day. Now everyone is gone except the janitor, who's sweeping the gym floor. I will have to wait until tomorrow to discover how Funky solves his dilemma.

Last week the cartoon focused on the overweight, sweatshirted, bewhistled coach who filled class time by showing movies. One day the principal was commenting on the coach and how he had already burned out three movie projectors during the year. Another day the students were discussing why the windows in the coach's classroom had been painted black—they concluded it was because the coach did nothing but show films.

These are funny scenarios—to some. For me, however, they hurt more than amuse. That's my profession, and those are my colleagues he is mocking. Obviously Tom Batiuk, the creator of the Funky Winkerbean cartoon, had some unpleasant experiences in physical education. Unfortunately, he's not the only one. All too many adults share his feelings about physical education classes.

This chapter focuses on those feelings and their development related to physical activity, including

- feelings about self,
- feelings about others,
- feelings of joy,
- feelings of satisfaction,
- feelings of pleasure,
- feelings of self-accomplishment, and
- developing positive perceptions of competence.

The list could continue. All of these feelings fall into the category of the affective domain: how children feel about themselves and about physical activity. There's a lot we don't know or understand about feelings. We do know, however, that participation in physical activity has the potential to create powerful and lasting impressions—both painful and joyous.

Our goal as physical educators is to create environments that are pleasant, warm, and caring—and that result in children developing positive attitudes. Perhaps if Tom Batiuk had been in such classes, Funky Winkerbean might find physical education more enjoyable, and the coach would be depicted as a caring, sensitive, and respected teacher.

This chapter focuses on pedagogical skills used by physical education teachers to create the types of environments that lead to the development of desirable attitudes toward physical activity and one's involvement in it. The chapter deals with the everyday things we do as teachers and how they influence children's feelings.

## After reading and understanding this chapter, the teacher will be able to

- describe the feelings of children that are related to experiences in physical education,

- analyze the intentional and unintentional actions of teachers that contribute to how children feel about themselves and physical activity,

- analyze games and activities taught in physical education and how they influence children's feelings,

- explain how games can be modified to de-emphasize competition,

- describe some of the ways teachers have found to avoid making children feel bad about testing and test results in physical education classes, and

- describe how teachers can help children get in touch with and understand their feelings about their involvement in physical activity.

# INTENTIONAL AND EVER PRESENT

When children come to physical education class they should feel good about the experience, not apprehensive or fearful of being embarrassed. They should feel that physical education class is a warm and caring environment that encourages and supports them in learning new and different skills and activities. They should also understand that mistakes will be made and that they are an important, and necessary, part of learning. These feelings translate into positive attitudes about themselves and physical activity, ideally contributing to the enjoyment of physical activity for a lifetime.

Teachers who help children create these positive attitudes tend to do two things:

▶ They make a special effort to create these positive attitudes every day for every class they teach—it's not simply an accident.

▶ Their effort is ever present, not just an aspect of a few games or activities that they do from time to time.

A number of texts (e.g., Flugelman, 1976; Glover & Midura, 1995a, 1995b; Grineski, 1996; Hichwa, 1998; Orlick, 1978a, 1978b; Turner & Turner, 1984) describe games and activities that promote cooperation and cooperative experiences. It seems, however, that developing positive attitudes involves more than simply playing "Hug Tug," "Frozen Beanbag," "Lap Sit," "Cooperative Musical Chairs," or "Long, Long Jump." It's an environment, created by the teacher, that says, "You're OK; I'm glad you are here even if you aren't very skilled or very fit. This class is to help you improve and enjoy physical activity, not to make you feel bad because you can't do something." To create such an environment, teachers use a variety of tools from their pedagogy tool box. Some are more subtle than others, but together they say to the children, "You belong here, and my goal is to help you feel good about yourself as you participate in physical activities."

## *Values of Physical Activity*

One part of the definition of a physically educated person (chapter 1) relates specifically to that person's feelings about the value of physical activity. Programs that are positive and considerate of children's feelings help them learn to value physical activity and its contributions to a healthy lifestyle. A physically educated person

• **demonstrates responsible personal and social behavior in physical activity settings;**
• **demonstrates understanding and respect for differences among people in physical activity settings; and**
• **understands that physical activity provides opportunities for enjoyment, challenge, self-expression, and social interaction (NASPE, 2004, p. 1).**

# TECHNIQUES AND STRATEGIES

Effective teachers use several techniques and strategies to assist every child, not just the highly skilled, to enjoy physical activity. These include providing choices, analyzing teacher–student interactions, asking about students' feelings, and analysis of teaching behaviors via audio or video. Successful teachers work hard to create an environment

that says, "It's OK to make mistakes in this class," and help children to understand that "sport" skills take a long time to learn and a lot of practice.

## Provide Choices

Poor Funky Winkerbean! His teacher provided no choice but for him to attempt to climb to the top of the rope, and he got stuck. A caring teacher would have provided Funky with several choices so that he would have been able to avoid the embarrassment of being asked to do something that he knew he couldn't do—but was required to do anyway (chapter 7).

When children are asked to play in a game that singles them out (e.g., batting in softball, dribbling in basketball, being the only one who is "it" in a game of tag), any feelings of inadequacy and incompetence are reinforced in a hurry if they fail by striking out, losing the ball, or being unable to catch anyone else. The entire class observes them fail.

Caring teachers work hard to create environments in which children are not singled out in front of the class and embarrassed by their awkwardness. Activities are designed and taught so that children can avoid these embarrassing situations (e.g., every child has a ball to dribble; there are three or four batters in several minigames; or there are three or four "its" in a game of tag). Teaching by invitation and intratask variation are also used to avoid placing children in uncomfortable situations by providing choices (chapter 7). Funky Winkerbean, for example, might have been invited to see if he could climb higher than he did last time—or climb to one of several sections on the rope marked by different colored tape.

## Interaction Analysis

Another way teachers avoid contributing to the development of negative attitudes toward physical education is to become aware of who they interact with, and how. If teachers interact differently with the skilled or attractive child compared to how they interact with the unskilled or unattractive child, a subtle message comes through to the children, reinforcing any tendency toward feelings of incompetence. There might also be a tendency to interact differently with boys and girls. The teacher might not be aware of her interaction patterns, but the children are! When teachers meet several hundred children a day, it's hard to make the hundreds, perhaps thousands, of interactions all ideal.

We hope that a single embarrassing or unfortunate incident won't instantly create a negative attitude for a youngster. However, several years of negative interactions and experiences will clearly contribute to feelings of inadequacy and incompetence. Figure 10.1, the feedback analysis form, helps to provide some insights about which children we are interacting with. It can easily be modified to answer different questions about which children we are interacting with and how.

## Taking Emotional Temperatures

Another pedagogical tool used by effective teachers is to assess children's feelings about physical education by simply asking them how they feel about what is being taught and how it is being taught—that is, checking the emotional pulse of the class (McCaughtry, 2004). Jan, the teacher in McCaughtry's (2004) study, had this to say about teaching students to throw a football: "How students feel about, say, throwing a football matters as much as whether they can throw it well. You see, if they hate football, or feel embarrassed at their throwing, or are continually bad, they will quit trying to learn . . . and if they learn how to throw it, but just don't care about it, then what's the reason for teaching it? They're never going to use it if they don't have that emotional bond." (p. 41)

She describes another example of checking the emotional pulse of a class when she asks a group playing a small-sided game of touch football how they feel about their game. They told her they were bored. So Jan watched their games for a few minutes and realized that the receivers were running too far downfield and the quarterbacks were unable to throw the ball that far. She used "play-teach-play" to practice shorter pass routes that had been taught in previous classes before they returned to the game. She employed techniques from her pedagogical tool box to assess her students' emotional state in order to better match the lesson and unit contents to the interests and abilities of her students.

## Recording

Another technique a teacher can use to ascertain the type of environment he is creating is to record a class, using either audio or video. You might strap a small audio recorder on your belt, attach the microphone to your shirt, and then record a lesson. When you listen to the recording, try to hear what you communicate to children about what is important to you.

> ▶ Do you provide feedback about knowledge of results (the ball went into the goal) or knowledge of performance (critical elements related to the movement)?
> ▶ Do you sound too demanding or too critical?
> ▶ Do you communicate a tone of warmth and caring to the children?
> ▶ Do you sound supportive? Encouraging? Understanding?
> ▶ Do you interact differently with boys than with girls? With high-skilled or low-skilled youngsters? With children who have physical disabilities?

When you listen to (or watch) the recording you will have to determine how you sound in relation to how you want to sound—the decision is yours. At times you might want to ask someone you trust to listen to part of the recording in order to help you interpret the affective messages you are communicating. Do not be too hard on yourself. Remember that teaching is a complex and difficult job.

# Mistakes-OK-Here Zone

Another way teachers help children feel good about themselves is to assist them to realize that learning inevitably involves mistakes. That's how we learn. We try not to make mistakes, but they happen—and that's OK.

One of the ways teachers do this is to declare the playground or gym a "mistakes-OK-here zone." It's expected that everyone, including the teacher, will make mistakes from time to time. It's normal—an important part of learning. When a mistake does occur, there's no reason to laugh at, ridicule, or single out any student. We accept it and understand.

Obviously the mistakes-OK-here zone can be described, but description is not enough. When a child does make a mistake and is ridiculed or laughed at, the teacher immediately stops the class and focuses on the idea of a mistakes-OK-here zone—to let children know that she will not accept criticism or sarcasm when a mistake is made.

The mistakes-OK-here zone is also created when children see the teacher making mistakes when he tries to learn something he has yet to master. Obviously, how and when this is done will depend on the teacher, the class, and other factors, but letting your students witness your mistakes is an important way of communicating the idea that learning involves trial and error. Children learn a great deal from watching someone they respect try to learn something. They begin to realize that skills are learned, not inherited, and that mistakes are part of the learning process, not something to become upset about.

# PE Teachers Are Superheroes

Many children, especially the youngest, regard their PE teachers as superheroes. They can do everything! Children don't realize that our physical adeptness came from lots of practice and hard work. They just assume we were born that way. We reinforce this perception when we demonstrate only the skills we can do well. Would it be beneficial to the children if we also let them know that there are some skills we don't do so well? Or do we want to preserve our superhero image?

# The "Yet" Intervention

Agnes Stillman (1989) described one of the ways she helps students feel positive about physical education. She has humorously titled it "The Stillman Two-Part 'Yet' Intervention."

Part 1—When a student forgets and says, "I can't," Stillman adds "yet" on the end of the comment. She concluded after 21 years that the phrase "I can't" will never be totally eliminated from the vocabulary of students.

Part 2—She makes a deal with the student. She asks the student to try the skill 37 times, and if it still can't be done, then she accepts the student can't do it.

The number 37 is arbitrary. Stillman's point is that she wants children to try—and try hard. But if they truly try and still can't do it, she accepts that and suggests something else for the student to try.

# *The "Yet" Intervention at Work*

"I can't!"

Hearing Ralph's voice attached to that, I turn to him and say (with my finger up),

"Ralph, what did I hear you say?"

"I can't . . . yet."

"Thank you. Now, how many tries have you made?"

"Eleven."

"So, how many more tries do you have?" (We can integrate math skills!)

"Twenty-six."

I give him some encouragement and then move on to Sarah and Sam. Sure enough, I look over at Ralph in time to see him execute the skill well enough that he is actually smiling about it. I've got him now.

I eventually get back around to Ralph.

"Well, what are we up to now?"

We both know he lost count. He creates a number—33. He could have said 37, but he's an honest kid. By saying 33, he knows he has only four more tries to close our deal. By now, however, he's not trying to prove me wrong. He has had some success, although he hates to admit it. I ask if I may watch his last four tries, which I point out should be his best efforts. And, of course, they're successful enough to bring praise, pats on the back, and high fives. Ralph heads for the locker room with a feeling of accomplishment and I say a quiet "thank you" and prepare for the next Ralphs to arrive.

Adapted, by permission, from A. Stillman, 1989, "The 'yet' intervention," *Strategies* 2(4): 17, 28.

# SELECTION OF ACTIVITIES

In addition to the actions of the teacher, the activities we select to teach and the way we group children also affect how children feel. Obviously we can select activities that will mean public failure (or success) for children. Picking teams, elimination games, and relays typically contribute to undesirable feelings for some of the children in a class—typically the poorly skilled children who stand to benefit the most from physical education (Williams, 1996).

## Captains Picking Teams

This section is probably unnecessary today—at least I hope it is. We now realize that asking children to form teams by selecting two captains and having them pick the children one at a time is excruciatingly painful to children and creates lasting, haunting impressions as adults (Graham et al., 1992; NASPE, 2008; Williams, 1996). This process should be banned from schools—against the law! It simply hurts too much to stand and wait, only to be picked last or next to last. Sadly, children don't understand that they are being picked last because they are unskilled; they think that they are picked last because they are unpopular, or bad, or ugly, or because of any number of self-imposed, harmful perceptions.

## Elimination Games

Another vestige from the past that I wish was gone forever is games in which children are eliminated. Who is eliminated first? The child who needs the most practice, of course. This is simply a prehistoric practice that needs to be stopped in schools, and not only in physical education (Graham et al., 1992; NASPE, 2008).

## Relays

A third type of activity that promotes feelings of inferiority in some children is relays (NASPE, 2008; Williams, 1996). Inevitably, the poorly skilled or overweight children end up at the back of the relay lines. They are the ones still lumbering along when the race has already been decided and, invariably, the last thing that happens in a game is remembered as the most important part. Thus the child who comes in last becomes the target of ridicule and is often blamed for the loss—even though the other team members were also slow. Again, this leads to lasting harmful feelings about physical activity and painful, unpleasant memories of physical education. How can such a situation possibly result in feelings of eagerness and enthusiasm toward participation?

Relays, picking teams, and elimination games are simply unnecessary. They are potentially damaging to a child's self-concept. We long ago developed superior approaches to selecting teams and motivating children to participate in physical activity.

## *Forming Teams in Physical Education*

Ideally, the formation of teams whereby one half of the class competes against the other half is a rare occurrence in children's physical education classes. There might be instances, however, when it is developmentally appropriate to divide a class into two teams. There are several ways to do so that are relatively quick and do not damage a child's self-esteem.

One of the easiest ways is to ask children to find a partner (don't tell them you are about to organize them into teams). Ask one partner to stand on the blue line and face her partner who is standing on the red line. All children will be standing on two lines, facing one another. The children on the blue line compose one team, the ones on the red line the other team. Interestingly, this is one of the quickest and easiest ways to form teams of equal ability because very often in physical education classes children pick partners of similar ability.

Another quick way to form teams is to ask children to "count off." The ones are on one team; the twos are on the other. Or you can ask them to "count off in fours"—ones and threes, for example, on one team, twos and fours on the other.

Another way to form teams is to ask children with birthdays in the first six months of the year (January through June) to stand on one line; those with birthdays in July through December stand on the other line. This should come out reasonably close in numbers.

## COMPETITION FOR CHILDREN

If a teacher isn't careful, competitive games can also be damaging to a child's perceived self-competence. At various times in physical education classes, there will be opportunities for children to participate in competitive games. Score will be kept and winners determined. Competitive games put pressure on children, especially the poorly skilled. Several alternatives allow a teacher to avoid putting pressure (and potential damage to

self-concept) on those children who do not enjoy competition. They include allowing children to choose the type of game they want to play, alternative scoring systems, and child-designed games.

## Decision Making by the Loudest

Have you ever watched a class of children respond to the question, "What game do you want to play today?" Invariably a few children respond quickly and loudly—"kickball" or "dodgeball" or "killerball." Especially to beginning teachers, it sounds as if the whole class is in agreement. In fact, the loud response is made by a few children—often the highly skilled, and they are forceful. Needless to say, those who really don't want to play those games keep quiet.

## Choice of Games

One alternative is simply to provide children with a choice: "We are going to play two games. In this game we are going to keep score; that game is just for fun—no score will be kept." Although some might think it difficult to have two games going on simultaneously, it is becoming increasingly common in physical education classes to see several games played at the same time.

## Alternative Scoring Systems

A second alternative is to change the scoring system to encourage a spirit of cooperation and support, thus avoiding the critical comments and harshness often observed in competitive games. For example, points can be awarded for instances of good sportsmanship. A positive comment made to an opponent, a gesture of sportsmanship, such as helping an opponent up after she falls, or an offer to show someone a trick to help them improve might all earn a point. Clearly, the scoring system needs to be developed with the students so they understand why it is necessary and feel a sense of ownership.

Alternative scoring systems are especially instructive to highly skilled, competitive children, who become so intensely involved in games in which a score is kept that they totally lose a sense of perspective, especially when they become frustrated with their poorly skilled classmates. My experience is that these children initially find it difficult to adjust to these alternative scoring systems; but these are often the children who need to develop a perspective on their behavior in competitive situations.

## Child-Designed Activities

Asking children to design their own games, dances, or gymnastics sequences encourages them to invent activities that match their own ability (chapter 11). Although the activity the children design will often be different from a teacher-designed activity, there is a certain degree of satisfaction and enjoyment derived from creating a new activity. This seems especially true for children who might not be highly skilled but who are terrific at inventing enjoyable sequences, games, and dances.

Once again, the teacher will need to decide when it is appropriate to include child-designed activities. Obviously children need a background before they can begin to design successful activities; they can't design out of thin air.

Although it might appear limiting, children seem to do better when the invention is directed by the teacher, such as in these instances:

▶ Make up a game with your partner. It needs to have kicking in it. You may use one or two foam soccer balls. There are also hoops and cones if you need them.

▶ Your game can be played with three or four people. The equipment is limited to a maximum of three cones, one ball, one hoop, and three carpet squares.

## *Competition for Children: Convincing the Skeptics*

Occasionally I encounter the view that competition for children is good for them. "They need to learn how to lose!" is the battle cry often emitted by the frustrated ex-athlete or wannabe superstar. There might be a grain of truth to the idea that children need to learn how to lose gracefully and with understanding, but I remain convinced that learning to cooperate with others is a far more important skill to learn than learning how to lose. An occasional loss might not be harmful to children. Losing every day, however, is certainly unpleasant, if not harmful. And if we're not careful and sensitive, some children can easily be placed in situations in which virtually every physical education class is a losing experience.

When people confront me on my views of competition for children, I refer them to classic books by Tutko and Bruns, *Winning Is Everything: And Other American Myths,* and *Joy and Sadness in Children's Sports* by Rainer Martens. I don't know if they read them, but I hope they do because these books create a powerful and sensitive portrayal of the damage an overemphasis on competition can do to a child's emerging self-concept.

# TESTING

In addition to competitive games, another way we can make a child feel inferior and physically inept is in testing situations. In the classroom, tests are relatively private affairs—only the teacher and student know if mistakes are being made on a math test. In physical education, however, results are public. All students know who came in last in the mile or who can't catch a ball. As physical education teachers, we need to be sensitive to this fact and be careful to minimize harmful effects that might influence the feelings of children. Fortunately, we have developed some ways to avoid placing children in uncomfortable situations, including ways to help them understand test results and set their own goals.

## Interpreting Test Results

Sometimes teachers will choose to share test scores with children. How this is done is important. Posting scores on a wall for everyone to see can quickly lead to ridicule and magnify feelings of incompetence for the unskilled child. Certainly we ask children not to discuss others' scores, but that's naive on our part. Children do compare scores.

It also seems that standardized norms and criterion scores are harmful to those children who know they are less skilled than many others in the class. What good does it do to reinforce feelings of inadequacy?

The most humane and sensitive approach to reporting test scores to children is to enable them to compare their current scores with their past scores. Is the child improving? That's the truly important score, and the one the child has the most control over. Probably the only advantage of being poorly skilled is that practice can rather quickly result in drastic improvements on sensitive tests (i.e., it's easier for the poorly skilled child to show improvement than it is for the highly skilled child). Using computers, it is easy to provide children with individual reports of their test results and to show them how they have improved since the last test.

## Setting Own Goals

Another way teachers help children feel good about themselves is by helping them set their own goals (Grineski, 1993). This works better with older children who can begin to understand that improvement takes time and practice. No matter how old the children are, at the beginning they will need help in setting realistic goals that can be accomplished in a relatively short period of time. Increasing the number of times they are able to jump a rope or dribble a ball or do sit-ups in 30 seconds is readily achievable. If we're not careful, however, children will set unreasonable goals that are simply unreachable, even in a year. For example, making 9 of 10 free throws or running a mile in under six minutes are goals that are difficult to attain, even for the highly skilled or fit child.

Over time, goals can become harder as children realize what is required to achieve various goals. Having decided to ask children to set their own goals, teachers must devote time to explaining the whole process of goal setting. They must also explain the meanings of success and failure and the idea that goals are for the children themselves, not to impress teachers or friends.

# UNDERSTANDING FEELINGS

One of the advantages of aging is that we can better understand our feelings. Children have a difficult time separating their feelings from their own self-worth. "I can only do a few push-ups and I miss the ball a lot when I am batting, so I must not be a very good person" is the way some children think. Over time they begin to realize that athletic prowess does not equate to self-worth, but this process can take a while. We can help children promote this understanding in physical education by asking children to keep student logs and by implementing discussion circles.

## Student Logs and Journals

Asking children to write about the feelings that arise from participating in physical education helps teachers become more in touch with children's feelings (Cutforth & Parker, 1996; Tjeerdsma, 1997). With the increased emphasis in elementary schools on "writing across the curriculum," more classroom teachers are willing to devote five minutes or so to allow children to write in their logs immediately after they return from physical education class.

A question such as "How do you feel about dance?" can often be answered better in a paragraph than a single word. The log allows a teacher to gain deeper insights about children that might otherwise go undetected.

Wentzell (1989) has suggested ideas for stimulating children to write about physical education. Many of these ideas can be adapted for children in grades four through six (box 12.1).

It seems to work best if only one or two classes at a time keep physical education logs and then only for a period of several weeks. When we teach 400 or more children, it is simply overwhelming (and not enjoyable) to spend an entire weekend reading logs. The purpose of the logs is to allow children to get in touch with their feelings and for you to better understand how children feel about your teaching and your program. This can be accomplished by reading the logs of a few children—not all 400. This also allows the teacher to make comments in the logs if she thinks it is appropriate and would be valued by the children.

It works best when children's journals are durable, especially if they will be writing outside. You want them to last several months. Some teachers use manila folders with papers inside. Others use college bluebooks or find ways to laminate covers and bind pages inside the journals (Cutforth & Parker, 1996). The advantage of a bound journal is that it is easier to avoid losing pages, especially outside on a windy day. The disadvantage is that it is hard to add pages to the journal. Journals can be kept in cardboard boxes, organized by class, or can be organized alphabetically. Writing tools can be stored in cups, shoe boxes, or bags (Cutforth & Parker, 1996). As with virtually everything we do in physical education, it is important to teach journal-writing protocols so children understand how to get out and put away their journals.

Box 12.1

# Ideas for Writing About Physical Education

- I felt prepared/unprepared for the lesson because . . .
- I was/wasn't motivated to participate in the lesson because . . .
- The most important thing I learned today was . . . , because . . .
- The lesson was well organized/needed more organization because . . .
- Too much time/not enough time in the lesson was spent on . . . (explain).
- I most liked/disliked . . . , because . . .
- Next class I would/wouldn't like to review . . . , practice . . . , experience . . .
- Physical education is/is not/should be . . .
- The two activities/sports in physical education that I feel most confident in are . . . , because . . . I feel most awkward in . . . because . . .
- I feel that students my age do/don't obtain enough exercise . . . , I suggest that . . .
- If I were the teacher of physical education this year, I would remove/add/make the following changes in the way the class is conducted . . .
- I believe that personal health/wellness is . . . My present health status is . . .
- If I desire to maintain/change my present state of health/wellness, I must . . .
- Personal health/wellness is/is not important to me because . . .
- Competition is good/not good because . . . Cooperation is good/not good because . . . I prefer competition/cooperation because . . .

Reprinted, by permission, from S.R. Wentzell, 1989, "Beyond the physical-expressive writing in physical education," *Journal of Physical Education, Recreation and Dance* 60(9): 19.

## Discussion Circles

Another way to get in touch with children's feelings is a discussion circle. Again, this can be done occasionally with a class or two. The purpose is to determine how children feel about physical education.

The children and the teacher sit in a circle and talk about how things are going in class (Tjeersdma, 1997). Specific questions seem to work best:

> ▶ "How do you feel about coming into the gym and getting started immediately?"
> ▶ "How do you feel about the way I ask you to find partners or form groups?"
> ▶ "Do you feel tired when you leave PE class?"
> ▶ "Is there some activity that you wish I would teach from time to time?"
> ▶ "This week we have been striking with rackets. Have you practiced that skill after school? Why or why not?"

For teachers who have never used a discussion circle, several techniques are important to note. For a discussion circle to be productive, the teacher needs to carefully plan any questions that will be asked and then be certain that the children don't wander too far off during the discussion. It also helps to set a time limit at the beginning so the children understand how much time is going to be spent in the discussion.

Second, children need to be encouraged to say what they feel. If the teacher becomes defensive or angry, the discussion circle will not succeed.

Third, these are children, and they will say what they think. If a teacher wants to hear only good things about the program, then it is probably not a good idea to use a discussion circle. Teachers who successfully lead discussion circles are able to remain objective about what children say and help them express their feelings about the program.

## LEARNED HELPLESSNESS

Often youngsters who do poorly in school, in any subject, fall victim to the learned helplessness syndrome (Martinek & Griffith, 1994). Youngsters feel that success or failure is beyond their control, so they quickly give up or quit trying because they believe they can't do anything to improve or succeed. Learned helplessness occurs as early as third grade (Martinek & Griffith, 1994). The comments that follow are vivid, yet painful, examples of learned helplessness and show how some youngsters feel about their chances of success in physical education:

"I always drop the ball because I am too slow." "Serving the ball is always hard for me because I can't hit the thing very well." "I have always been clumsy . . . that's why I have a hard time doing gymnastics." (Martinek & Griffith, 1994, p. 119)

Clearly, these youngsters believe they can't succeed in these activities because of their lack of ability. When these statements are contrasted with the following statements made by children who are "mastery oriented" (Martinek & Griffith, 1994), the concept of learned helplessness becomes even clearer. Children who are mastery oriented make self-critical but positive statements:

"I did not do good on that task, but I think I can do it if I keep practicing at it." "I did terrible on this (the bump). I would miss it at first, but after a while I started trying . . . it started to come." "I had trouble with the headstand last week. I am trying to strengthen my stomach muscles so I can do it." (Martinek & Griffith, 1994, p. 119)

# CONCLUDING THOUGHTS

The examples of sensitive teaching in this chapter don't require a new curriculum. What we teach doesn't necessarily have to be changed, although the way we teach certain activities might be altered.

The message of this chapter is that we need to be sensitive to all children in our classes so they are comfortable and feel our support. When children come to physical education class, we want them to feel secure while they are with us. We want them to trust that we will try not to embarrass them or put them in uncomfortable situations. We want our classes to be a special place where children feel good about themselves—and about physical activity.

Funky Winkerbean got down from the rope with the help of the custodian. He was embarrassed, but he made it. The coach is still showing movies to his classes. In some schools physical education is still being taught the way it was 30 years ago, but there is a growing revolution in physical education. I hope this chapter will contribute to these changes so that the Funky Winkerbeans of the future will no longer be placed in embarrassing situations that lead to a dislike of physical activity and contribute to the development of a poor self-image.

# SUMMARY

Physical activity has a powerful influence on how children feel about themselves. As physical education teachers, we must do everything we can to be sensitive to how our students feel and help them build positive feelings about their involvement in physical activity. Teachers who help children build positive attitudes are constantly aware of children's feelings and consciously modify and select activities that are considerate of both the highly skilled and the poorly skilled, the enthusiastic and the reluctant, and the physically fit and less fit. They understand that competition might cause some children to turn off to physical activity, so they provide alternatives to games that emphasize winning and score keeping. They also try to make any testing they do positive for children and make specific attempts to understand the feelings of children.

# QUESTIONS FOR REFLECTION

1.  Think back to your experiences in physical education classes. Try to recall three examples of teachers being unpleasant or even harmful to the poorly skilled or unfit children in your classes. Why do you think teachers weren't sensitive to these children?

2.  Reflect on your own teaching. Do you think you tend to favor any certain group of children—high- or low-skilled? Attractive or unattractive children? Boys or girls? What do you do, as you teach, to be sensitive to your tendency to favor a certain group?

3.  Think about your friends or acquaintances who have been turned off to physical activity. Do you know why this is so? Why do they find it so hard to exercise regularly? Can any of these feelings be traced back to their experiences in physical education classes?

4. In physical education, it is difficult to make testing private. Describe some ways teachers might test in physical education to help ensure the relative privacy of the test. Do you think children can test one another? Why or why not?

5. Children have different levels of experience and understanding than adults do. Can you recall two examples of how you saw something differently as a child and now as an adult? Briefly describe the change in feelings or attitude.

# REFERENCES

Cutforth, N., & Parker, M. (1996). Promoting affective development in physical education: The value of journal writing. *Journal of Physical Education, Recreation and Dance, 67*(7), 19–23.

Flugelman, A. (Ed.) (1976). *The new games book.* Garden City, NY: Doubleday.

Glover, D.R., & Midura, D.W. (1995a). *More team building challenges.* Champaign, IL: Human Kinetics.

Glover, D.R., & Midura, D.W. (1995b). *Team building through physical challenges.* Champaign, IL: Human Kinetics.

Graham, G., Castenada, R., Hopple, C., Manross, M., & Sanders, S. (1992). *Developmentally appropriate physical education for children: A position statement of the Council on Physical Education for Children (COPEC).* Reston, VA: National Association for Sport and Physical Education.

Grineski, S. (1993). Achieving educational goals in physical education—a missing ingredient. *Journal of Physical Education, Recreation and Dance, 64*(5), 32–34.

Grineski, S. (1996). *Cooperative learning in physical education.* Champaign, IL: Human Kinetics.

Hichwa, J. (1998). *Right fielders are people, too: An inclusive approach to middle school physical education.* Champaign, IL: Human Kinetics.

Martens, R. (Ed.). (1978). *Joy and sadness in children's sports.* Champaign, IL: Human Kinetics.

Martinek, T.J., & Griffith, J.B. (1994). *Journal of Teaching in Physical Education, 13,* 108–122.

McCaughtry, N. (2004). The emotional dimensions of a teacher's pedagogical content knowledge: Influences on content, curriculum and pedagogy. *Journal of Teaching in Physical Education, 23,* 30–47.

National Association for Sport and Physical Education (NASPE). (2004). *Moving into the future: National standards for physical education.* 2nd ed. Reston, VA: NASPE.

National Association for Sport and Physical Education (NASPE). (2008). *Appropriate Practices for Elementary Physical Education.* Reston, VA: NASPE.

Orlick, T. (1978a). *Cooperative sports and games books.* New York: Pantheon.

Orlick, T. (1978b). *Winning through cooperation.* Washington, DC: Acropolis Books.

Stillman, A. (1989). The "yet" intervention. *Strategies, 2*(4), 17, 28.

Tjeerdsma, B. L. (1997). A comparison of teacher and student perspectives of tasks and feedback. *Journal of Teaching in Physical Education, 16*(4), 388–400.

Turner, L.F., & Turner, S.L. (1984). *Alternative sports and games for the new physical educator.* Palo Alto, CA: Peek.

Tutko, T., & Bruns, W. (1976). *Winning is everything: And other American myths.* New York: Macmillan.

Wentzell, S.R. (1989). Beyond the physical—expressive writing in physical education. *Journal of Physical Education, Recreation and Dance, 60*(9), 18–20.

Williams, N. F. (1996). The physical education hall of shame: Part III: Inappropriate teaching practices. *Journal of Physical Education, Recreation and Dance, 67*(8), 45–48.

## Chapter 13

# Assessing and Reporting Children's Progress

*When I was 8 months pregnant I went with the fifth grade to camp for 4 days. When I returned from camp, a kindergartner said, "Did you have your baby?" Another kindergartner responded by saying, "Duh, it's still in her shirt!"*

**Mary Driemeyer, Sappington Elementary, St. Louis, Missouri**
Reprinted with permission from PE Central (www.pecentral.org).

Since chapter 2 (planning), each of the chapters has presented a variety of active teaching skills for your pedagogy tool box—the skills that teachers use (pedagogy) when they are actually with their students. In this chapter we will focus on another aspect of teaching, one carried out both with students and in the teacher's office or home. Essentially, we attempt to answer the question, "How can I realistically determine if students are learning what I want them to learn as a result of my teaching?"

## After reading and understanding this chapter, the teacher will be able to

▶ explain why assessment is an important part of a quality program of physical education,

▶ define alternative assessment and its characteristics,

▶ provide examples of scoring rubrics,

▶ describe realistic and practical approaches to assessing children's improvement and understanding related to motor skills,

▶ describe practical ways of assessing children's cognitive understanding related to various physical education concepts,

▶ describe practical ways to assess children's attitudes and feelings related to various aspects of physical education,

▶ describe ways of reporting progress to parents based on student assessments,

▶ explain the difference between formal and informal assessments, and

▶ provide examples of informally assessing youngsters as a part of checking for understanding and during closure.

# WHY ASSESS?

Why do we need to assess the children we are teaching? There are at least four reasons.

One reason is that assessment forces us to look carefully at every child in a class, at least for a few moments. This allows us to briefly reflect on that child and how well he is able to do on a particular assessment. Most of the time we are reasonably accurate about our subjective assessments of the ability of our students. There are surprises, however, and testing helps to uncover them.

Another benefit to assessing is that assessments done in fifth or sixth grade provide an overall analysis of the success of our program. They allow a teacher to determine if her program is truly instructionally aligned and to answer the all-important question, Am I meeting the goals and objectives for my program? Assessment allows us to gain insights on what our students have and haven't learned in five or six years (assuming we have been teaching at that school that entire time). It also increases our credibility as professionals (Arbogast & Griffin, 1989; Doolittle, 1996; Hopple, 2005; NASPE, 2004; Schiemer, 2000). Parents and administrators expect us to be able to assess, and report, the progress of children. Third, when we have an assessment program in place with some recorded evidence about the progress our students are making, we can make more informed, sounder decisions about the individual children in our program. This is in contrast, for example, to the teacher who is asked about a child by a parent and has no recorded evidence except what she can (or cannot) remember about the child.

A fourth benefit is that assessment, as described in this chapter, becomes a self-imposed accountability measure. I suspect that every teacher has been surprised at one time or another by what her students didn't know—even after the teacher thought a lesson was taught so well and so clearly that no one could possibly have missed it. When teachers test the things they have taught, not the things someone else thinks they ought to test, it can be a real eye opener.

These are four reasons it makes sense for teachers to assess the progress of their children. The next important question is how to assess realistically in an elementary school setting to determine

▶ individual progress the children are making and

▶ the influence of our program on the children after five or six years.

# GRADING

Grading and assessment are often confused. They have very different purposes. Assessment is used as a way to determine how well children are learning the content you are teaching. Grading is a way to tell parents how well their child is doing in your class. Of course children also pay attention to their grades (some more than others!).

Many schools provide teachers with relatively limited opportunities for physical educators to inform parents about how well their child is doing. Some physical educators, for example, report student progress by checking one of three categories:

▶ Excellent

▶ Satisfactory

▶ Needs Improvement

This is all the information parents receive on how their children are doing in physical education. Needless to say, limited choices like these are unsatisfactory to teachers. Ideally, there is a broader range of choices for the teacher. Better yet, the teacher is not confined to reporting progress in one of three categories but has the opportunity to report student progress on a variety of skills and concepts taught during that grading period. The ideal way of reporting is to provide parents with information about the progress their child is making—what they have accomplished and what they need to work on. The ideal approach to reporting how well students are doing is when assessments are reported directly to parents as a measure of student progress (Shellhase, 1998).

# NEW WAYS TO ASSESS IN PHYSICAL EDUCATION

Since the first edition of this book was published in 1992, a radical change has occurred in the process teachers use to assess students. Today many teachers design their own assessments (Schiemer, 2000). Teacher-designed assessments are also referred to as alternative assessment (Hopple, 1997; Joyner & McManis, 1997; Melograno, 1997; Schwager, 1996), authentic assessment (Lund, 1997; NASPE, 1995), and performance assessment (Westfall, 1998). Essentially, these terms refer to teacher-designed assessments that truly assess student progress in areas important to the teacher and are congruent with the specific goals of the district or school curriculum (NASPE, 1995; 2004). These relatively new approaches to assessment are based in part on the development of curricular standards for many of the subject areas, including physical education (NASPE, 2004), that specifically describe what students are expected to learn. Teacher-designed assessments were also developed as a reaction to the traditional summative assessments often administered at the end of an academic year, on content the teacher might or might not have taught, and in ways that are often uninteresting and stressful to students.

Alternative assessments, often called formative assessments, give teacher and student insight on progress being made. Alternative assessment techniques have six characteristics (Lund, 1997):

1. Alternative assessment tasks are designed to be meaningful and genuine to youngsters, not contrived. Multiple choice tests, for example, do not meet these criteria. Nor do traditional physical fitness tests. Good alternative assessments are more like an interesting problem for youngsters to solve.

2. Alternative assessments require youngsters to use higher-order thinking skills because tasks are often complex and require critical thinking (chapter 11) to correctly solve a problem.

3. Children know the criteria for scoring the assessment in advance of the assessment. The criteria are called rubrics and allow youngsters to self-evaluate their performance progress because they clearly articulate what youngsters are expected to learn (NASPE, 1995). Box 13.1 is an example of a scoring rubric for the overhand throw. It uses the categories of *Exemplary, Acceptable,* and *Needs Improvement,* providing criteria for each category (Smith, 1997).

Teachers typically create a variety of rubric categories depending on the concept or skill to be assessed (Schiemer, 2000). Ardovino and Sanders (1997), like Shellhase (1998) and Smith (1997), use three categories in their rubric for assessing the underhand throw: *Achieving, Developing,* and *Not Yet* (box 13.2). Westfall (1998) suggests achievement levels for degrees of quality, frequency, and expertise on a four-point scale teachers might use to record student progress (table 13.1).

**Box 13.1**

# Example of a Rubric Scale for the Overhand Throw for Distance

## Exemplary
- The student stepped in the direction of the target with the leg opposite the throwing arm.
- The student visually focused on the target being thrown at.
- The student used sequentially coordinated musculature to maximize motor function relative to the throwing task.
- The student adjusted the force with which he or she threw to maximize both distance and accuracy.

## Acceptable
- The student stepped with the leg opposite the throwing arm.
- The student visually focused on the target.
- The student used entire body (legs, torso, and arm) in the throwing motion.

## Needs improvement
- The student did not step when throwing (kept feet planted).
- The student used only the arm to throw.

Reprinted, by permission, from T.K. Smith, 1997, "Authentic assessment: Using a portfolio card in physical education," *Journal of Physical Education, Recreation and Dance* 68(4): 46-52.

**Box 13.2**

# Scoring Rubric for Kindergarten Children on the Underhand Throw

## Achieving

- Always faces target when throwing underhand
- Always swings arm back ("tick")
- Always swings arm forward ("tock")
- Always steps with the opposite foot
- Always watches the target

## Developing

- Sometimes faces target when throwing underhand
- Sometimes swings arm back ("tick")
- Sometimes swings arm forward ("tock")
- Sometimes steps with the opposite foot
- Sometimes watches the target

## Not Yet

- Does not face target when throwing underhand
- Does not swing arm back ("tick")
- Does not swing arm forward ("tock")
- Does not step with the opposite foot
- Does not watch the target

Reprinted, by permission, from L. Ardovino and S. Sanders, 1997, "The development of a physical education assessment report," *Teaching Elementary Physical Education* 8(3): 24.

**Table 13.1** Assessing the Overhand Throw

|  | SIDE TO TARGET | HIGH ELBOW | STEP WITH OPPOSITE FOOT | THROW BALL FORWARD | POINT TO TARGET |
|---|---|---|---|---|---|
| David |  |  |  |  |  |
| James |  |  |  |  |  |
| Julien |  |  |  |  |  |
| Michelle |  |  |  |  |  |
| Robin |  |  |  |  |  |
| Scott |  |  |  |  |  |
| Shannon |  |  |  |  |  |

Reprinted, by permission, from S. Westfall, 1998, "Setting your sights on assessment: Describing student performance in physical education," *Teaching Elementary Physical Education* 9(6): 7.

4. Alternative assessments are designed to assess the curriculum the teacher is actually teaching. For this reason, assessments often seem to the children to be a part of a regular lesson. When assessments truly reflect what is being taught in a program, the teachers literally "teach to the test"—to the benefit of students.

5. Because the criteria for the assessment are known by students in advance (scoring rubric), the teacher can assume the role of coach or ally as opposed to test administrator. Although this is a subtle difference, it is one that many teachers enjoy because they can actively root for youngsters to succeed.

6. Finally, when assessments are authentic, many of them also become public. It is understood that they will be shared with others. This becomes clearer when examples are provided in the section "How to Assess," which provides examples of a variety of alternative assessments.

## WHAT TO ASSESS

Before a teacher can decide how to assess, she needs to make a decision about what to assess (instructional alignment). This is an obvious starting point for thinking about the purposes and goals of a physical education program (chapter 2) and answering the question, "What are the outcomes we want to accomplish in our physical education program?" This question is recommended as the first step in the curriculum design process (Hopple, 2005).

Once the overall K–12 program goals have been decided, the next step is to "design down" from these outcomes by determining grade-level outcomes and then developing the themes or units for the year, followed by specific lessons that will lead to the accomplishment of these outcomes (Hopple, 2005). Figure 13.1 depicts this design-down process.

Once a teacher makes a decision on what to teach at various grade levels, she then needs to decide which outcomes will be assessed because, given the limited amount of time allocated for physical education in most districts (chapter 2), it is unrealistic to think that every outcome could be assessed. Guides and standards published by national associations, in all subject areas, provide good places to start making these decisions—but these are typically wish lists because there is not enough time to provide effective learn-

## The design-down process

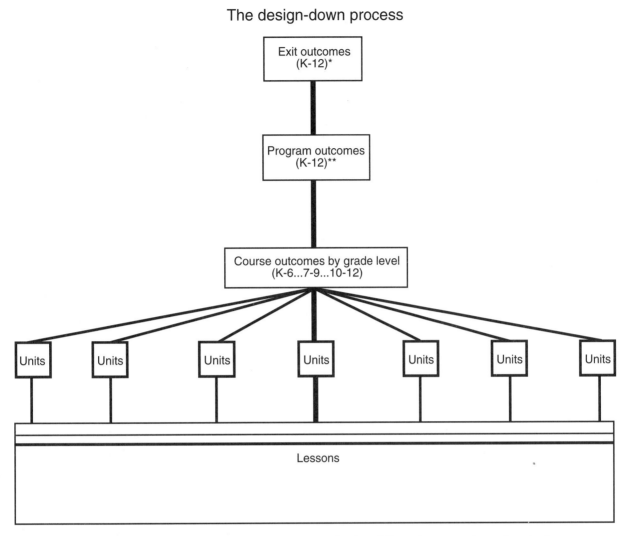

*Exit outcomes are often intended to demonstrate application skills and are generic to all content areas.

**Program outcomes refer to skills, knowledge, and behaviors of specific content areas.

**Figure 13.1** Illustration of the design-down process.
Adapted, by permission, from C. Hopple, 2005, *Elementary physical education teaching and assessment*, 2nd ed. (Champaign, IL.: Human Kinetics), 12.

ing. Today most states have developed standards (www.pecentral.org); there are also national standards (NASPE, 2004) on which many state standards are based. Once a teacher has decided what to assess, the next step is to figure out how to best assess various learning outcomes.

# HOW TO ASSESS

Fortunately, a physical educator today has a plethora of performance or alternative assessments to choose from (Hopple, 2005; NASPE, 1995; Schiemer, 2000) in addition to the fitness and skill tests and checklists used for many years by physical educators. These assessments can be classified into products, portfolios, written products, and performance tasks (Hopple, 1997).

# Products

Student-generated products are assessments completed by students that take the form of an exhibition or display. Examples of this type of assessment include science fair projects, photography collections or exhibits, artwork, drawings, video and audio recordings, models, posters, slide shows, collages, and banners (Hopple, 1997). Based on the outcome to be assessed, the teacher might decide to use one of these types of assessments and then create a rubric describing the criteria for the project. These types of assessments are especially valuable when students can complete them as homework or in another class as an art, science, or writing project.

# Portfolios and Other Written Products

Because written assessments require skills highly valued across the curriculum, portfolio or written assessment can often be completed in a classroom (Fortman-Kirk, 1997). In fact, some classroom teachers welcome the opportunity to have students write essays or reports on topics that are of special interest to the students. Some of the forms that written assessments might take include essays, stories, poems, research papers, portfolios, learning logs, personal fitness and activity plans, self-assessments reported in writing, advertisements, brochures, checklists of cues or critical elements, editorials or opinion pieces, and newspaper articles or proposals (Hopple, 1997).

# Performance Tasks

A third type of alternative assessment requires performances by youngsters as a way to demonstrate their understanding of the criteria described in the rubric. Some examples of performance tasks include musical or dramatic performances; dance, gymnastic, or movement sequences; officiating games; fitness and skill tests; debates or interviews; oral presentations or reports; skills checks during game play; skits or dramatizations; and peer tutoring (Hopple, 1997).

One of the most interesting examples of a performance assessment is a system for assessing improvement in 13 fundamental motor skills (Shellhase, 1998). Shellhase provides performance standards for grades K–6 in a logical progression based on the National Standards (NASPE, 1995) and skill themes (Graham, Holt/Hale, & Parker, 2007), along with teaching cues for each of the skills. She has devised a reporting system, using the assessment rubric for each of the motor skills, which she sends home to parents to apprise them of their children's progress. The entire system is stored on a computer disk to allow modifications as necessary. The system can also be readily used with a personal digital assistant (Wegis & Van der Mars, 2006) and then downloaded so that a teacher can avoid the plethora of paperwork that is so difficult to manage when teaching several hundred children a week.

# Assessments on PE Central

As we mentioned earlier, PE Central (www.pecentral.org) is a Web site for K–12 physical educators. The site contains a wealth of information for teachers, including examples of assessments that can be downloaded for free and adapted for use with all grade levels (Werner, 1997). The table of contents on the front page of PE Central will guide you to the assessment examples.

# REPORTING WHAT HAS BEEN ASSESSED

Once a teacher has decided what to assess, and has selected or devised an assessment task and a scoring rubric, the next step is to devise a way to report to parents or guardians on the progress students are making (Allen, 1997; Ardovino & Sanders, 1997; Hopple, 1997; Shellhase, 1998). Alternative assessments lend themselves to comprehensive reports that are easily understood and appreciated by many parents (Doolittle, 1996).

Because criteria for each assessment are spelled out in a rubric, a teacher can provide parents, and administrators, a clear description of what is expected of the children and the progress they are making. Ardovino and Sanders (1997) adopted the criteria from their scoring rubric into a progress report to parents (figure 13.2), which was used by Shellhase (1998) in her assessment system:

▶ Not yet developed the skill

▶ Developed the skill

▶ Achieved the skill

## Just to let you know what we are doing in physical education

Name_____ Date_____

This week we learned the *underhand throw.* The underhand throw should include the following components:

- Face the target (K-2).
- Swing your arm back "tick" (K-2).
- Swing your arm forward "tock" (K-2).
- Watch the target (K-2).
- Step with the opposite foot (1-2).
- Bend the knees as you step (3-4).
- Point your fingers to the target (3-4).

Helpful hints for the underhand throw include: Make sure the arm comes just past the knee ("tick") and forward ("tock"); to make the ball go straight toward the target, point the hand right at the target.

**Your child has**

- not yet developed the skill.
- developed the skill.
- achieved the skill.

Next week we will be working on the *overhand throw.* Some helpful hints for the overhand throw include:

- Throw hard.
- Bring arm way back just near the ear.
- Step with opposite foot.
- Follow through.

Please discuss this skill with your child and return this to me.

Parent's signature_____

**Figure 13.2**   Example of a progress report to parents for young children.

Reprinted, by permission, from L. Ardovino and S. Sanders, 1997, "The development of a physical education assessment report," *Teaching Elementary Physical Education* 8(3): 23–25.

Figure 13.2 contains an example of Ardovino and Sanders' parent report, entitled "Just to let you know what we are doing in physical education." Hopple (1997) also suggests three criteria for her parent reports (figure 13.3):

**M**—Child has *mastered* the skill or concept.

**P**—Child is *practicing on/working toward* mastering the skill or concept.

**B**—At the present time, child is *below developmental level* regarding this skill or concept.

Hopple's parent report includes concepts of body awareness and space awareness, as well as kicking skills, punting skills, and behavior.

## A Frightening Thought

Increasingly, schools are being held accountable for what children are or are not learning. I am frightened that if we don't design our own ways of assessing children a test battery will be handed to us, similar to the standardized tests used in many classrooms today, and we will have to administer those tests to every child. In some districts and states this has already happened with the physical fitness tests. Although fitness is an important part of what we teach in physical education, good programs certainly do more than just attempt to improve fitness (NASPE, 2004). We need to begin to discover ways of assessing our children in all domains, not only fitness; otherwise, the success of our programs will be measured only by how many pull-ups children can do or how fast they run a mile. Is that truly the important measure of a physical education program? Do we want this to be the sole measure of our effectiveness as physical educators?

# INFORMAL ASSESSMENTS

So far, we have discussed formal assessments designed to systematically determine, and in some cases report, the progress youngsters are making in physical education. Teachers, however, often use informal assessments as a way to quickly judge how students are doing—but this is for their own information, in order to determine whether students are grasping the important concepts and skills and if they are enjoying physical education. Such informal assessments can be designed to determine students' improvement in performance and motor skills, their grasp of cognitive concepts, and their attitudes. Two examples of physical, cognitive, and affective assessments are described for each of these three domains.

## Informally Assessing Motor Skills

There are times when a teacher asks, "Do students seem to be grasping this concept? Should I move on or stay with this task or cue?" In this case the teacher is not attempting to assess the progress individual children are making but is rather asking a broader question about the progress being made by an entire class (chapter 8). Scanning and videoing are two useful techniques in getting answers to these questions.

### Scanning

One method of scanning involves providing a task for students and then observing a single critical component by visually scanning students in a 10- to 15-second visual sweep

## Physical education report
### Grades 1st-2nd—1st nine weeks

Dear parents: Below you will find a listing of the skills and concepts your child has been working on in our physical education class for the first nine weeks. Before each skill or concept, you will find either an "**M**," which denotes your child has *mastered* this skill or concept; a "**P**," which means your child is *practicing on/working toward mastering* this skill or concept; or a "**B**," which means your child is, at the present time, *below developmental level* in regard to this skill or concept. An item preceded by a double asterisk (**) means it is appropriate for your child to show mastery of this item *at the present time* (we will continue to work toward mastering the skills not marked with a double asterisk, as well as additional skills not listed here, throughout the year).

Should you have any questions regarding this or any other matter related to physical education, please feel free to write or contact me at school. *Thank you.*

Sincerely, *Christine J. Hopple*
Physical education teacher

### *Body awareness* and *relationship* concepts

Involves having an understanding and awareness of the different body parts, their relationship to each other, and the ability to move the body in relation to others and objects. Acquiring this knowledge is a fundamental component of all games, dance, and gymnastic activities.

**It is expected that your child be able to understand the concept of and:**

____ **Identify the different parts of the body (e.g., foot, head, knees, etc.).
____ *Grade 2 only:* must be able to distinguish between right and left side of body.
____ **Move the body in relation to objects or others (e.g., over, under, beside, between, behind, in front of, etc.).

### *Space awareness* concepts

Awareness of where the body and/or an implement is moving through space. Every sport or game involves the use of differing combinations of space awareness concepts; mastery of these concepts is important if students are to succeed in physical activities. In addition, having a cognitive understanding of these concepts of movement is also needed so students have a basis on which to modify and improve their performance in physical activities.

**It is expected that your child be able to understand the concept of and:**

____ **Find a self-space in a large empty area where he/she cannot touch anybody or anything.
____ **Move through general space in a large group with control (i.e., without moving into others; can find the empty areas to move into).
____ **Move his/her body in different directions at a given signal; forward, backward, sideways, to the left and right, up, and down. *(Grade 2: clockwise and counterclockwise introduced.)*
____ **Move his/her body through general space while making different pathways (i.e., straight, curved, zigzag, or angular. For example, soccer and football require students to move while making zigzag pathways.)

### *Kicking* and *punting*

Understanding the fundamentals of how to kick and being able to practice this skill multiple times gives students competence and the confidence not only to "play" at kicking, but also to participate in sports such as soccer.

**It is expected that your child be able to understand the concept of and:**

____ Consistently kick a ball using the instep of the foot ("shoelaces"). This kick is used for covering a long distance and moving the ball into the air.
____ Consistently use the inside of the foot to "tap" (foot dribble) a ball through general space, while keeping it under control.

### Behavior

Each day, your child rated his/her behavior on a scale of 1 to 4 (level 4 behavior includes cooperating with others, listening and following all directions, using all equipment safely and properly, and not keeping others from doing their work; level 1 is the opposite). This self-check is based on a widely accepted model for self and social responsibility.

The average behavior level your child exhibited this past nine weeks was:____

### Additional comments:

Comments to Miss Hopple:

(Have your child return this to me; I'll contact you and return this sheet to you.)

**Figure 13.3** Example of a report to parents assessing progress on movement concepts and kicking and punting.

(chapters 8 and 9). For example, the task might be to see how many times students can strike a ball against a wall using a racket. Once children begin, the teacher scans to see if they are turning the appropriate side to the wall (forehand or backhand) as they strike. Using this technique, a rough estimate of the number of children who are turning their sides appropriately can be obtained in a short time.

Some qualitative components are more easily assessed than others by using live observation. For example, it is relatively easy to observe whether, when catching, children use their hands appropriately (thumbs together for a catch at high level; little fingers together for a low-level catch). Other critical components, such as sequential hip and shoulder rotation, are harder to observe in a live setting unless the teacher has had a lot of practice in live observation of a particular skill.

## Videoing

Videoing a class can be useful in assisting a teacher to observe how well students are grasping a critical component, especially one that is difficult to observe in a live setting (Doering, 2000). A camera using a wide-angle setting can be placed in one corner of the gym or playground and turned on for several minutes during a lesson. Later the teacher can view the video and assess student use of the critical components. This is especially interesting when children are playing games because some students tend to forget some of the critical components during the excitement of a game. Some teachers replay the video in a later class to show students what they are forgetting during game play. This has to be done carefully, however, to avoid embarrassing youngsters who are not skillful.

## Digital Cameras

Digital cameras are commonly used by physical educators during assessment, to spruce up newsletters, to illustrate stations or learning centers, to help them memorize student names, and to enhance student portfolios, posters, bulletin boards, and school Web sites (Ryan, Marzilli, & Martindale, 2001). Digital cameras within cell phones are popular, and it won't be long before most teachers have their cell phone, digital camera, and personal digital assistant in a single device.

# Informal Cognitive Assessments

As we know, accomplished physical educators focus on youngsters' cognitive understanding of various concepts, in addition to their physical abilities (NASPE, 1995). Quick written tests and checking for understanding are two techniques teachers use to informally assess if youngsters are grasping critical concepts.

## The Quick Written Test in the Gym

The standard paper-and-pencil test comes to mind when we think of assessing children's cognitive understanding. The process, however, need not take a long time (Griffin & Oslin, 1990; Lipowitz, 1997). One technique for children that is easily done on a cafeteria floor or blacktop playground is to ask the children to "Help your friend, Murgatroid . . ." Here's how it works.

Before one or two classes (not necessarily every class taught that day), set out paper and pencils for each child in the class in an area away from the actual activity. Sometimes five-by-eight-inch index cards work better if you are outside. At some point in the lesson, ask students to go to this area and respond to a scenario, such as, "Your friend Murgatroid doesn't know how to dribble a ball. List up to five things (cues) you would tell her so that she can become a good dribbler." As soon as the children are finished, they can resume activity. This takes less than five minutes and provides valuable information on what children have learned. The example provided in figure 13.4 was given to a group of fourth-grade children several days after they finished a sequence of lessons on dribbling with their hands. The information provided the teacher with a measure of how effective he had been in teaching his students the critical elements (cues; chapter 9) of dribbling.

Another example of a paper-and-pencil assessment that can be quickly administered is a catching assessment for young children from PE Central (Werner, 1997). This assessment uses drawings of faces and asks children to draw a picture of themselves catching a ball (figure 13.5).

1. To use the finger pads of your hand not the palm

2. Not to <u>hit</u> the ball down, push it so you will stay in control

3. Don't have your wrist like a piece of metal but don't have it so loose you can't keep control of it

4. Keep your eyes looking in front of you to make sure you don't run into anything

5. Don't bash the thing so hard it goes above your head, keep it at your waist

**Figure 13.4**   Your friend Murgatroid doesn't know how to dribble a ball with her hands. List five things to help her become a good dribbler.

## PE Central catching assessment

Student name_____ Grade_____

**Physical education catching assessment**

Fill in the faces by drawing a happy face if you feel good about or you agree with the sentence, a straight line if you are unsure, or a frown if you don't feel good about or disagree with the statement.

1. I am a good catcher.

2. I think I could help someone else learn how to catch better.

3. My classmates are good catchers.

4. I always put my pinkies together when catching at a low level.

5. I always put my thumbs together when catching at a high level.

6. To be a better catcher, I need to continue practicing.

This is a picture of me "catching" in physical education class:

**Figure 13.5**  Physical education catching assessment from PE Central.
Reprinted, by permission, from P. Werner, 1997, "Using PE Central and the National Standards to develop practical assessment instruments," *Teaching Elementary Physical Education* 8(3): 12.

## Checking for Understanding

Another quick way to learn how well children understand a concept is to use the technique of checking for understanding. When used at the end, or closure, of a lesson, this method is called closure assessment (Marks, 1988). Ask students to show you their understanding of a particular cue (critical component) or concept you have taught. For example, when students are assembled around you, ask them to do the following:

▶ "Show me how your hands should look when you are trying to catch a ball at high level."

▶ "Show me one good way to stretch your lower back muscles."

▶ "Show me how your knees should look after you land from a jump."

A quick visual survey will tell you how well students have understood the concept. Of course, simply because they can show you they understand doesn't mean that they will always do it, but understanding is a necessary first step. This also serves as an excellent way to conclude the lesson and review the one or two cues (reminder words; chapters 6, 9, and 10) emphasized in the lesson. Some cognitive concepts can be assessed this way; others can't. These ideas, however, suggest ways that teachers can assess the cognitive understanding of their students.

# Informal Attitude Assessments

In addition to assessing physical performance and cognitive understanding, there are several ways teachers can begin to gain insights into the attitudes of their children toward physical activity and toward themselves. Many of us feel that the attitudes of children are important barometers for determining their proclivities for developing active, healthy lifestyles that endure into adulthood. This assessment can also be done using exit polls, which take little time, or with paper and pencil.

## Exit Polls

One simple, albeit somewhat imprecise, way to learn how children feel is an exit poll. For example, a teacher can laminate a number of faces: "smiley," neutral, and "frowny." As children leave the gym, they are asked to pick a face that best represents their feelings about their ability, their enjoyment, or the lesson from one of the three shoe boxes by the door (one contains the smiles, another the neutrals, and a third the frowns) and deposit it in the ballot box. Some sample questions are

> ▶ "How do you feel about your ability to strike a ball with a bat?"
> ▶ "How do you feel about doing sit-ups over the weekend?"
> ▶ "How do you feel about continuing to work on designing your own dances next class?"
> ▶ "How do you feel about today's lesson?"

## Paper-and-Pencil Attitude Assessments

As with the questions assessing cognitive understanding, the attitude questions can also be asked effectively as part of paper-and-pencil tests. These assessments can be very revealing.

In one study (Graham, Metzler, & Webster, 1991), students were asked to circle one of three faces, indicating their feelings about various subjects taught in physical education (questions 6-11 in figure 13.6). They consistently circled smiley faces until they came to the question on their feelings about dance and gymnastics. Then many circled neutral or frowny faces. This suggested that the dance and gymnastics programs needed to be reevaluated because, apparently, they were turning children off, rather than on, to these activities. Unfortunately, boys tended to circle frowny faces on the questions related to dance. A number of sample questions are provided in figure 13.6 to suggest ways that teachers might assess the feelings and attitudes of their children.

Logs, journals, and discussion circles also provide valuable insights on how and what children are (and aren't) learning in physical education classes (chapter 12).

1. I would rather exercise or play sports than watch TV.

    Yes     No

2. People who exercise regularly seem to have a lot of fun doing it.

    Yes     No

3. In school I look forward to attending physical education class.

    Yes     No

4. During physical education class at school I usually work up a sweat.

    Yes     No

5. When I grow up I will probably be too busy to stay physically fit.

    Yes     No

6. How do you feel about your ability to strike a ball with a racket?

7. How do you feel about your ability to kick a ball hard and hit a target?

8. How do you feel about your ability to run a long distance without stopping?

9. How do you feel about your ability to play many different games and sports?

10. How do you feel about your ability to participate in gymnastics?

11. How do you feel about your ability to participate in dance?

**Figure 13.6** Sample questions designed to understand children's feelings and attitudes toward physical activity.
From G. Graham, 2008, *Teaching Children Physical Education*, 3rd ed. (Champaign, IL: Human Kinetics).

# FITNESS TESTING

Although an increasing number of teachers are using alternative assessments as suggested by the National Association for Sport and Physical Education (NASPE, 2004), many states and districts still require a physical fitness test—although for many children such tests make for unpleasant and meaningless experiences (Hopple & Graham, 1995). Today there are several versions that a teacher might use. Typically they include a distance run and a measure of flexibility and upper-body and abdominal strength. Regardless of the version a teacher uses, there are ways to save time administering the tests and to make them more valuable for your students.

# Self-Testing

One way to save time is to teach upper-grade children to test themselves or one another. Yes, some time will need to be spent teaching them the proper way to administer and perform the tests. Will this work with every class in every school? No. Will it succeed with many classes? Yes, depending on the children and how well they are taught the process of self-testing.

Ultimately the most important part of any test is to let students know how they are improving in relation to their past performances—their progress. Children can be taught to measure their own progress, and, for this reason, it is important to emphasize recording honest scores. This works especially well if there is no pressure to compare scores with other students in the class (chapter 12). Self-measuring also allows teachers to test various items throughout the year rather than only once a year in the spring, for example. In some cases, youngsters can be taught to enter their own scores into a class computer. Needless to say, having youngsters handle this responsibility saves you a lot of time and also emphasizes self-responsibility.

During the year, a teacher might need to turn in an official set of scores. These scores might need to be administered by the teacher or at least be more closely supervised than some of the more informal tests done by students.

Another advantage of teaching students to test themselves is that they can do it on those days when the classroom teacher is responsible for physical education. This allows more time for instruction and practice during the days scheduled with the specialist (Parker & Pemberton, 1989). When the fitness sheets are kept in the classroom, it also makes for less bookkeeping for the PE teacher.

# Broad Categories

An easy way to streamline the fitness testing process is to insert scores into broad categories. For example, whether a child runs a mile in 9:15 or 9:25 is important to the child but not very important in assessing his or her cardiovascular fitness (based on the assumption that the mile run is a valid measure of that component of fitness). Categories of fitness require a lot less bookkeeping and yield a much quicker assessment. For example, as children complete a mile run, their times can be placed in three categories: under 7:30, between 7:31 and 9:30, and 9:31 and over. Sit-up scores might be recorded as under 10, 11 to 40, and over 40.

# Outside Help

A third method of saving time in fitness testing is not new, but it is effective. Recruit parents, classroom teachers, high school or university students, or retirees to volunteer to help with testing (East, Frazier, & Matney, 1989). Once volunteers are contacted and trained, you can save a lot of time on the days the tests are administered.

Any one of these ideas will save time and probably be more effective than when teachers try to administer an entire fitness test battery by themselves. This also allows teachers more time to use other types of assessment. Currently the emphasis in our profession seems to be primarily on physical fitness testing. Most programs, however, do more than simply try to enhance fitness performance scores; many teachers and children want to know about the progress they are making in other areas.

# SUMMARY

The examples provided in this chapter are more than any teacher would use in a year. Some you might never use. Others you might use occasionally or frequently. In any case, as teachers, we need to be smart about assessment. When it is overwhelming, it becomes a burden. We need to figure out ways to determine how our students are progressing without allowing assessment to become so time-consuming that we abandon the entire process. What seems to work best is to test or assess different classes at various times. Some classes will do well with some aspects of assessment, and others won't. Some classes are terrific in discussion circles, for example, whereas others do a poor job at self-testing. The program is voluntary (it is for your information), so there is no need to test every child in every grade. Sample the classes intelligently, based on their characteristics and your time.

There's an expression people use when they are overburdened with work: "My plate is full." Many of the children's physical educators I work with have plates that are overflowing. Developing, administering, and scoring tests for their students will just add to the overflow. That's why I have tried to stress in this chapter that any assessment—of physical fitness, motor skills, cognitive skills, or attitudes—needs to be conducted efficiently and intelligently.

A well-planned assessment program has two benefits. First, it provides valuable insight on our students that we wouldn't have otherwise. Second, in this era of increasing school accountability, an assessment program allows us to share some relatively objective information regarding what children are learning and thinking as a result of our programs. Without assessment, it is much harder to defend our programs when they are questioned, and with increasing budget constraints, they often are. Assessment programs do not have to be ornate or comprehensive to demonstrate the value our programs have for our students.

# QUESTIONS FOR REFLECTION

1. It is generally agreed that elementary school physical education teachers do not typically test their children to any great extent. In this era of accountability, why do you think this is true? Do you have any evidence that this is changing?
2. Children can learn to test themselves on various fitness and motor skills. Discuss the pros and cons of this process and the circumstances under which it would (and wouldn't) work.
3. Typically, we have relied on a few standardized items to test physical fitness. Describe several other ways, beyond the current methods used, that we might assess physical fitness.
4. Is it important to assess the critical components of motor skills? Why or why not?
5. This chapter describes a variety of ways that a teacher might realistically assess the progress children are making in physical education. Of all the ways, which ones do you think you are most likely to use? Which ones are you least likely to use? Why?

6. What do you think are the potential consequences of simply not assessing children?

# REFERENCES

Allen, V. (1997). Assessment: What to do with it after you've done it. *Teaching Elementary Physical Education, 8*(6), 12–15.

Arbogast, G.W., & Griffin, L. (1989). Accountability: Is it within reach of the professions? *Journal of Physical Education, Recreation and Dance, 60*(6), 72–75.

Ardovino, L., & Sanders, S. (1997). The development of a physical education assessment report. *Teaching Elementary Physical Education, 8*(3), 23–25.

Doering, N. (2000). Measuring student understanding with a videotape performance assessment. *Journal of Physical Education, Recreation and Dance, 71*(7), 47–52.

Doolittle, S. (1996). Practical assessment for physical education teachers. *Journal of Physical Education, Recreation and Dance, 67*(8), 35–37.

East, W.E., Frazier, J.M., & Matney, L.E. (1989). Assessing the physical fitness of elementary school children: Using community resources. *Journal of Physical Education, Recreation and Dance, 60*(6), 54–56.

Fortman-Kirk, M. (1997). Using portfolios to enhance student learning and assessment. *Journal of Physical Education, Recreation and Dance, 68*(7), 29–33.

Graham, G., Holt/Hale, S., & Parker, M. (2007). *Children moving: A reflective approach to teaching physical education.* 4th ed. Mountain View, CA: Mayfield.

Graham, G., Metzler, M., & Webster, G. (1991). Specialist and classroom teacher effectiveness in children's physical education [Monograph]. *Journal of Teaching in Physical Education, 10*(4), 321–426.

Griffin, L., & Oslin, J. (1990). Got a minute? A quick and easy strategy for knowledge testing in physical education. *Strategies, 4*(2), 6–8.

Hopple, C. (2005). *Elementary physical education teaching and assessment.* 2nd ed. Champaign, Il.: Human Kinetics.

Hopple, C., & Graham, G. (1995). What children think, feel and know about fitness testing. In Graham, G. (Ed.) Physical education through students' eyes and in students' voices. *Journal of Teaching in Physical Education, 14*, 408–417.

Hopple, C.J. (1997). The real world process of assessment. *Teaching Elementary Physical Education, 8*(4), 4–7.

Joyner, A.B., & McManis, B.G. (1997). Quality control in alternative assessment. *Journal of Physical Education, Recreation and Dance, 68*(7), 38–40.

Lipowitz, S. (1997). Integrated assessment: Sue Schiemer makes assessment a regular part of her program. *Teaching Elementary Physical Education, 8*(3), 16–18.

Lund, J. (1997). Authentic assessment: Its development and applications. *Journal of Physical Education, Recreation and Dance, 68*(7), 25–28.

Marks, M. (1988). A ticket out the door. *Strategies, 2*(2), 17, 27.

Melograno, V.J. (1997). Integrating assessment into physical education teaching. *Journal of Physical Education, Recreation and Dance, 68*(7), 34–37.

National Association for Sport and Physical Education (NASPE). (1995). *Moving into the future: National standards for physical education.* St. Louis: Mosby.

National Association for Sport and Physical Education (NASPE). (2004). *Moving into the future: National standards for physical education.* 2nd ed. Reston, VA: NASPE.

Parker, M., & Pemberton, C. (1989). Elementary classroom teachers: Untapped resources for fitness assessment. *Journal of Physical Education, Recreation and Dance, 60*(6), 61–63.

Ryan, S., Marzilli, S., & Martindale, T. (2001). Using digital cameras to assess motor learning. *Journal of Physical Education, Recreation and Dance, 72*(8), 13–16, 18.

Schiemer, S. (2000). *Assessment strategies for elementary physical education.* Champaign, IL: Human Kinetics.

Schwager, S. (1996). Getting real about assessment: Making it work. *Journal of Physical Education, Recreation and Dance, 67*(8), 38–40.

Shellhase, K. (1998). *Grades K–6 assessment system: A complete assessment package for the K–6 physical education teacher.* Blacksburg, VA.: www.pecentral.org.

Smith, T.K. (1997). Authentic assessment: Using a portfolio card in physical education. *Journal of Physical Education, Recreation and Dance, 68*(4), 46–52.

Wegis, H., & Van der Mars, H. (2006). Integrating assessment and instruction. *Journal of Physical Education, Recreation and Dance, 77*(1), 27–35.

Werner, P. (1997). Using PE Central and the National Standards to develop practical assessment instruments. *Teaching Elementary Physical Education, 8*(3), 12–14.

Westfall, S. (1998). Setting your sights on assessment: Describing student performance in physical education. *Teaching Elementary Physical Education 9*(6), 5–9.

## Chapter 14

# Continuing to Develop as a Teacher

*I had first graders using the pedometers, many for the first time. After working hard to get as many steps during class as they could, one of the students turned to me and said, "Guess how hot I am." After replying that I didn't know, he said, "Well, my 'thermometer' says 4-7-4 . . . that's HOT!!!"*

**Vicki Staso, Russell Elementary School, Missoula, Montana**
Reprinted with permission from PE Central (www.pecentral.org).

*"Those who can, do. Those who can't, teach. Those who can't teach, teach physical education."*

**Woody Allen**

We began this book with the same quote by Woody Allen. I hope that, by now, you have been stimulated to think about many of the ways that teachers have found to avoid turning kids like Woody Allen off to physical activity—and on to learning and enjoying physical activity.

I hope, too, that you have recognized many of the skills and approaches you already use as a teacher and that you have been stimulated to expand your pedagogical tool box with some of the skills introduced to you. Effective or successful teaching, as described in the last 13 chapters, isn't easy. It's darned hard work! The purpose of this final chapter is to describe some of the ways that teachers have found to maintain their enthusiasm for teaching and continue to develop as professionals, so that they avoid the stagnation and fatigue that eventually come to any professional who settles into a comfortable routine that remains unchanged year after year.

## After reading and understanding this chapter, the teacher will be able to

▶ describe the three stages of a teaching career and their influence on the way we teach,

▶ analyze the various ways teachers continue to improve and learn throughout a career, and

▶ explain why it is important that teachers continually strive to remain current and improve their teaching ability.

## STAGES OF TEACHING

As teachers of children, it is important that we know and understand how children develop. This knowledge allows us to comprehend why children are able (or unable) to learn various skills or movements at various ages and stages. Knowing that, we can design and implement experiences that are developmentally appropriate for children.

It is also helpful to understand how teachers develop so we can better understand our own feelings, attitudes, and professional growth. It makes sense for us to know and understand the developmental stages of teaching.

▶ Why is the first year of teaching typically the most difficult?

▶ How do experienced teachers seem to know so much?

▶ Why do beginning teachers seem to have more discipline problems than veterans?

▶ How do teachers improve and develop?

▶ How can teachers retain their freshness and eagerness throughout a career?

▶ Are there actually stages in a teaching career?

This chapter is the only one in the book that is not directly about teaching children. It is a significant chapter, however, in that it addresses those of us who do the teaching.

Feiman-Nemser (1983) suggests three stages of teacher development. Her analysis provides a starting point for a discussion of the types of things teachers do to remain current and enthusiastic about their teaching and to improve over the course of their careers.

In a rather simplified overview, Feiman-Nemser (1983) suggests that teachers pass through two stages on the way to mastery, the third stage in her developmental analysis. The initial stage is induction, and the second stage is a period of consolidation.

## Induction Stage

Undergraduate practicum experiences in schools, student teaching, and the first year of teaching are all included within the category of induction. For many of us, the first year is the most challenging year of teaching for three reasons:

- In most cases, we are alone with little or no collegial support.
- Much of what we do is brand new: discipline, unknown children, unfamiliar school and colleagues, new boss (principal), and content that must be developed for an entire year rather than for a few weeks.
- The daily schedule demands a great deal of time and energy.

One challenge of the induction year is simply to learn how to talk to various ages of children so they will listen and understand. We quickly learn, for example, that telling a class of kindergarten children to form a circle outside on the grass is futile—for both the teacher and the children. So is a direction such as, "Stand with your right side facing the wall," or "Read the directions written on the board." As we watch their perplexed faces and disorganized responses to our statements that they are not yet ready for, we learn a lot about teaching.

During the induction year we also begin to learn which content is appropriate for which grade level, how long to spend at various tasks, what to do when one child refuses to be a partner to another child, effective ways to deal with tattling, ways to quickly organize children to avoid pushing and shoving, and techniques for explaining the qualities of various movements and skills. For these reasons and numerous others, the first year of teaching is often considered a survival year.

# *Wet Blankets and Mentors*

In the first year of teaching, often during the first few days of school, you might encounter at least one veteran teacher who wants to tell you "what it's really like teaching today." Often these veterans are dissatisfied with their careers and quickly proceed to tell you all they see wrong with kids today, the principal, and the parents. They also quickly add all the reasons why what is currently being taught at universities won't work in the real world. Be ready for these wet blankets. They are the type of people who doubted that airplanes could fly, that televisions would be in every home, and that the Internet would become part of daily life. My recommendation is that you listen politely to the wet blanket, refrain from arguing, and then continue to do what you were doing.

Not all experienced teachers are wet blankets, however. In fact, most are not. It is wise to find one, or more, that you really connect with and use him or her as a mentor for the countless questions that arise in the first few weeks of school: How do you complete this form? Which meetings are important to attend? How does the school deal with parent complaints? In elementary schools your mentor will typically not be another physical educator, but his wisdom and experience about youngsters, how schools work, and getting along with the principal and parents might prove invaluable. And you will need a mentor—no matter how well you are prepared for your first year of teaching, there are always questions that arise. It is comforting to be able to ask a mentor you can trust, who is also positive, for the answers that you need right then—not tomorrow, or next week.

Throughout induction, especially toward the beginning, two questions that were addressed in chapters 3 and 4 seem to dominate our thoughts about teaching:

▶ "Do the children like me?"

▶ "How can I find better ways to ensure that children behave?"

# Consolidation Stage

During the next phase of teaching, the consolidation stage, these questions become less common and are replaced by concerns related to learning how to accommodate the varying skill levels of children in a single class and how to make the best of the time available to enhance children's learning. This holds especially true for teachers who see their students only once or twice a week.

During this stage, teachers' knowledge of pedagogical content truly begins to develop—knowledge that cannot be learned at universities but is attained only through years of working in schools with children. This is when we begin to learn to use many of the tools in our pedagogical tool box.

▶ We begin to understand how a 5-year-old is different from an 8-year-old, who is different from an 11-year-old. Our lessons become more developmentally appropriate.

▶ We begin to recognize tasks that will succeed with third-graders and those that won't, and we no longer have to rely on the first one or two lessons of the day to adjust the lesson (chapter 9) (Graham, Hopple, Manross, & Sitzman, 1993).

▶ The "functional fixedness" of the induction phase dwindles, and we become comfortable exploring different ways to use the equipment and facilities (Housner & Griffey, 1985). For example, we are no longer devastated when we discover, five minutes before a class is scheduled to begin, that the indoor facility is in use for the winter play rehearsal.

▶ We learn that children will still like and respect us even when we are firm and demanding (chapters 3 and 4).

▶ Our observational skills become much sharper (chapter 8); we can quickly scan a class and analyze what is (or isn't) going on (Housner & Griffey, 1985).

▶ We know the content better because of the lessons we have taught and reflected on; we change tasks less and focus more on student learning. We become adept at small task changes that actively involve youngsters in practicing the tasks and skills that need to be practiced (Graham, Hopple, Manross, & Sitzman, 1993).

As a result of our experience and hard work, the satisfying feeling that we are doing a good job comes more frequently. We know when an unsuccessful lesson was a result of poor teaching and when it was a result of external circumstances (a substitute teacher, Halloween, or dogs or bees on the playground) (Tjeerdsma, 1995). We realize that we still have a lot to learn, but we also understand how much we have learned since the induction stage.

## Mastery Stage

Feiman-Nemser (1983) suggests that after several years some teachers begin to approach mastery. They are able to effectively orchestrate and use many of the teaching skills described in the previous 13 chapters.

Master teachers have learned through experience and hard work to develop lessons that are enjoyable and beneficial for children. Their lessons have definite and clear purposes that mesh with the long-term goals of their programs (chapter 2). Whether they're teaching dance, games, gymnastics, or fitness concepts, they have mastered the process of presenting the content (chapters 6 and 9) so that children are interested, challenged, and successful (chapters 5, 7, and 11). Master teachers are able to observe and understand children as they move (chapter 8) and to improvise appropriately based on their vast storehouses of knowledge and information accumulated in earlier years of teaching (Borko & Livingston, 1989). Discipline problems are minimal, and when they do occur they are dealt with effectively and humanely (chapters 3 and 4). Feedback is both useful and pervasive (chapter 10). Children view physical education class as a warm and supportive experience that they enjoy and look forward to (chapter 12).

In contrast to the consolidation-stage teacher, the majority of the lessons taught by a master teacher are effective and satisfying for both teacher and students. There are surprises, but a master teacher's past experience and hard work help her to deal with many of the problems that every teacher encounters—and to deal with them in ways that are beneficial to the children and personally fulfilling to the teacher.

People aren't born master teachers. They might have many of the characteristics that allow one to succeed at teaching, but it is only through experience and constant effort that they gain mastery. One prevalent characteristic of highly successful teachers is their inquisitiveness and ability to analyze and reflect on their own teaching (Schon, 1990). When they might be satisfied, they are instead constantly trying to improve their teaching and their programs. This point is poignantly made by David Hawkins, observing a veteran teacher of 35 years and a student teacher:

The veteran teacher commented that what held her to teaching after all these years was that there was still so much to be learned. The student teacher responded in

*(continued)*

*(continued)*

amazement that she thought it could be learned in two or three years (Feiman-Nemser, 1983, p. 150).

Teaching is a dynamic, ongoing journey that never ends. Although it's possible to teach the same content, using the same process, essentially repeating the first year 30 times, most of us desire more from our careers. We want to improve, learn, develop, change; we want to explore new ideas and approaches—to become better teachers than we were the year before. How do children's physical education teachers do this?

# TECHNIQUES FOR CONTINUING TO IMPROVE AS A TEACHER

They work at it! They purposely search for ways to remain refreshed and excited about their teaching year after year. In this section I will briefly describe some of the more common techniques teachers use to remain current in and energized about their profession (Docheff, 1992; Markos, Walker, & Colvin, 1998; Raxter, 1992).

## Reading

One way to remain current is to read. Some teachers purchase one new elementary school physical education textbook every year and read it as a way of keeping up with what is going on. Some prefer to read journals such as *Strategies* or the *Journal of Physical Education, Recreation and Dance* (JOPERD). Others locate books on physical activity in bookstores and keep current that way. In recent years DVDs and the Internet have provided teachers with opportunities to learn techniques and strategies used in different sports and to apply this information toward upgrading their teaching.

It saddens me when I meet teachers who haven't remained current. They just aren't abreast of recent developments. They know it. Their older students know it. And, unfortunately, the principals of their schools and the parents of their students know it. Needless to say, that hurts our profession because it reflects on our image as physical educators. Comedians like Woody Allen and cartoonists like Tom Batiuk are living testimony to these poor teachers' ineffectiveness and the harmful effects of being in their classes.

## Conferences and Workshops

Attending conferences and workshops is another way teachers gain new ideas. They are harder to schedule and more expensive than reading, but some find that interaction with colleagues a great way to replenish their supply of teaching energy. Most states have annual conferences. See www.pecentral.org for a listing of state associations that host conferences each year.

Veteran teachers report that the most advantageous part of attending conferences is the opportunity to meet others and share ideas and concerns. They might not go to many sessions, but they learn a lot from these discussions.

## Support Groups

The ability to share ideas and concerns with other teachers seems especially important for elementary school PE teachers because they are so alone and isolated in their schools. Classroom teachers have chances throughout the day to vent their emotions, celebrate their small victories, and generally be sociable with other teachers in similar situations. For many PE specialists, the majority of their adult interactions during a school day are with the cooks in the cafeteria or the custodian.

Some physical education teachers form support groups with other specialists. They meet monthly, sometimes weekly, in person or over the phone, to share ideas and provide emotional support for one another. In recent years I have become increasingly convinced that these opportunities to gain and give support are vital for teachers to reach full potential. The support might come from a spouse or a friend, but, given the challenges of teaching children's physical education, teachers who remain enthusiastic about teaching seem to find ways to get support.

The Internet offers a plethora of ways to remain current about new trends and issues in physical education. It is also a forum for an online support group. Interestingly, when the first edition of *Teaching Children Physical Education* was published in 1992, the Internet was not even mentioned. How quickly times change! As I have mentioned, probably the most comprehensive and widely used Internet site for K–12 physical educators is PE Central (figure 14.1; www.pecentral.org). The PE Central Web site includes

**Figure 14.1** Home page of PE Central.
Used by permission of PE Central (www.pecentral.org), the premier web site for physical education teachers.

hundreds of lesson ideas, examples of assessments, and descriptions of best practices. PE Central is also an excellent source for publications and music related to your physical education program.

In addition to Web sites such as PE Central, the Internet provides another popular way for teachers to remain current and connected through e-mail discussion groups. One of the more widely used e-mail discussion groups is NASPE-L, sponsored by the National Association for Sport and Physical Education. Instructions for subscribing to NASPE-L can be found at www.naspeinfo.org. Other good references using technology are www.pelinks4u.org, an online newsletter for physical educators developed by Steve Jefferies at Easter Washington University and Bonnie Mohnsen's technology newsletters available at www.pesoftware.com.

## Teachers Visiting Teachers

Obviously, the Internet allows physical educators throughout the world to share the latest information. You can also ask and answer questions related to your teaching, and do so rather quickly. Some teachers, however, are fortunate to have colleagues close by, and a visit to observe them teaching can be especially valuable. In fact, some teachers find a visit more valuable than attending conferences or reading. These visits typically reinforce some of what a teacher already does while also stimulating new ideas. Unfortunately, many school administrators have yet to see the value of teachers visiting teachers, so release time may be hard to obtain.

## Sharing Videos

Sharing videos of lessons is another way teachers gain fresh approaches to teaching. A recorded lesson on dance, task sheets, or intratask variation can be traded with or borrowed from another teacher. An advantage to this approach is that teachers don't need to be close by—discussions and questions can occur over the telephone.

If a teacher has viewed several DVDs and has developed a support group, he might be willing to take a risk and explore a new way of teaching. Many veteran teachers, for example, find it difficult to use a scattered formation in which every child has a ball and is moving at the same time. The transition from lines to scattered formations is not an easy one. When a teacher has watched a video, for example, and developed a relationship of trust with a colleague, he might be more willing to experiment with a scattered formation or another new method.

We often read about an idea or hear it described at a conference but remain unwilling to try it. When we see the idea come to life on video, however, and know that we can call a friend and ask, we are often more willing to try that new idea.

## Committee Work

Some teachers remain current by serving on physical education committees within a district or at the state level. Occasionally the committee work itself is stimulating; more often, the interaction with other teachers is the valuable part of committee work. The value, of course, is that it allows teachers to hear other viewpoints and ideas. For most teachers a little committee work goes a long way, but it can be helpful for opening new horizons. Not surprisingly, it's usually easy to serve on a committee—volunteers for committee work are about as rare as lottery winners.

## Supervising Student Teachers

Supervising student teachers or serving as a mentor for beginning teachers are other opportunities to gain new ideas and insights by working with someone fresh out of college. Invariably, when a supervisor is conscientious as she works with her student teacher, she reflects on how she teaches, what she teaches, and why she has done it that way over the years—a learning experience in itself. Good supervision is time consuming; it's also professionally stimulating.

## Making Presentations

Making presentations is motivating for some teachers. Others hate even thinking about it. It's nerve wracking and time consuming, but an occasional presentation about an idea or activity that has been successful is also a stimulant for personal growth. I have been told countless times by teachers that they have nothing of value to share. After some prodding and encouragement, they realize that they have an idea or two that just might benefit others. When teachers make slides or a video of their kids, the time flies by—and the audience benefits.

## Graduate School

The degree of stimulation teachers find in graduate courses depends on the content of the course, the professor, and the personal motivation of the teacher taking the course. It seems that teachers who have been instructing for several years derive more benefits from returning to school than do those who have just finished their degree. They seem to know the questions they want to ask and to appreciate being back in school. If they are able to explore ways to apply the course work to their teaching, they often notice an improvement.

## Continuing Education Credit

Many states are increasingly providing alternatives to graduate courses for teachers who wish to obtain recertification. This provides teachers with some interesting ways of recharging batteries (e.g., some states give recertification credit for attending conferences, writing an article, or participating on state committees). The temptation, of course, is to take the easy way out and simply do what's quickest and requires the least amount of work. This is understandable but certainly doesn't lead to improvement in one's career.

# SEVEN HABITS OF HIGHLY EFFECTIVE TEACHERS

You might have read the best-selling book by Stephen R. Covey called *The 7 Habits of Highly Effective People.* The book is about the habits of successful people and how they lead their personal and professional lives. Martin (2004) has applied the habits described by Covey to physical educators.

1. Be proactive. Base your work on your goals and accept responsibility for the outcomes; don't blame others when things don't work out. Instead ask what you might do different in the future.
2. Begin with the end in mind. The key question is "What type of teacher do I want to be remembered as at the end of my career?" and then work toward the answer throughout your years in the profession.
3. Put first things first. Be clear about your goals and be certain that you make time to spend on them. This can be especially difficult given the busy schedules of teachers, but it is an important part of becoming the type of teacher you want to become.
4. Think win–win. Try to engineer solutions to problems whereby all involved feel good about the solution. This can be especially important when working with other teachers and administrators so it feels that you are all on the same team.
5. Seek first to understand, then to be understood. This habit involves learning to listen to others so you understand them and, in turn, they understand you. This is a crucial part of the previous strategy of win–win.
6. Synergize. This habit can be summarized as the "whole is greater than the individual parts." It involves working with others to accomplish common goals that could not be accomplished individually—at least not as well as they can be done by a group.

7. Sharpen the saw. This final habit involves taking good care of yourself, including your physical, mental, social, emotional, and spiritual dimensions. This is what enables someone to be effective and productive.

## WHAT TYPE OF TEACHER WILL YOU BECOME?

Teachers who do the hard work necessary to develop and improve their careers are naturally inclined to participate in some of the activities I have described to enhance their teaching. No doubt they also find other ways to improve. Obviously, not every suggestion will be worthwhile for every teacher.

In our profession, as with most others, it is essentially up to the individual to remain current and continue to develop. There are easy ways to satisfy professional growth requirements imposed by a state accrediting agency, but they might be of virtually no worth to professional growth as a teacher. The same is true for physicians, attorneys, and accountants. It seems, however, that if a teacher wants to be truly successful, he will continue to study and learn and try new ideas throughout his career—not because he has to but because he wants to (Martin, 2004). When this doesn't happen, the teacher might decline in effectiveness or perhaps simply never become very adept at teaching. Some will become lifetime members of physical education's Hall of Shame (Williams, 1996). Others will be known for rolling out the ball rather than as being role models for youngsters (Spencer, 1998).

## PARTING THOUGHTS

Good teaching is hard work. Part of the hard work is continuing to grow and develop as a teacher. There are times when we all ask the questions, "Is it worth it? Why am I working so hard when others don't seem to care?"

When I ask these questions, I remember three quotes that inspire me to do the best job I can for my students. One quote is from President John F. Kennedy: "Children are our most important natural resource and our best hope for the future." That reminds me of the importance of my job—and what I have dedicated my life to professionally.

In fact, when I reflect on these words, I realize that no job, no matter how much it pays or what status it carries, is more important than teaching.

A second thought I reflect on from time to time is one that helps me realize that I am not the only one who is tempted to say, "What the heck? Why work so hard?" This quote is from Bobby Kennedy. He wrote:

> Sometimes it seems to me that it doesn't matter what I do, that it is enough to exist, to sit somewhere, in a garden, for example, watching whatever is to be seen there, the small events.
>
> At other times, I'm aware that other people, possibly a great number of other people, could be affected by what I do or fail to do, that I have a responsibility, as we all have, to make the best possible use of whatever talents I've been given, for the common good.
>
> It is not enough to sit in that garden, however restful or pleasurable it might be.
>
> The world is full of unsolved problems, situations that demand careful, reasoned, and intelligent action.

The final quote accompanies a photograph of a young boy looking out over a lake. The quote reads:

> A hundred years from now it will not matter what my bank account was, the sort of house I lived in, or the kind of car I drove. But the world may be different because I was important in the life of a boy. (Witcraft, 1950, p. 2)

As children's physical education teachers, we influence hundreds of children a year. When we're successful and work hard, we do our part to make the world a better place for children to grow up in. I hope that by writing this text I have helped you to become a better teacher and a positive influence on many children throughout your career in teaching.

## QUESTIONS FOR REFLECTION

1. Why is it important for a teacher to continue to work at improving throughout a career? What are the consequences of not remaining current and enthusiastic?
2. This chapter describes three stages of teaching: induction, consolidation, and mastery. Do you agree with these divisions? Why or why not? How might they be expanded to include five or six stages?
3. The cartoon on page 218 depicts a hypothetical teacher expressing her views on how things change in physical education. What would you say to that individual?
4. A variety of techniques for remaining current and enthusiastic about teaching are included in this chapter. Which ones appeal to you most? Least? Why? Do you think your view might change over your career?
5. Seven habits of highly effective teachers are described near the end of the chapter. Select three of those seven habits and describe an example from your

personal life that illustrates how you exemplify that habit—or what you might do differently to increase your effectiveness for that habit.

6. In the final section of this chapter, I shared three quotes that are personally motivating to me. Do you have any quotes that you find encouraging? Would you want to share them with other teachers?

# REFERENCES

Borko, H., & Livingston, C. (1989). Cognition and improvisation: Differences in mathematics instruction by expert and novice teachers. *American Educational Research Journal, 26*(4), 473–498.

Covey, S. R. (1989). *The 7 Habits of Highly Effective People.* New York: Fireside.

Docheff, D.M. (1992). Are you a good teacher? *Strategies, 6*(2), 5–9.

Feiman-Nemser, S. (1983). Learning to teach. In L. Shulman & P. Sykes (Eds.), *Handbook of teaching and policy.* 150–170. New York: Longman.

Graham, G., Hopple, C., Manross, M., & Sitzman, T. (1993). Novice and expert children's physical education teachers: Insights into their situational decision-making. *Journal of Teaching in Physical Education, 12*, 197–217.

Housner, L.D., & Griffey, D.C. (1985). Teacher cognition: Differences in planning and interactive decision-making between experienced and inexperienced teachers. *Research Quarterly for Exercise and Sport, 56*(1), 45–53.

Markos, N.J., Walker, P.J., & Colvin, A.V. (1998). Professional practice: Elementary "think tank." *Strategies, 11*(4), 7–8.

Martin, L. (2004). The seven habits of highly effective physical educators. *Journal of Physical Education, Recreation and Dance, 75*(2), 47–52.

Raxter, L.M. (1992). Keeping your edge: Maintaining excellence. *Strategies, 5*(8), 24–26.

Schon, D. (1990). *Educating the reflective practitioner.* San Francisco: Jossey-Bass.

Spencer, A. (1998). Physical educator: Role model or roll the ball out? *Journal of Physical Education, Recreation and Dance, 69*(6), 58–63.

Tjeerdsma, B.L. (1995). "If-then" statements help novice teachers deal with the unexpected. *Journal of Physical Education, Recreation and Dance, 66*(6), 22–24.

Williams, N.F. (1996). The physical education hall of shame: Part III: Inappropriate teaching practices. *Journal of Physical Education, Recreation & Dance, 67*(8), 45–48.

Witcraft, F.E. (1950). Within my power. *Scouting Magazine,* October, 2.

# Appendix

## Students' use of time coding form

Teacher _____ Coder _____

Date _____ # of students _____ over 50% of students _____

*Time analysis codes:* Decision is based on what 51% of the observed students are doing at the time.

M = Management: Time when *most* students (over 50%) are *not* receiving instruction or involved in lesson activity (e.g., changing activities, getting out or putting away equipment, listening to behavior rules or reminder).

A = Activity: Time when most students (over 50%) are involved in physical movement (e.g., catching a ball, throwing at a target, running).

I = Instruction: Time when most students (over 50%) are receiving information about how to move or perform a skill (e.g., how to move using all the space, watching a demonstration, listening to instructions).

W = Waiting: Time when most students (over 50%) are *not* involved in the other categories (e.g., group activity but only one or two are participating, waiting for a turn, off-task behavior, waiting for the teacher to give directions).

| 1 | 2 | 3 | 4 | 5 | 6 | 7 | 8 | 9 | 10 |
|---|---|---|---|---|---|---|---|---|---|

| 11 | 12 | 13 | 14 | 15 | 16 | 17 | 18 | 19 | 20 |
|---|---|---|---|---|---|---|---|---|---|

| 21 | 22 | 23 | 24 | 25 | 26 | 27 | 28 | 29 | 30 |
|---|---|---|---|---|---|---|---|---|---|

Percent of M time = _____ ÷ _____ = _____ %
Total M seconds     Total lesson seconds

Percent of A time = _____ ÷ _____ = _____ %
Total A seconds     Total lesson seconds

Percent of I time = _____ ÷ _____ = _____ %
Total I seconds     Total lesson seconds

Percent of W time = _____ ÷ _____ = _____ %
Total W seconds     Total lesson seconds

From G. Graham, 2008, *Teaching Children Physical Education,* 3rd ed. (Champaign, IL: Human Kinetics).

Teacher's name_____ Observer_____

Class taught_____ Date_____

Lesson focus_____

*Directions:* Write down the statements the teacher makes to the entire class—not to groups or individuals—about motor skills—not about behavior or management. At times you may need to abbreviate, but try to capture the intent of the meaning. When the lesson is over, classify each statement as extending (tasks), refining (cues), or applying (challenges). Then graph the statements in the order in which they occur. You may need to use the back of the sheet to record all of the statements.

1.

2.

3.

4.

5.

6.

7.

8.

9.

10.

(continue on back)

```
Extend
 (tasks)      |
              |
              |
Refine        |
 (cues)       |
              |
              |
Apply         |
 (challenges) |
              |_____
               1  2  3  4  5  6  7  8  9  10 11 12 13 14 15 16 17 18 19 20
```

From G. Graham, 2008, *Teaching Children Physical Education,* 3rd ed. (Champaign, IL: Human Kinetics).

# Feedback analysis form

Date_____ Class_____ Grade_____

Topic of lesson_____

| Names | General feedback | Specific feedback | | | | | | | |
|---|---|---|---|---|---|---|---|---|---|
| | | Behavior | | | Skill | | | Cong | |
| (May not want to list entire class) | (No specific referent) | + | 0 | — | + | 0 | — | Yes | No |
| 1. | | | | | | | | | |
| 2. | | | | | | | | | |
| 3. | | | | | | | | | |
| 4. | | | | | | | | | |
| 5. | | | | | | | | | |
| 6. | | | | | | | | | |
| 7. | | | | | | | | | |
| 8. | | | | | | | | | |
| 9. | | | | | | | | | |
| 10. | | | | | | | | | |
| 11. | | | | | | | | | |
| 12. | | | | | | | | | |
| 13. | | | | | | | | | |
| 14. | | | | | | | | | |
| 15. | | | | | | | | | |
| 16. | | | | | | | | | |
| 17. | | | | | | | | | |
| 18. | | | | | | | | | |
| 19. | | | | | | | | | |
| 20. | | | | | | | | | |
| 21. | | | | | | | | | |
| 22. | | | | | | | | | |
| 23. | | | | | | | | | |
| 24. | | | | | | | | | |
| 25. | | | | | | | | | |
| 26. | | | | | | | | | |
| 27. | | | | | | | | | |
| 28. | | | | | | | | | |
| 29. | | | | | | | | | |
| 30. | | | | | | | | | |

From G. Graham, 2008, *Teaching Children Physical Education,* 3rd ed. (Champaign, IL: Human Kinetics).

# Index

*Note:* The letters *f* and *t* after page numbers indicate figures and tables, respectively.

# About the Author

**George Graham, PhD**, has been on the faculty at Pennsylvania State University in the department of kinesiology since 2002. He was on the faculty at Virginia Tech for 17 years, where he was a member of Virginia Tech's Academy of Teaching Excellence. He began his career teaching and coaching in the public schools of California and Oregon and served on the faculties of the University of Georgia and the University of South Carolina before moving to Blacksburg, Virginia.

Since its inception in 1996, Dr. Graham has served as the senior advisor for PE Central (www.pecentral.org), the most widely used Web site by physical educators in the United States.

Dr. Graham has published extensively on physical education teacher effectiveness and physical education for children; he has more than a dozen books, monographs, and journal features and more than 50 articles, monographs, and videotapes to his credit. He is a sought-after speaker and consultant, having delivered presentations at more than 100 conferences throughout the world, including over 60 keynote speeches and feature addresses. He has served as a consultant to more than 70 school districts, the United States Tennis Association, and the Professional Golf Association. He continues to work as a consultant to schools and districts throughout the United States.

In 2007, Dr. Graham was inducted into the National Association for Sport and Physical Education (NASPE) Hall of Fame. He is also a fellow in the American Academy of Kinesiology and Physical Education (2005) and the North American Society of Health, Physical Education, Recreation and Dance Professionals (2004). Dr. Graham has also received the Margie Hanson Honor Award presented by the Council on Physical Education for Children in 1997 and the NASPE Curriculum and Instruction Academy Honor Award in 1996. He served as the executive director of the United States Physical Education Association. With his graduate students, he wrote the first developmentally appropriate document for NASPE. With his undergraduate students, he spends several weeks each semester in elementary schools teaching children physical education.

You'll find other outstanding
physical education resources at
**www.HumanKinetics.com**

In the U.S. call . . . . .1.800.747.4457
Australia . . . . . . . . . 08 8372 0999
Canada. . . . . . . . . 1.800.465.7301
Europe . . . . .+44 (0) 113 255 5665
New Zealand . . . . . . 0800 222 062

**HUMAN KINETICS**
*The Information Leader in Physical Activity & Health*
P.O. Box 5076 • Champaign, IL 61825-5076

# DVD User Instructions

The reproducible worksheets on this DVD-ROM can only be accessed using a DVD-ROM drive in a computer (not a DVD player on a television). To access the reproducible worksheets, follow these instructions:

## Microsoft Windows

1. Place DVD in the DVD-ROM drive of your computer.
2. Double-click on the "My Computer" icon from your desktop.
3. Right-click on the DVD-ROM drive and select the "Open" option from the pop-up menu.
4. Double-click on the "Worksheets" folder.
5. Select the reproducible worksheet that you want to view or print.

## Macintosh

1. Place DVD in the DVD-ROM drive of your computer.
2. Double-click the DVD icon on your desktop.
3. Double-click on the "Worksheets" folder.
4. Select the reproducible worksheet that you want to view or print.

*Note:* You must have Adobe Acrobat Reader to view the reproducible worksheets.